"The church and its ministries will be very grateful for this book! It provides an accessible and thorough account of how we can enact care and protection from abuse in the church. Readers can study the content, learn a great deal, and implement new ideas that will safeguard and then set the stage when healing is needed. I warmly recommend this book for any Christian context where there is a commitment to respond differently to the all-too-common issue of abuse."

Paul Loosemore, director of the Counseling Department at Covenant Theological Seminary

"This book covers extensive ground and will serve not only as a training manual for safeguarding officers but also as a text for any leader seeking to make church a safer place and to better respond to survivors and victims. *Skills for Safeguarding* should be required reading for those training for ministry—both lay and ordained. It is an excellent resource for all safeguarders in the church."

Julie Conalty, bishop of Birkenhead and deputy lead bishop for safeguarding in the Church of England

"In *Skills for Safeguarding*, Compton and Patterson have brought clarity and process to the role of safeguarding that make it much more accessible. They give us key warnings and tie the work of safeguarding to our biblical callings. The applications and reflections ensured that I was thinking about how this all applied to me in my context. A wonderful addition to kingdom work of bringing shalom to a troubled world."

Vern Salter, director of care and director of the John Powell Institute at Mission Training International

"*Skills for Safeguarding* is a unique resource that offers an in-depth understanding of abuse from the perspectives of both the abuser and the abused. This book features data and case studies from numerous experts, helping readers comprehend the grooming process used by abusers, which enables them to identify potential issues before the issues lead to victimization. Individuals who are supporting abused persons throughout the healing process can gain insight into the abused persons' thought processes and actions as well. I highly recommend ministries use *Skills for Safeguarding* as valuable training material for their staff and volunteers."

Denise O'Donoghue, director of biblical womanhood and target learning at Iron Academy / Academy 31

"A timely, much-needed book chock-full of practical wisdom about abuse prevention and response for church communities. This carefully constructed set of resources is a must-read for all church leaders if the church is to address the tragic reality of abuse in its midst and intentionally work toward becoming communities of healing."

Amanda W. Benckhuysen, author of *The Gospel According to Eve: A History of Women's Interpretation*

"More than a practical textbook for safeguarding, this is a theologically grounded call for advocacy. Richly informed by leading specialists, it offers not only a multiangled approach to understanding abuse and the effect it has on survivors but also a guide to self-care in developing the necessary skills for safeguarding. With helpful questions for both personal reflection and wider application, this is a book we should all lean into."

Marcus Pound, associate professor of theology and assistant director of the Centre for Catholic Studies at Durham University

"Compton and Patterson offer a clear vision and practical strategies for addressing the trust deficit in churches and religious institutions. This indispensable resource provides leaders with the biblical and psychological categories and competencies necessary for safeguarding Christ's body, highlighting the beauty of the *imago Dei*. Written with care and compassion, this robust educational resource focuses on preventing abuse and mitigating the collateral damage when abuse is exposed. If you aspire to be a trustworthy leader, devoted to the peace and purity of the church, this book is replete with reliable behaviors and skills you can employ. I will be using this resource to train leaders for years to come."
Clifton Roth, executive director of CrossPoint

"*Skills for Safeguarding* is a timely and helpful resource for any organization that works with children or other vulnerable populations. While there is not a perpetrator under every rock, abuse is far too common around the world, and the evil one knows all too well that if he wants to 'steal and kill and destroy' (John 10:10), abuse is a highly effective weapon. Bravo to these editors and contributors, or as Jesus said in Matthew 25:40, 'Truly I tell you, whatever you did for one of the least of these brothers and sisters of mine, you did for me.'"
Kenyon Knapp, licensed professional counselor and dean of the Liberty University School of Behavioral Sciences

"*Skills for Safeguarding* is a call to action for leaders everywhere! With a heart for healing the hurting and a desire to protect the integrity of every organization, Dr. Lisa Compton and Taylor Patterson provide relevant information along with scriptural support to practically equip and inspire leaders to proactively safeguard all who are in their care. This book will become a roadmap for churches and ministries everywhere to create thriving, healthy, and safe environments for everyone!"
Katie Samuel, pastoral team member at The Chapel in Midlothian, Virginia

"*Skills for Safeguarding: A Guide to Preventing Abuse and Fostering Healing in the Church* is an invaluable resource for anyone dedicated to the crucial work of safeguarding within faith communities. Authored by a panel of experts, including licensed professionals and seasoned practitioners, this book is notable for its comprehensiveness and interdisciplinary approach. The structured sections, enriched with real-life case studies and practical tools, provide clear guidance and actionable insights, making complex safeguarding concepts accessible and implementable. The emphasis on self-care, acknowledging the emotional and psychological demands placed on those in safeguarding roles is a crucial aspect of this book. This holistic perspective ensures that safeguarders are not only equipped to protect and support victims but also maintain their own well-being. As someone deeply involved in safeguarding work, I find this resource both relevant and impactful. It is a comprehensive guide, blending best practices with compassionate care, making it a must-read for church leaders, mental health professionals, and laypersons committed to creating safe and healing environments."
Daniele Donnini, director of Align Safeguarding and regional expert for the Pontifical Commission for the Protection of Minors

SKILLS *for* SAFEGUARDING

A GUIDE *to* PREVENTING ABUSE *and* FOSTERING HEALING *in the* CHURCH

DR. LISA COMPTON *and* TAYLOR PATTERSON

Academic

An imprint of InterVarsity Press
Downers Grove, Illinois

InterVarsity Press
P.O. Box 1400 | Downers Grove, IL 60515-1426
ivpress.com | email@ivpress.com

InterVarsity Press® is the publishing division of InterVarsity Christian Fellowship/USA®. For more information, visit intervarsity.org.

All Scripture quotations, unless otherwise indicated, are taken from The Holy Bible, New International Version®, NIV®. Copyright © 1973, 1978, 1984, 2011 by Biblica, Inc.™ Used by permission of Zondervan. All rights reserved worldwide. www.zondervan.com. The "NIV" and "New International Version" are trademarks registered in the United States Patent and Trademark Office by Biblica, Inc.™

The publisher cannot verify the accuracy or functionality of website URLs used in this book beyond the date of publication.

Cover design: David Fassett
Interior design: Jeanna Wiggins
Image: © MirageC / Moment / Getty Images

ISBN 978-1-5140-1073-0 (print) | ISBN 978-1-5140-1074-7 (digital)

Printed in the United States of America ♾

Library of Congress Cataloging-in-Publication Data
Names: Compton, Lisa, editor. | Patterson, Taylor (Taylor Ann), 1995-
  editor.
Title: Skills for safeguarding : a guide to preventing abuse and fostering
  healing in the church / edited by Dr. Lisa Compton and Taylor Patterson.
Description: Downers Grove, IL : IVP Academic, [2024] | Includes
  bibliographical references and index.
Identifiers: LCCN 2024019174 (print) | LCCN 2024019175 (ebook) | ISBN
  9781514010730 (print) | ISBN 9781514010747 (digital)
Subjects: LCSH: Church work with children. | Child sexual
  abuse–Prevention. | Sexually abused children–Pastoral counseling of. |
  Sexually abused children–Rehabilitation. | Church management. |
  Corporations, Religious–Safety measures. | BISAC: RELIGION / Christian
  Ministry / Counseling & Recovery | RELIGION / Christian Church /
  Administration
Classification: LCC BV639.C4 S538 2024 (print) | LCC BV639.C4 (ebook) |
  DDC 259/.2–dc23/eng/20240605
LC record available at https://lccn.loc.gov/2024019174
LC ebook record available at https://lccn.loc.gov/2024019175

31 30 29 28 27 26 25 24 | 13 12 11 10 9 8 7 6 5 4 3 2 1

This book is dedicated to

the trauma survivors who have bravely shared

their stories with us, inspired us with their resilience,

and allowed us to be a part of their healing journey.

We also would like to express our gratitude

to all the expert contributors who gave

their efforts to this project.

CONTENTS

SECTION V: SKILL DEVELOPMENT

SECTION VI: CARE FOR SAFEGUARDERS

LIST OF CONTRIBUTORS

Dr. Lisa Compton is the director of the PhD in Counselor Education and an associate professor at Regent University. She has over twenty-six years of experience as a Licensed Clinical Social Worker, Certified Trauma Treatment Specialist, and compassion fatigue educator. Dr. Compton has appeared on CBN News and has spoken internationally on trauma and abuse. She is the coauthor of the book *Preparing for Trauma Work in Clinical Mental Health* and has also published several journal articles related to trauma and absorption vulnerability in *Traumatology and the Journal of Creativity in Mental Health*. She is the cofounder of *The Helper's Coach*, an agency providing vitality training and consultation for helping professionals.

Rev. David Cook is an adjunct professor in the psychology department at Gordon College, an ordained Presbyterian minister, and a Licensed Mental Health Counselor in Massachusetts. He has worked in private practice providing court-mandated outpatient treatment to registered sex offenders for over ten years and as a consultant on inpatient sex offender treatment with the Massachusetts Department of Public Health for over seven years. Research interests include gender identity, sexually deviant behaviors, toxic shame and guilt, and effective clinical training and supervision.

Dr. Kristi Cronan is a Licensed Professional Counselor, Approved Clinical Supervisor, and Registered Play Therapist who partners with children, adolescents, and adults. In her clinical work, she has partnered with thousands of people to support healthy individual and family development from an ethical, multiculturally competent, trauma-informed, and attachment-driven perspective. She has served as adjunct professor at Regent University and Townsend Institute at Concordia. Her dissertation research was an analysis of evangelical purity culture on gender-based beliefs.

Dr. Gabriel Dy-Liacco is the founder of the Catholic Safeguarding Institute, associate professor at Divine Mercy University, a Licensed Professional Counselor, and an organizational consultant for leadership in the Catholic church. In 2014, Pope Francis appointed Dr. Dy-Liacco to the Pontifical Commission for the Protection of Minors as a founding member to advise him in developing the Catholic church's policies on safeguarding and to build capacity among local churches. His many other professional roles include serving on the scientific advisory board of the Pontifical Gregorian University's Centre for Child Protection, as board director for MAGIS Creative Spaces, and as reviewer for journals on psychology and spirituality.

Dr. Kathie T. Erwin is a professor at Divine Mercy University, a Fulbright Specialist for teaching and research at the University of Iceland, and chair of the Institutional Review Board. She is a Florida Licensed Mental Health Counselor and Qualified Supervisor who has worked in private practice and developed geriatric group programs over the past twenty-five years. Dr. Erwin is the author of six professional books on gerontology/aging issues and practice development. She serves as president of the Florida Mental Health Counselors Association, board member of the Green Cross Academy of Traumatology, and a guest lecturer for University of Iceland and the International Institute of Postgraduate Education in Ukraine.

Cynthia Malcolm Fisher is a Licensed Marriage and Family Therapist and a Licensed Mental Health Counselor in Massachusetts, and she received graduate training from Gordon-Conwell Theological Seminary. Cynthia has been counseling for over twenty-five years and works with clients with complex trauma backgrounds and intimate partner violence in faith-based marriages. Cynthia is the clinical director of a group private practice north of Boston, Massachusetts, and is an adjunct professor at Gordon-Conwell Theological Seminary. Her crosscultural experiences include supervising Ukrainian counselors in training and co-conducting a study of supervisory competencies during the outbreak of war in Ukraine. Cynthia is a PhD candidate at Regent University.

Dr. Kristy M. Ford is an associate professor and program director for Liberty University's CACREP-accredited clinical mental health counseling online program. She is a Florida Licensed Mental Health Counselor, specializing in clinical supervision and counseling research, with more than twenty years of clinical experience. Dr. Ford's research has focused on trauma-informed care, attachment-based treatments, adverse childhood experiences, and religious accommodation in evidence-based practice, and she has published research and presented findings at multiple international, national, and regional conferences. She is the practice owner and clinical director of Hope Springs Counseling Group in Marianna, Florida.

Dr. Crista Glover is an assistant professor at Regent University, a Licensed Professional Counselor in Virginia, and an approved clinical supervisor. She specializes in therapy for women and has over fifteen years of clinical experience treating women recovering from sexual abuse, assault, and intimate partner violence. In her time working in college mental health, she served as a Title IX coordinator, a women's center liaison, and community partner with the YWCA. Her research focuses on health-promoting behaviors to recover from relational injury and painful life events.

Dr. Danielle H. Johnson is on the faculty at Grace College and Theological Seminary and an adjunct instructor at Divine Mercy University. She is a Licensed Professional Counselor, Approved Supervisor in addictions and professional counseling, and chair of the graduate student committee for the International Association for Resilience and Trauma Counseling. Dr. Johnson holds a Certificate of Graduate Studies in Trauma and is a Certified Trauma Healing Group facilitator and trainer through the American Bible Society's Trauma Healing Institute. She has conducted a trauma awareness training for pastors in the Dominican Republic and strives to reduce the stigma surrounding mental health and substance use treatment, particularly within marginalized and faith-based communities.

Dr. Vanessa Kent is an assistant professor and clinical director for the Master's Counseling Program, Regent University. She is dually licensed as a Licensed Marriage and Family Therapist and Clinical Mental Health Counselor. As a clinician/supervisor for over twenty-five years, she specializes in complex trauma and adoption support, reproductive trauma, and women/couples. She is trained in EFT, attachment-focused EMDR and Trust-Based Relational Interventions. She was a consultant for Child Protection Team, leading therapy groups for child incest victims in military families. She is a trainer/consultant for church-based trauma support group for victims of rape/incest. She developed/teaches attachment and emotional regulation curricula.

Dr. Pensiri Kongkaw-Oden is a faculty member in the department of psychology and counseling at Gannon University. As a Licensed Practitioner, educator, and multicultural individual, Dr. Kongkaw-Oden is adept at teaching complex counseling skills and has presented internationally on transformative listening. Having grown up in both Thailand and Texas, she considers herself a third-culture kid (TCK) and serves as a consultant for the TCK Holistic Care Project, an international, interdisciplinary group dedicated to developing evidence-based assessments and curricula to provide the best support for TCKs. Her research interests include trauma, compassion, multicultural competencies, transracial adoption, and intersectionality.

Dr. Cindy Palen is a Licensed Professional Counselor in Arkansas and a nationally certified counselor. She is an assistant professor at Liberty University and works as a supervisor for the International Institute of Postgraduate Education in Ukraine. Dr. Palen's recent publications in the *Journal of Creativity in Mental Health*, *Play Therapy Magazine*, and her dissertation research with war-torn Ukraine speak to her passion for trauma-focused counseling practices. Dr. Palen's primary clinical and research interests are trauma-related, including PTSD, sexual abuse, dissociative disorders, eating disorders, wartime trauma, and EMDR. Dr. Palen works in private practice at Oaks Counseling in Arkansas.

Taylor Patterson is a Licensed Professional Counselor in Virginia and received her graduate training in trauma-informed counseling services and spiritual integration from Reformed Theological Seminary. She has provided counseling services to survivors of domestic violence, sexual assault, human trafficking, and clergy abuse in outpatient and residential settings. Her cross-cultural experiences include providing trauma-focused counseling through an interpreter to Spanish-speaking clients, facilitating transnational supervision to masters-level counseling students in Cairo, Egypt, and teaching English to refugees in the United States. She is currently a PhD student in counselor education and supervision and has recent publications in *Counseling Today* and *Traumatology*. She is the cofounder of *The Helper's Coach*, an agency providing vitality training and consultation for helping professionals.

Dr. Angela Rinaldi serves at the Institute of Anthropology at Pontifical Gregorian University in Rome (Italy), where she coordinates the English safeguarding programs. She holds a PhD in social teaching of the church and public ethics. She has published on sexual abuses of minors within the Catholic church, abuse of power, the culture of safeguarding, and human formation. She authored three books: *Hacia una Iglesia que proteja a los más pequeños*, *Una migrazione che dà speranza. I minori non accompagnati in Italia*, and *Dalla parte dei piccoli. Chiesa e abusi sessuali*. She researches the consequences of the misuse of power on vulnerable people and their consciences, and social agency from the perspective of church social teaching and ethics.

Dr. Kathryn Stamoulis is an Educational Psychologist and Licensed Mental Health Counselor based in New York who specializes in adolescent sexual development. She has served as an expert witness in cases involving the sexual abuse and grooming of minors. Committed to public education, her work has appeared in numerous publications and media outlets. She was featured in the Netflix docuseries *Filthy Rich: Jeffrey Epstein* and in sources including *The New York Times*, NPR, MSNBC, and *Today*.

Dr. Kaitlyn Callais Stafford is an assistant professor and the interim director of the counseling programs at the Townsend Institute at Concordia University Irvine. She is a Licensed Clinical Social Worker and EMDR certified therapist and consultant. Dr. Stafford has served as a faculty member, supervisor, and consultant for the International Institute of Postgraduate Education in Ukraine, as chair of the Ukraine Aid Coordination Team, and as fundraising coordinator and expert advising board member for the Ukraine Institute of Traumatherapy. Dr. Stafford specializes in working with military service members, veterans, and adults with complex trauma histories.

Dr. Karen J. Terry is a professor in the department of criminal justice at John Jay College of Criminal Justice and on the faculty of the Criminal Justice Doctoral Program at the Graduate Center, CUNY. She holds a doctorate in criminology from Cambridge University. Her primary research interest is sexual offending and victimization, particularly abuse of children in an institutional setting, and she has received nearly $4 million in federal and private grants. Most significantly, she was the principal investigator for two national studies on sexual abuse of minors by Catholic priests in the US.

Dr. Mary L. Troy is an assistant professor in the Department of Counseling and Human Services at the University of Scranton. Dr. Troy is a national board-certified counselor and a Licensed Professional Counselor in Pennsylvania. She also works as an LPC in a private counseling practice, where she has helped many clients heal from sexual trauma. Dr. Troy regularly lectures on child abuse issues which include physical and psychological signs/effects of abuse, mandated reporting, and how to help survivors of childhood abuse.

INTRODUCTION

DR. LISA COMPTON AND
TAYLOR PATTERSON

EVERY BELIEVER IS CALLED to use their voice to advocate for those in need (Proverbs 31:8-9), seek justice on behalf of others (Isaiah 1:17), and demonstrate their religion by acting on behalf of vulnerable groups (James 1:27). In short, every believer is called to safeguard. The care we provide to the most vulnerable and powerless among us is counted as service to the Lord (Matthew 25:40; Mark 9:37). This protective service is rewarded by God: "Blessed are those who have regard for the weak; the LORD delivers them in times of trouble" (Psalm 41:1). On the other hand, there is severe punishment for those who harm children and other vulnerable members of society: "It is impossible that no offenses should come, but woe to him through whom they do come! It would be better for him if a millstone were hung around his neck, and he were thrown into the sea, than that he should offend one of these little ones" (Luke 17:1-2 NKJV). Those of us with power and influence are called by God to sacrificially serve and protect those who are more vulnerable. As we will learn in subsequent chapters, every human being is made in the image of God; therefore, we all have some measure of power and agency that we are responsible for stewarding faithfully. Adults in the church have a clear obligation to honor the vulnerability of children and are commissioned by God to use their influence to act on their behalf.

Safeguarders can be individuals hired by the church in a vocational safeguarding role, but they can also be pastors/priests/clergy and other church leaders, laity, mental health professionals, and anyone who desires to promote a safe environment, prevent abuse, and facilitate healing from abuse and trauma. Ideally, every adult in the church acknowledges their responsibility to safeguard and seeks to grow in safeguarding skills to better serve abuse survivors and cultivate a culture of safety for the vulnerable. Examples of abusive situations that safeguarders may encounter include:

- a person who was abused by a stranger, acquaintance, or friend
- a person who was abused by a family member outside of the church
- a person who was abused by a family member inside the church
- a person who was abused by a leader in the church

All of these cases provide an opportunity for the church, the body of Christ, to actively participate and fulfill our divine mandate to serve in this protective role.

WHAT IS SAFEGUARDING?

According to Dr. Angela Rinaldi, a lecturer at Pontifical Gregorian University in Rome, safeguarders are people who recognize their responsibilities and roles in setting up safe environments. This means that safeguarders are people able to prevent abuses and act when abuse happens. Safeguarding actions include:

- **Look**
    - identify signs and indicators of abuse
    - recognize possible risk and protective factors of abuse
- **Listen**
    - listen to victims' stories in an empathetic, nonjudgmental, supportive manner
    - provide safe places for individuals and families to share their stories
- **Equip**
    - share tools that promote healing with survivors and their families
    - teach others to build healthy relationships
    - connect primary and secondary victims to appropriate resources
- **Speak Out**
    - speak publicly against abuse
    - report abuse to law enforcement based on local laws
    - advocate to those in authority positions to promote safety

Safeguarders look, listen, equip, and speak out in various capacities as they work with individuals, families, churches, communities, and organizational systems. In order to function properly, all members of the church must devote themselves to the work of safeguarding within the confines of their roles and expertise in partnership with other members of the body (1 Corinthians 12:21-31). Mental health professionals are skilled in addressing the mental health needs of trauma survivors, including addiction recovery, suicidality, severe emotional dysregulation, self-harm, and dissociation. Church leadership provides compassionate care that emphasizes spiritual development and care for the trauma survivor. Lay people can use their vocational expertise to provide for survivors' practical needs and can provide a safe, supportive community in which survivors experience healthy and reparative relationships. No one person or profession can alone accomplish the work of safeguarding. It is necessary that all parts of the body of Christ work collaboratively with one another to create church communities that prevent abuse and foster healing for trauma survivors. This text will train you in the knowledge and skills needed to perform these functions and form multidisciplinary partnerships.

VALUED ROLE

You are the most valuable asset of the church. You are the hands, feet, and mouthpiece of Jesus on this earth against the evil principalities and powers that plot to bring harm and destruction. That statement may sound grandiose but will be validated as you read the chapters outlining the unconscionable reality of abuse, particularly against children. As is often quoted, "The only thing necessary for the triumph of evil is for good men to do nothing." For too long, abuse in the church has been concealed not only by perpetrators but also by others who choose to look the other way or even enable the harmful behaviors to continue. Based on Matthew 25:45-46, what we fail to do for the powerless, we fail to do for the Lord. However, when godly women and men take action against abuse and its destruction, evil will no longer flourish.

This is the opportune time to become involved in safeguarding. Modern society has over-sexualized children, and child pornography and human trafficking are at epic proportions (Woldehanna et al., 2023). There are even marginal secular groups that seek to normalize pedophilia as an alternative sexual preference that they claim people should be free to act on. The church should be a pillar of sexual morality and a safe refuge for all people, but too often, it has been a place where people have used their power and spiritual authority to exploit others. We have repeatedly seen the pervasive evil of sexual abuse in the church and subsequent coverups publicly exposed by courageous survivors and diligent investigative journalists. It is time for the church to take its rightful place on the front lines against all forms of abuse—both in the community and within its own walls. We need to be so appalled by evil that we use our voices, our energy, and all our resources to expose what is hidden in darkness, stand with those who have been harmed, and bring those who perpetrate harm to justice.

TRIGGER WARNING

This work is worth doing, and it will cost you. It will require you to turn toward the reality of trauma rather than looking away. You will be challenged to courageously advocate for the voiceless, sometimes even at personal cost. As you engage in this work and seek to do good, you will clearly see the evil in the world. It will change you. You will feel overwhelmed by the harsh reality that trauma is a global pandemic and that abuse is prevalent across gender, race, ethnicity, socioeconomic levels, nations, religions, and church denominations. The fact that so many precious, innocent children have been violated in youth programs, vacation Bible schools, summer camps, church settings, and Christian homes by those who claim to serve in the name of Jesus will incite disgust and rage. Use your rage to fuel your mission, and use your anger to advocate for those without a voice. We must work to strengthen our ability to "not be overcome by evil, but overcome evil with good" (Romans 12:21).

This text is not only a guide on how to help others but also a source of vital information to help you care for yourself while doing this divine work. In order to experience longevity in your ministry and personal wellness, you will need tools to reduce psychological and emotional harm from secondary trauma exposure. Proverbs 4:23 warns us to guard our hearts. As you work through this text, be aware of your own reactions to this challenging topic and take breaks as needed. This will help you meaningfully engage with and retain the information presented in this text and prepare you to regulate your own emotions as you sit before real survivors telling their stories of horrific abuse. We recommend you be intentional about how you read this text. For example, it is likely not wise to read portions of this text right before you go to bed. Some readers may prefer to read this text while in the library or coffee shop rather than in their homes because being in public helps them to stay grounded. Others may prefer to read in the comfort of their homes as it provides a quiet, peaceful place to digest the information. Regardless of your preference, be mindful of its impact. It may also help to take walks outside as nature can be very grounding or stretch your body to reduce muscle tension. You may want to skip ahead to the chapter on emotion regulation strategies to develop those skills first.

OVERVIEW

The chapters are structured so that this book can be used as a textbook in an academic setting or as a general knowledge text for anyone who realizes their safeguarding responsibility and wants to grow in the necessary skills. Safeguarding in the church is a complex topic that requires expertise in multiple areas, including power dynamics, trauma responses, perpetrator characteristics, vulnerable populations, and foundational helping skills. In order to provide depth to the text, we recruited authors with unique expertise in their chapter topics. However, we wanted this book to read as one cohesive text, rather than a collection of essays with different writing styles and voices. To accomplish this, we edited each chapter to match one consistent voice and structured the material so that the topics build on one another. Although no stories represent actual clients, we have included many illustrations of abuse that come from our work with trauma survivors. Each chapter includes:

- content expert section on the chapter topic
- questions for self-reflection
- questions for group discussion

We also want to provide a brief note about terms. There is no one label that accurately reflects both the destructive nature of trauma and the incredible resilience of those who have been abused. For example, the term *victim* rightly recognizes the significant harm that is done by abuse and places the responsibility for that harm on the perpetrator. However, people who have experienced abuse often do not want to maintain *victim* as a long-term identity marker. On the other hand, the term *survivor* is grounded in a strengths-based perspective and highlights the resilience of those who have been abused. We also recognize that some who have experienced trauma do not wish to be called *survivor* because they feel this term overemphasizes the trauma as part of their identity and life experience. We seek to honor the dignity of all people and have taken care throughout the text to choose terms carefully based on the context of each sentence. The term *victim* will be used to reference those who have been abused when discussing perpetrator dynamics and the immediate aftermath of abuse. *Survivor* will be used when engaging with the strategies people implement to manage the long-term effects of abuse and their efforts to heal from traumatic experiences. We chose to use the term *perpetrator* throughout to represent those who enact the abuse.

CONCLUSION

Trauma work is a heroic adventure—a battle against destructive forces and an incredible effort to pursue healing. At the heart of the evil of abuse in the church, particularly child sexual abuse, is the profound abuse of power and a system that enables this harm through the conspiracy of cover-up (Doyle, 2006). This book provides thorough training to equip an army of protectors and trauma responders. This text will prepare you for safeguarding work as well as provide you with skills to reduce your own risk of compassion fatigue, both necessary components of spiritual formation for every person who serves in any ministry capacity.

Safeguarding will be a multigenerational mission of change. It requires an army of laborers committed to advocating for the vulnerable for the rest of their lives to reverse a culture of complicity that suppresses the truth to preserve power and protect an institution. Equipping the saints with tools to prevent abuse and care for survivors will take time. However, significant systemic change for the church is possible. Training in safeguarding skills is a crucial step in this journey. When reflecting on the presence of evil and the justice of God, the psalmist writes, "The wicked plots against the righteous, and gnashes his teeth at him; but the LORD laughs at the wicked, for he sees that his day is coming" (Psalm 37:12-13 RSV). We can be confident that ultimate victory is with the Lord. We will win the war against abuse through our obedience to the Lord's calling to serve and by the guidance and power of his Holy Spirit.

REFERENCES

Doyle, T. P. (2006). Clericalism: Enabler of clergy sexual abuse. *Pastoral Psychology*, *54*(3), 189-213. https://doi.org/10.1007/s11089-006-6323-x

Woldehanna, S., Powers, L., Bouché, V., Bright, K. T., Call, T., Chen, M., Fasthorse, H., Fattah, T. B., Gix, L. T., Jacobs, E., Jacobs, F., Maha'a, A., Marsh, E., Nolan, B., Singh, N. S., Snyder, K., Vincent, K., Vollinger, L., & Watters, C. (2023, January). In harm's way: How systems fail human trafficking survivors. *Polaris Project: National Survivor Study*. https://polarisproject.org/wp-content/uploads/2023/07/In-Harms-Way-How-Systems-Fail-Human-Trafficking-Survivors-by-Polaris-modifed-June-2023.pdf

SECTION I

REALITY
OF ABUSE

1

FOUNDATIONAL KNOWLEDGE OF SAFEGUARDING AND ABUSE

TAYLOR PATTERSON

A WOMAN CRIES AS SHE CONFIDES in a friend about ongoing domestic violence in her home and is rebuked for not submitting to her husband's leadership. A young boy whispers reluctant agreement when he is told by his youth pastor that he surely misunderstood his teacher's actions because only girls are sexually abused. A family is excommunicated from a church for expressing discomfort with the authoritarian leadership style. A young pastor feels unappreciated and overworked but finds comfort in sexual fantasies about a grieving congregant to whom he is ministering; he insists she needs frequent prayer meetings and pastoral counseling sessions to spend more time together. A teenage girl bravely reports abuse perpetrated by a church deacon but hides in shame when her Sunday school teacher responds with encouragement to dress more modestly. The church has too often abandoned its charge to reflect the character of God, promote truth, and pursue righteousness. Instead, we have directed our efforts toward cover-up and self-preservation.

In her discussion of David and Bathsheba, Jacqueline Grey (2019) writes, "When leaders and institutions prioritize their reputation over truth it results in the perpetuation of one transgression after another" (p. 22). The abusive act itself is one transgression; the culture that enabled the abuse to fester is another; the complicity, or turning away, of others after indications of abuse are revealed is another; and the ensuing institutional efforts to cover up abuse is another. The work of safeguarding requires us all to commit ourselves to the mission of the church by repenting of the ways we have turned away from the suffering of the vulnerable and courageously advocating for truth and righteousness in our communities.

SAFEGUARDING THROUGHOUT SCRIPTURE

Though it is a more recent term, safeguarding is not a new work. Throughout human history, men and women have used their power in a way that harms others and serves themselves, and people have turned away from injustice to preserve their comfort. In response, God has raised up advocates who execute justice, defend the vulnerable, and call others to repentance. Consider the following biblical accounts of leaders and institutions being held accountable by God's chosen safeguarding advocates.

King David, lauded as a "man after [God's] own heart" (1 Samuel 13:14; Acts 13:22),[1] was anointed by God to rule over Israel, and from his lineage Jesus the Messiah was born (Matthew 1). However, David used this power and influence to meet his own needs when he commanded his messengers to take Bathsheba from her home to have sex with him (2 Samuel 11:4). David's transgressions multiplied when he responded to Bathsheba's pregnancy by using his military authority to orchestrate the death of her husband and cover his sin (2 Samuel 11). These cascading abuses of power angered God. In response, God charged Nathan with the task of safeguarding and commanded him to boldly confront the King of Israel. This could have resulted in a great personal cost to Nathan, as David had already facilitated a murder to cover his sins, but Nathan was committed to justice and obedient to God's commands. Nathan rebuked David and warned him of the coming judgment. This judgment was not done in secret; instead, God tells David, "You did it secretly, but I will do this thing before all Israel and before the sun" (2 Samuel 12:12). Grey (2019) writes that it "is not defending God's repute by covering unethical behavior; in fact, we are undermining the justice of God" (p. 25). Nathan is a model for us as we seek to grow in courage for the work of safeguarding to hold our leaders accountable to God's standard of humility and service.

God's commitment to justice and care for the vulnerable is not limited to individual leaders but extends to nations and institutions that are commanded to represent his character. The Old Testament prophets were raised up by God to call the nation of Israel to repentance for forsaking God and his commands.

---

[1]Scripture quotations in this chapter are from the ESV unless otherwise indicated.

Isaiah 1 describes God's displeasure with Israel's half-hearted worship, as evidenced by their lack of attention and care for the vulnerable. Isaiah 1:16-17 charges Israel to "wash yourselves; make yourselves clean; remove the evil of your deeds from before my eyes; cease to do evil, learn to do good; seek justice, correct oppression; bring justice to the fatherless, plead the widow's cause." Israel's rebellion incurred the wrath of God. However, God was also committed to rebuilding his people into an institution that reflected its original design. The prophet Isaiah writes, "Afterward you shall be called the city of righteousness, the faithful city" (Isaiah 1:26). God is not afraid to dismantle and rebuild his established institutions for his glory. When we see patterns of abuse in the church, we are called to be like the prophets, calling leaders to repentance and working for the good of the community and the glory of God.

These accounts emphasize that no leader is too powerful and no institution is too large to be rebuked when the vulnerable are being harmed. The church must take God's glory too seriously to sit idly by while cultures of abuse fester within the household of God. Psalm 72:14 describes God's safeguarding character: "From oppression and violence he redeems their life, and precious is their blood in his sight." God has called us to join in this work and be agents of that redemption. We must not turn away. Instead, we must (1) lean in by learning about the impact of trauma, developing skills for engaging with survivors, and courageously advocating for safe communities; and (2) look within by facing our own susceptibility to use power for selfish gain, soothing our discomfort as we bear witness to suffering, and healing from wounds that prompt us to employ unhealthy strategies for meeting our own needs.

LEAN IN: UNDERSTANDING ABUSE

To effectively *lean in* to the work of safeguarding our communities, we must have a proper understanding of abuse that unveils quietly lurking evil. Unfortunately, most abuse is committed by a person in a position of trust—a parent, family member, teacher, coach, or religious leader. These instances of abuse and subsequent cover-up exist in all types of institutions—parachurch ministries, Catholic churches, Protestant churches, and nondenominational churches. No institution or denominational affiliation is immune to the potential abuse of power. The public exposure of widespread instances of child sexual abuse in the Catholic church perpetrated by priests was an *enormous* step in the direction of holding our religious institutions accountable and helping our communities be safer. However, there is a danger that we might see these instances of grievous abuse and praise God we do not "sin like they do," while ignoring the wickedness in our own hearts and institutions. Learning about complicity and the different types of abuse helps us attune to the potential evil in our midst.

Disclaimer: The following discussion includes both abuse that is criminal in many jurisdictions and abuse that is not legally reportable but still extraordinarily harmful. In instances of criminal abuse (such as child abuse), we *must* follow all reporting laws. The church does not replace legal institutions, and they could put others in harm if criminal abuse is not reported. While not every type or instance of abuse in this discussion is a criminal offense, they are *all* grievous sins against God and those made in his image; therefore, they must be confronted by the church. Jurisdictions may vary in their determination of legally reportable abuse, but God's law is consistent in what is evil in his sight.

Complicity. When conceptualizing abuse in the church, we must first face our own complicity. We are complicit when we create environments that make abuse possible or turn away from indications that abuse is happening. For example, if a school custodian walks by a classroom, sees a teacher kissing a young boy through the classroom window, and chooses not to speak up, he is complicit in her actions. Scripture clearly states our responsibility to do good and not turn away from injustice. James 4:17 says, "So whoever knows the right thing to do and fails to do it, for him it is sin." There are varying degrees of complicity, ranging from failure to confront questionable policies that have yet to result in an act of abuse to knowingly facilitating a perpetrator's access to a child. It is common for trauma survivors to feel most betrayed by those who could have stopped the abuse but chose not to.

Gregory Mellema (2008) elaborates on the concept of complicity by summarizing Thomas Aquinas's discussion of how people can enable wrongdoing and the ensuing moral responsibility. These include nine areas of complicity:

1. by command—someone in a position of authority commands another to commit wrongdoing
2. by counsel—advising another to commit wrongdoing
3. by consent—condoning or giving permission to another to commit wrongdoing

4. by flattery—commending the consideration or the carrying out of wrongdoing

5. by receiving—covering up knowledge of wrongdoing or protecting the person who committed it

6. by participation—joining in wrongdoing

7. by silence—discovering wrongdoing and saying nothing

8. by not preventing—not taking reasonable steps to guard against wrongdoing when one has the ability and responsibility to do so

9. by not denouncing—acknowledging that the wrongdoing took place but not condemning it as morally unacceptable

Safeguarding would also add to Aquinas's model not helping the victim(s) pursue healing as an area of complicity. Abusive religious systems often utilize shame to silence members' internal, Spirit-led sense of right and wrong, fostering a culture that breeds complicity. When describing the relationships between shame and religious trauma, Alison Downie (2022) writes, "In such contexts, truth is always and only external. Truth is received by submission to authority, by conformity. It is not known from within" (p. 925). If "truth" is only received from the religious authorities who are enabling, perpetrating, and covering up abuse, then how does a person attune and respond to conviction from the Holy Spirit? The following section is designed to help sharpen our awareness of right and wrong so we will feel emboldened to speak out on behalf of victims despite potential pressure from religious systems to keep silent. We will outline the various types of abuse and include an application case study following one family, the Jeffersons. In the case study, we will demonstrate how the abuse unfolds within the system and identify those with some degree of complicity. Proverbs 3:27 tells us, "Do not withhold good from those to whom it is due, when it is in your power to do it." These stories will help us to honestly reflect on where it was in our power to act on another's behalf but we failed to do so.

Emotional and verbal abuse. Emotional abuse can be challenging to identify, as it is often subtle. Emotional abuse involves a "sustained pattern" of controlling, degrading, or coercive language that quietly erodes the victim's confidence (Francis & Pearson, 2021, p. 5). The perpetrator does not have to use harsh language or yell and scream to be considered emotionally abusive. Verbal abuse is similar to emotional abuse but has a larger emphasis on aggressive, hurtful language toward another person or verbal threats of violence. Victims of emotional and verbal abuse can experience severe self-doubt, to the point of questioning their own perception of reality. Examples of this type of abuse include:

- guilt trips
- extreme jealousy
- constant monitoring
- name-calling
- insults
- sarcastic or humiliating "jokes" used to show contempt
- threats of physical harm

Application. Derrick and Susan Jefferson had a whirlwind romance. Their dating and engagement relationship lasted about six months before they raced to the altar, excited to pledge their lifelong faithfulness to one another before God and their church. Derrick served as a youth pastor at their local church where Susan also worked part time as an administrative assistant. During their dating relationship, Derrick seemed easygoing. He was attentive and caring, often surprising Susan with small gifts to display his love for her. Now that they were married and living together, Derrick seemed different. He was particular about what Susan wore in public and communicated that a faithful wife ensured she did not steal the gaze of other men. Susan wanted to serve and honor her husband, so she adjusted her wardrobe and behavior according to his preferences. Still, Derrick seemed annoyed and impatient.

As his jealousy escalated, Derrick frequently accused Susan of having an affair. To prove her trustworthiness, Derrick demanded that Susan let him go through her text messages, track her location through her phone's GPS, and monitor her use of their credit card. Susan began withdrawing from her other friendships out of fear that Derrick might think she was betraying his trust. Over the years, Susan withdrew from her community to focus on ensuring Derrick was happy.

Susan got pregnant and gave birth to two beautiful children, Josie and James. She felt hopeful their marriage was turning a corner and that her humble submission was finally paying off. However, after they emerged from the postpartum daze, Derrick got angry with Susan more frequently. What was once expressions of jealousy and suspicion turned into yelling, name-calling, and verbal threats of violence. It was not uncommon for Derrick to yell, "I should kill you for the way you talk to me!"

In a moment of bravery, Susan confided in her coworker through tears, trying to gauge if this was normal in a marriage. Her coworker and fellow church member reminded Susan how lucky she was to have a husband who loves the Lord and serves the church faithfully. She told Susan that Derrick is a good man and that she should be careful not to provoke him to anger. Susan was reminded to show him grace and be eager to serve him, as it can be difficult to be the head of the household.

Derrick's interactions with Susan display all the hallmarks of emotional and verbal abuse. He belittles her, speaks to her as if she is crazy, monitors her every action, and threatens to harm her. Susan desires to be a dutiful, faithful wife and wants a marriage in which she feels safe and connected. Her coworker practices complicity when she excuses Derrick's behavior on the grounds of his service to the church. She reinforces Susan's fear that she is responsible for the abuse and loses a significant opportunity to support Susan and confront Derrick for the sake of the health of their marriage.

Physical abuse. Physical abuse includes intentionally injuring another's body or purposefully making someone physically uncomfortable. Examples include:

- slapping or punching
- strangling
- confinement or unlawful restraint
- burning

Application. As time goes on, Derrick's yelling and name-calling became scarier and more frequent. One night in February during an argument, Derrick slapped Susan and locked her outside in the snow while barefoot in her pajamas. She was outside for two hours begging to be let inside before a neighbor heard her. Susan played it off as an unfortunate accident to avoid Derrick's escalating rage, claiming she went outside to check the mail and forgot to bring her key. The neighbor used his phone to call Derrick, explained the "accident," and asked him to let her inside. Derrick unlocked the door and made small talk with the neighbor, laughing about his wife's mistake. When Susan entered the house, Derrick said, "I hope that taught you not to disobey me."

Susan was committed to healing her marriage and convinced Derrick to see their pastor, John, for marriage counseling. In their sessions, Derrick turned on the charm. He laughed with Pastor John about how hard it is to be married and the difficulty of practicing patience with a wife who can be so frustrating. The night before one of their sessions, Derrick got enraged in front of the children. When Susan tearfully asked him to go into the other room so the children wouldn't see them fighting, Derrick put his hands around her neck and yelled, "I swear I will kill you if you keep disrespecting me in front of my children!" This emboldened Susan to confess to her pastor in their marriage counseling session what was happening in the house and that she was afraid he would hurt the children. When Susan was finished talking, Pastor John took a deep breath and said, "Derrick is the best youth pastor in town. He works with children all the time; you do not need to worry that he will hurt the children." He encouraged Susan to "win him with gentleness," and said that if she obeyed God and was more respectful, Derrick would not act out.

Susan decided to take her pastor's advice and tried to live peaceably with her husband as best she could. She would be vigilant about what she said and how she behaved around Derrick, staving off his abuse for a few weeks. Eventually, something would set him off, and he would physically harm her. The next day, he would bring her flowers and apologize, saying, "If you did not make me so mad, I would not have hurt you."

Derrick's escalation from emotional and verbal abuse to physical abuse displays a common progression seen in domestic violence. It is not uncommon for the perpetrator to act out in an abusive incident (e.g., hitting or slapping the victim) and follow up with "love-bombing" tactics, or grand gestures of affection, such as lavish gifts, seemingly sincere apologies, or excessive flattery (Arabi, 2023). These strategies make it difficult for the victim to trust their survival instinct to leave and pursue safety. When Derrick brings flowers to Susan and attempts to apologize for his actions (though his apology lacks a genuine acceptance of responsibility), she is lured back into a relationship with him, hopeful that maybe this time will be the last time.

To a small degree, the Jeffersons' neighbor could be considered complicit in the abuse if he noticed a continued pattern of incidents similar to the one described above and did not seek to support Susan. The more egregious act of complicity comes from the Jeffersons' pastor, John, who refuses to denounce the abuse. Instead, he counsels Susan to continue to endure Derrick's abuse, even suggesting that she is at fault. If John had a thorough understanding of physical abuse and the courage to perform his safeguarding role, he would have rebuked Derrick for his actions, urged him to participate in long-term treatment aimed at stopping the cycle of abuse, validated Susan's right to go to the police, and helped her establish a plan for safe housing for her and her children.

Spiritual abuse. Spiritual abuse is the perversion of religious or spiritual beliefs and/or power to exert control over someone else (Ellis et al., 2022). This is particularly harmful to victims, as it inherently suggests their abuse is permissible or approved of by God. Spiritual abuse also creates an environment that allows other types of abuse to fester, namely sexual abuse perpetrated by religious leaders. Spiritual manipulation and control foster a culture of absolute obedience to leaders and loyalty to the institution that makes people vulnerable to grooming tactics and silences victims. Examples include:

- misusing Scripture to coerce followers to give away all their possessions
- claiming absolute authority over people's basic life decisions, such as how to dress, where to live, and who to marry
- elevating the spiritual leader as one who "speaks for God" and demanding unquestioned submission from the congregants or parishioners
- communicating a behavior-based acceptance model that conflates a person's worth in the kingdom of God to their service to the church

Application. Susan and Derrick's church grew exponentially, and Derrick was promoted to assistant pastor. They developed a close friendship with Pastor John and his wife and really believed in the mission of the church. John was charismatic and made the congregants believe they were part of the exciting work God was doing in their city. He would describe their congregation as "the only church in town that preaches the true gospel." He preached with authority as he warned against false teachers and those who would try to divide the congregation and thwart the advancement of the kingdom of God.

Susan led the church's women's ministry and met weekly with the pastor to discuss ministry events. In their weekly meetings, John would ask Susan to "keep a look out" for congregants who were seeking to divide the church. He asked her to inform him of anyone who was critical of the church's teaching, as they could be a "wolf in sheep's clothing." Susan felt uncomfortable with his request but wanted to stay in his good favor. When her friend, Jacqueline, expressed discomfort with the pastor's teaching methods and claim to authority over virtually every aspect of their lives, Susan encouraged her to submit to her elders and trust the leadership God put over them. Susan told John about Jacqueline's concerns and her encouragement to obey leadership. John commended Susan on a job well done.

Three weeks later, John told Susan that Jacqueline and her family had been removed from church membership. "I tried to call her to repentance for her disobedience, but she was not responsive. We cannot have any divisions in the church," he explained. Susan felt sad, confused, and guilty, but she believed she could not risk voicing her concerns. What would she do if she were kicked out of the church?

One of the primary goals of spiritual abuse is to extinguish dissension to increase the power of the spiritual leader, which cultivates complicity in the congregation. In this case, Susan functioned as a "spy" for the spiritually abusive leader, making her a complicit party in the harm done to Jacqueline. It is important to note here that Susan was also at risk of spiritual harm if she denounced the abuse and advocated for Jacqueline. However, as we recall from the story of David and Nathan, God sometimes calls us to obedience even at a potential personal cost. One of the most effective ways a church can prevent spiritual abuse is by seeking leaders with integrity over talent, character over charisma, and maturity over verbal eloquence.

Sexual abuse. Sexual abuse is any use of another person's body for one's own sexual gratification without their consent. It also includes *any* sexual activity perpetrated by an adult with a child under the age of eighteen, regardless of the perpetrator's perception of the child's consent. As we will explore in later chapters, sexual abuse often begins with nonsexual touch (such as putting a hand on a person's knee or the small of their back) and sexually suggestive remarks. Sexual abuse includes:

- molestation and rape
- showing children or vulnerable adults pornography
- recording consensual sexual activity without permission
- voyeurism—watching others while they are naked, dressing, or having sex without their knowledge or consent
- exhibitionism—revealing one's genitals in public or without the other's consent
- frotteurism—rubbing one's genitals against another person without their consent (e.g., in a crowded subway car)

Application. The Jeffersons moved in next door to Pastor John and his family. Their children were of similar ages, and Susan felt so grateful to have extra support given the tension she felt with Derrick. They spent the whole summer in John's backyard swimming pool, laughing and enjoying one another's company.

The Jefferson's daughter, Josie, was thirteen years old and loved spending time with John's kids. One day, Josie was in John's daughter's bedroom changing out of her bathing suit. John walked in while she was changing; she quickly grabbed her towel to cover up, thinking this was just an embarrassing mistake. John sat on his daughter's bed and told Josie that it was okay and to continue changing. Josie was confused and uncomfortable but thought, he is a pastor; this must be okay. As she took her bathing suit off, John told her how beautiful she was. Josie did not know what to do, so she apprehensively thanked him for the compliment and quickly put her clothes back on.

Josie felt unsure about what happened and wanted to talk to someone about it. She knew her parents loved and defended Pastor John, so she described her experience to her small group leader instead. Her youth leader told her that Pastor John was under a lot of stress and that Josie should wear more modest swimwear to prevent him from "lusting" after her. Josie felt embarrassed but took her mentor's advice to heart. She started wearing a T-shirt and shorts over her swimsuit when they went to John's house to swim. But John continued to watch her change and touched himself while she took her clothes off.

Josie felt ashamed, and she wanted John to stop. She eventually tried telling her mom, Susan. Susan dismissed Josie's concerns, thinking she had to be mistaken and knowing the consequences of accusing the pastor of sexual sin. The abuse continued and eventually escalated to the point where John was regularly raping Josie. One day, Josie's younger brother, James, walked in while John was fondling Josie's breasts. James ran out of the room and immediately told his mom. Susan finally believed Josie.

Susan and Derrick brought the incident to the church elders, hoping they would give advice on how to proceed. The elders told them that this issue should not be taken to the police and must be handled within the church. They said they would talk to Pastor John and put him on administrative leave for one month while he got "treatment." He would then be restored to leadership. Susan and Derrick were encouraged to talk to Josie about God's command to forgive others. They were warned that if they reported the incident to the police, it would be seen as an attempt to disgrace John and the church, and they would be removed from church membership.

This case highlights how sexual abuse flourishes in an environment of complicity. Josie's small group leader justified the pastor's actions, blamed Josie, and disobeyed her legal responsibility to report instances of child abuse. Susan shut down her daughter's plea for help by dismissing her concerns and fearing the personal consequences of speaking against their spiritual leader. The church elders failed to denounce the abuse and initiated a cover-up attempt, using their spiritual authority to silence the victims. Additionally, commanding survivors of abuse to forgive privately without publicly acknowledging the institution's complicity or the perpetrator's responsibility is another form of spiritual abuse (Arms, 2003).

LOOK WITHIN: REFLECTION AND REPENTANCE

It is important that we do not stop at leaning in and learning about how others use their power to harm. It would be a shame if we read this book saying, "Praise God that I do not sin like they do." We all have the ability to use our power to exploit or harm, therefore we must also *look within* and be vigilant about identifying our own sinful tendencies so we can be safe for survivors of abuse. If not conducted in the context of safety, church responses to abuse and attempts to care for victims can cause further harm instead of healing. Victims may experience retraumatization and alienation from churches and other ministry institutions, which hinders their recovery process and potentially causes a systemic rupture throughout the church community. Preventing the retraumatization of abuse victims and preserving the dignity and respect of all trauma survivors begins with a recognition of relational safety.

The Tripod of Relational Safety Model (TRSM) is a comprehensive framework to understand the necessary components for safeguarding vulnerable persons developed by Dr. Gabriel Dy-Liacco. Among his many international roles, Dr. Dy-Liacco was appointed by Pope Francis to the Pontifical Commission for the Protection of Minors (PCPM) as a founding member to directly advise the pope and others on safeguarding issues. TRSM's concept of relational safety refers to a sense of safety people experience when relating with others, including their own selves. When people feel respected, listened to, and free to be their authentic selves, they can interact without fear of threat or harm. Relational safety is required on all levels of human relationships—with self, with others, within institutions, and with God—in order to make a meaningful impact. This comprehensive focus is evident in the three legs of the model: safe self, safe community, and safe ministry (see figure 1). All three components are born out of a relationship with God, which provides a template for goodness and drives our beliefs, meaning making, and values. This model illustrates how each person can manifest God's love to ourselves, each other, and the world.

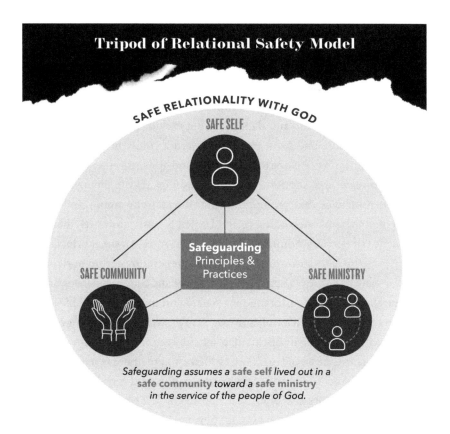

Figure 1. Tripod of Relational Safety Model. Used by permission of Catholic Safeguarding Institute

Safe self. Self-reflection is a key skill for functioning as a safe self. To care for the vulnerable without using power to meet their own needs, safeguarders must develop an awareness of their own wounds, triggers, emotional states, strengths, and challenges. This understanding fosters emotion regulation and self-compassion that enables meaningful and healthy connection with others. If a person has not developed a "safe self," he is at risk of causing harm to himself and others. For example, if a safeguarder experiences intense anxiety at the thought of conflict as a result of unhealthy conflict resolution patterns within her family of origin, she may find herself unwilling to practice courageous confrontation when witnessing signs of abuse. Or if a spiritual leader experiences a deeply felt sense of unworthiness or self-criticism, he might use his spiritual authority to find validation through the obedience of his congregants. The movement toward a safe self is an individual's journey toward personal maturity in all areas of functioning, including thoughts, emotions, sexuality, and spirituality.

Safe community. The safe community functions as a person's home base and a place where members are accepted as their authentic selves. This can include friend groups, family, geographic communities, and religious communities. These groups avoid gossip and slander, do not exclude members based on differences of opinion, and work together toward a common good. These are places where members are free to both rejoice and grieve together, trusting they will receive care and support. Safe communities also implement trauma-informed principles that promote healthy interactions among individuals, groups, and systems. According to the United States' Substance Abuse and Mental Health Services Administration (SAMHSA, 2014), these principles include (1) safety, (2) trustworthiness and transparency, (3) peer support, (4) collaboration and mutuality, (5) empowerment, voice, and choice, and (6) awareness of cultural, gender, and historic issues. Safe communities enforce these principles and act swiftly when a violation occurs to protect the victim. For example, child sexual abuse should be disclosed to law enforcement, and victims of sexual abuse should never be forced to interact with their perpetrator (even a repentant one), whether in the context of a family, community, or church setting.

Safe ministry. Safe selves who are supported by safe communities can then properly engage in safe ministry. Safe ministry involves a "victims-first" approach where individuals, especially those who are vulnerable, are prioritized over ministry projects and reputations. According to Scripture, our Christian service should benefit the most vulnerable members of society. This service should not be motivated by selfish ambition or involve any corruption. James 1:27 confirms this ministry model: "Pure and undefiled religion before God and the Father is this: to visit orphans and widows in their trouble, and to keep oneself unspotted from the world" (NKJV). Safe ministry is a natural overflow of safe selves and safe communities, as it requires leaders and members of faith communities to shepherd, encourage, and advocate for one another without selfish and harmful attempts to meet their own needs.

Safe ministry also involves careful application of theology and "rightly handling the word of truth" (2 Timothy 2:15). According to Rachael Denhollander, attorney and advocate for sexual abuse survivors and the first person to file charges against USA Gymnastics' doctor Larry Nasser, theological distortions elevate the risk of abuse in ministry settings. She highlights the following common areas where ministries may unintentionally misrepresent these good and God-honoring concepts in a way that could make people more vulnerable to abuse and silence victims (Daye, 2019; Vernick, 2023):

- **Unity.** Emphasizing the *agreement* of fellow believers over the pursuit of truth and labeling people who may speak out in dissent as "divisive."
- **Authority.** Emphasizing the *submission* of women and children over personal safety and agency.
- **Conceptualization of sin as ubiquitous.** Emphasizing the concept that *all people sin* over holding those who harm others accountable for their actions.
- **Commission priorities.** Emphasizing the mission to *maximize the number of church attendees* over the mission to protect individuals from harm and provide care for those who have already been wounded.
- **Sufficiency of Scripture.** Emphasizing the use of Scripture as the *totality of counsel* needed to the exclusion of wisdom from other sources (such as doctors) and any community collaboration.
- **Forgiveness and justice.** Emphasizing not only forgiving but also *forgetting, moving on, reconciling*, and *handling matters outside of court* which can silence victims, increase their risk of revictimization, and prevent accountability for perpetrators.
- **Piety.** Emphasizing that Christians should *not gossip* over the church community speaking truth and pursuing understanding and accountability.
- **Faithfulness.** Emphasizing service and loyalty *to the organization and its leaders* over care for individuals, particularly those who are vulnerable and without their voice in their own protection.

Correct teaching on these topics promotes safe ministry culture, while distortions in these theologies allows Scripture to be weaponized for control and harm instead of being used to bring freedom and righteous living as God intended.

CONCLUSION

Will you be a courageous prophet, speaking up for the vulnerable and preserving the integrity of the church? Or will you be like the Pharisees, a "whitewashed tomb" who turns away from injustice toward comfortable religion (Matthew 23:27)? Maya Angelou is attributed with saying, "I did then what I knew how to do. Now that I know better, I do better." This book is intended to lift the veil from our eyes, revealing the places of wickedness that we might know better, and it is designed to equip you to do better through practical skills for preventing abuse and supporting trauma survivors.

> His divine power has granted to us all things that pertain to life and godliness, through the knowledge of him who called us to his own glory and excellence, by which he has granted to us his precious and very great promises, so that through them you may become partakers of the divine nature, having escaped from the corruption that is in the world because of sinful desire. For this very reason, make every effort to supplement your faith with virtue, and virtue with knowledge, and knowledge with self-control, and self-control with steadfastness, and steadfastness with godliness, and godliness with brotherly affection, and brotherly affection with love. For if these qualities are yours and are increasing, they keep you from being ineffective or unfruitful in the knowledge of our Lord Jesus Christ. For whoever lacks these qualities is so nearsighted that he is blind, having forgotten that he was cleansed from his former sins. (2 Peter 1:3-9)

We pray that as you read this text, you will be empowered by God to grow in faith, virtue, knowledge, self-control, steadfastness, godliness, brotherly affection, and love so the church might be effective and fruitful in its ministry as evidence of our salvation in Christ and a reflection of the heart of God.

PERSONAL REFLECTION

1. What thoughts, feelings, and physical sensations did you experience as you read about the Jefferson family? Were there any aspects of their story that were more challenging to read?

2. What personal transformation do you hope to experience as you read this text?

3. Where do you feel tempted to look away from harm or injustice?

GROUP DISCUSSION

1. How does the Tripod of Relational Safety Model reflect God's design for the church?

2. Consider the impact of complicity on the survivors of abuse within the church. How does complicity contribute to their sense of betrayal? What

role can leaders and members of the church play in supporting survivors?

3. Consider the ethical responsibilities of people within the church when confronted with knowledge of abuse. How does Scripture inform how you navigate these situations?

REFERENCES

Arabi, S. (2023). Narcissistic and psychopathic traits in romantic partners predict post-traumatic stress disorder symptomology: Evidence for unique impact in a large sample. *Personality and Individual Differences, 201,* 111942. https://doi.org/10.1016/j.paid.2022.111942

Arms, M. F. (2003). When forgiveness is not the issue in forgiveness: Religious complicity in abuse and privatized forgiveness. *Journal of Religion & Abuse, 4*(4), 107-28. https://doi.org/10.1300/J154v04n04_09

Downie, A. (2022). Christian shame and religious trauma. *Religions, 13*(10), 925. https://doi.org/10.3390/rel13100925

Ellis, H. M., Hook, J. N., Zuniga, S., Hodge, A. S., Ford, K. M., Davis, D. E., & Van Tongeren, D. R. (2022). Religious/spiritual abuse and trauma: A systematic review of the empirical literature. *Spirituality in Clinical Practice, 9*(4), 213-31. https://doi.org/10.1037/scp0000301

Francis, L., & Pearson, D. (2021). The recognition of emotional abuse: Adolescents' responses to warning signs in romantic relationships. *Journal of Interpersonal Violence, 36*(17-18), 8289-313. https://doi.org/10.1177/0886260519850537

Grey, J. (2019). A prophetic call to repentance: David, Bathsheba and a royal abuse of power. *Pneuma, 41*(1), 9-25.

Mellema, G. (2008). Professional ethics and complicity in wrongdoing. *Journal of Markets and Morality, 11*(1), 93-100.

SAMHSA (2014). SAMHSA's concept of trauma and guidance for a trauma-informed approach. HHS Publication No. (SMA) 14-4884. Rockville, MD.

2

ABUSE OF POWER

THE EFFECTS OF ABUSIVE RELATIONSHIPS ON CONSCIENCE

DR. ANGELA RINALDI

ABUSE SURVIVORS' COURAGE in sharing their experiences of manipulation, grooming, and exploitation has sparked a growing awareness of the severe consequences of abuse of power. This has rightfully caught the attention of religious and secular institutions with hierarchical structures, such as universities, churches, schools, workplaces, and others. Abuse flourishes within a system that emphasizes the absolute power of leaders, encourages the unflinching submission and obedience of followers, and avoids meaningful accountability. Because abuse often occurs within a malfunctioning system, safeguarding must include efforts to heal the system through interdisciplinary collaboration. In the church, there is a need for people who help believers think critically about ecclesiology and are able to accompany them through difficult spiritual questions. On the other hand, people also need to be trained to understand the potential corruption of their power and the serious consequences of abuse of power on victims and communities. All people, especially the ones with leadership responsibilities, should have a primary role in actively preventing abuse and caring for trauma victims. In order to effectively improve the culture of the church as a structure, we need to fully understand the concept of power, making also reference to Scripture, deepening some of its anthropological and ethical elements. This chapter will cover the topic of power and the role of the conscience, relational dynamics, and perpetrator grooming.

POWER AND AUTHORITY

Power and authority are two related concepts. Romano Guardini defines power as "the ability to set reality in motion" (1951, p. 118). It involves a person or institution's ability to exercise agency over their circumstances. Plato, in the *Sophist*, defined power as "the ability to influence another or to be influenced by another" (247e). So, it implies the presence of an unbalanced relationship of influence between two persons. But are power and authority the same thing? According to Mounier, "Authority is the foundation of power and power is the visible instrument of authority" (2003, p. 87).[1] In other words, authority is the "source" of power, and this power can be executed by "authorities" who act on behalf of the authority (D'Ambrosio, 2021, p. 20). For example, consider a mother who is cooking dinner while her children play outside. As dinner is nearing completion, she sends out one of her children to gather the rest, instructing them to put their toys away, wash their hands, and get ready for dinner. While the child exercises power as he gathers his siblings, the mother is the authority who has commissioned him to act on her behalf.

For Christians, we could say that the *authority* is God and *authorities* the tradition, institutions, or even people chosen to lead a community (D'Ambrosio, 2021, pp. 20-21). It is not uncommon for individuals and communities to think and accept—perhaps because of the education they have received—that the consecrated or religious leaders are themselves the authority, rather than considering them to be people commissioned by God to act on his behalf. Talking about religious contexts, power is not "ours" but is given by God to men and women through the mandate to "rule" over creation. If the source of power is God, then the way a person exercises power must necessarily be in line with that source. If the child in the previous example used his delegated power to communicate the mother's instructions harshly (or outside the character of her authority) or incorrectly, this would be an inappropriate use of his borrowed power. This is an enormous responsibility for those who hold positions of power in religious (or church) contexts. If they do not exercise their borrowed power in a way that *responds* to others' needs or exigences and is in line with God's teaching, they are misrepresenting the authority's message. Moreover, when that behavior injures the dignity of the person, they should be

---

[1] It has been translated from the Italian version: "l'autorità è il fondamento del potere e il potere è lo strumento visibile dell'autorità."

prosecuted, as Pope Francis says in his Apostolic Letter, "Vos estis lux mundi" (2023, art. 3). Unfortunately, we know from history that this often did not happen, and the abuses still occurring in institutions are proof of this.

Power as responsibility. The use of power as representatives of God has ethical implications that increase people's responsibility to work for the good of others and creation. As we mentioned, humankind was "commissioned" by God to exercise dominion over the earth: "Rule over the fish in the sea and the birds in the sky and over every living creature that moves on the ground" (Genesis 1:28). However, the divine invitation is not solely to "rule over" but to "rule for" goodness and the betterment of all creation.

In *Redeeming Power: Understanding Authority and Abuse in the Church,* Diane Langberg writes,

> Note the stunning omission in God's directive: nowhere does he call humans to rule over each other! The man is not told to rule over the woman; neither is the woman to rule over the man. They are to rule together, in a duet, over all else God has created. They are to take the power God granted them and use it for good. (2020, p. 20)

This responsibility extends to a call to work for the good of the community and to be of help in case of need—a responsibility of each person and all the people in the community. Belonging to the body of Christ—as the church says— implies a personal responsibility for its well-being. Every person and all the people in a community, therefore, are commissioned by God to use their power and influence to work in collaboration with others for the community's flourishing. Honoring the dignity of all humans and upholding our responsibility for their care and protection is at the heart of safeguarding. People who abuse their power to exploit someone deny the victim's inherent dignity and treat her as an instrument for their own personal gratification.

Power as relationship. Power is inherently relational and implies the presence of an unbalanced relationship between two persons within a context or between individuals and institutions. For example, when a pastor or priest communicates to their church members a spiritual truth, they exercise power and influence on the people that will impact the members' thoughts, feelings, and behaviors. Or, when a student exerts her influence by writing a negative evaluation of her teacher, the teacher may change his teaching methods, feel defensive about the feedback, or experience negative consequences with his employer. This relational lens is necessary to properly understand the social role and implications of power. People and institutions do not exercise their agency in a vacuum, but they are in a mutual relationship of influence; the person has power, or agency, to influence the social structure—or the system—and the latter has an influence on the person (Boudon, 1991). As people play their roles in interpersonal relationships, they have the ability to effect change within the community as a whole.

When power is understood in the context of relationships, it is necessary to be aware of vulnerability, which develops within particular contexts where two or more people relate to each other. For example, in a medical context, the physician can evaluate a patient's complaints, assign a diagnosis, and prescribe treatment. In this context, the physician is considered the stronger party (powerful). The physician has the choice to steward this power graciously or wickedly. He can humbly listen to the patient's complaints, gently ask clarifying questions, and commit himself to relieving the patient's suffering. On the other hand, the physician could lord his power over the patient, dismissing her complaints, refusing to treat her ailments, or even causing physical harm. The exercise of power can have positive or negative connotations depending on how the "stronger" side leads in the relationship and so uses his power.

The person who exercises power must be aware of (a) the extent of the power he or she holds, (b) the fact that this power necessarily has effects and consequences to which that person has to be held responsible and accountable, and (c) that this power affects a person who, in that context, is "vulnerable" and therefore can suffer if there is an abusive exercise of power.

This vulnerability has objective and subjective elements. Role and rules are objective elements that may contribute to making a person vulnerable. For example, in structural hierarchies where the rule says that disobeying the superior is forbidden, the "weaker" person in the relationship might be objectively vulnerable. It may also happen between employer and employee or in a parish church between the priest and the faithful. Fear and trust might be considered subjective elements of vulnerability. For example, in the case of personal relationships, it might occur that a child completely trusts his mother, accepting everything she says as the truth. In this case, the mother holds a power that is almost "absolute," and might use it to harm the child. This kind of vulnerability may also occur between two friends where one of them discloses some problems or issues; the other can misuse this trust and make his friend feel ashamed, and so on. In church environments, it may happen not only in one-to-one relationships, like the trust a faithful member feels for a priest or a sister, but also when the church member is led to accept everything the priests/religious people say as the truth. That creates a vulnerability in the members. Power and vulnerability are inherent in all of our relationships and, when stewarded appropriately, create opportunities for meaningful connection and trust building. However, when power is abused, it harms the vulnerable ones, making them more and more vulnerable and at risk of being abused.

Everyone experiences varying degrees of vulnerability in relationships. That vulnerability increases when there is a larger power differential. As vulnerability increases, a person's agency to resist the various forms of abuse decreases. Depending on the significance of the power differential in a relationship, the vulnerable person is at risk of being in a situation where it is impossible to say no or oppose possible abuse. The wider the power differential, the more responsibility the stronger party has to steward their power faithfully. For example, in a one-to-one relationship where one person has significant spiritual authority, as in the case of spiritual accompaniment, an abusive use of power can have more weight and harsher consequences, making the gap between the powerful person and the one accompanied higher and so dangerous.

Even safeguarders can exercise significant power in their interactions with abuse survivors. Consider the following scenario:

> A young man, Mario, nervously approaches the parish safeguarding officer after a Sunday church service. He sees Mario fidget uncomfortably and asks if he needs to speak. Mario tells the safeguarder that he is scared to speak in the church and that he wants to do it in a neutral environment. The safeguarder tells Mario that he is in a hurry and would prefer Mario to just tell him now. Mario begins to cry, disclosing his experience of a local priest making sexual advances. He tells the safeguarder he is the only person he has told because he feels so ashamed. The safeguarder knows the priest personally and is not sure if he believes Mario. Moreover, the safeguarder is worried that if Mario's words are true, he will be perceived as a traitor for exposing the church. He tells Mario that he may have misunderstood the priest's actions and to stay away from the priest if he feels uncomfortable around him.

Thinking about Mario's vulnerability and the power exerted by the safeguarder, we can state that (a) Mario had the courage to approach the safeguarder with the goal of seeking comfort in his distress; (b) Mario attempted to exercise his agency requesting to meet more privately; (c) the safeguarder was in a position to exercise a stronger influence and insisted Mario disclose in a context in which he felt exposed. As Mario shares his experience with the priest, he is searching for someone who will listen to him. A safeguarder has the power to comfort Mario and gently empower him to discern his next steps. Instead, in this case, this opportunity to collaboratively promote Mario's well-being and the good of the community was lost due to fear of personal consequences, perhaps related to a lack of formation or awareness.

ABUSE OF POWER AND IMPLICATIONS ON THE CONSCIENCE

To engage with the impact of abuse on a person's body, mind, and spirit, we first need to identify the impact of the abuse of power on a person's conscience. The abuse of power, especially in relationships that are supposed to be safe and trustworthy, can disrupt the relationship of trustworthiness and confidence with God.

Conscience as a place where the relationship with God develops. To properly understand the significant impact of abuse of power, it is necessary to define what the conscience is. Due to the aim of this book, we view the conscience through a Christian lens, but it might be interesting to investigate how other contexts reflect on and explain what conscience is.

Pius XII defines the conscience as "the most secret core and sanctuary of a man" (1965, n. 16).[2] Using the term "sanctuary" highlights the conscience as the site of the encounter between God and the person. This emphasizes the depth and intimacy of such a "sanctuary," and thus, the importance of it remaining intact. The conscience also has moral values and guides a person's choices, informed by his commitment to being virtuous and doing good. It is necessary to protect and safeguard the integrity of conscience.

According to the church's theology, God is the source of good, and the conscience is the place where God speaks (Guardini, 1987, p. 45). There, the person develops his perception of right and wrong, even following the Scriptures and Christ as a model, and it is also the place where God guides the person through the Holy Spirit. Therefore, if for Christians the goal of life is to follow God's teachings, then it is in conscience itself that the person experiences a

---

[2]It has been translated from the Italian version: "La coscienza è come il nucleo più intimo e segreto dell'uomo."

relationship with God and guidance in life. Guardini says: "Conscience is, therefore, the organ for the eternal need for good. . . . Conscience is for a man like a window open on eternity" (1933, p. 26).[3] God provided human beings with a conscience to always be in contact and in relationship with him. Within this relationship, we may say that God exercises power and offers a model to follow: to accompany people to reflect, discern, and decide freely and responsibly. It is on this basis and for these purposes that power should be used: to honor people's responsibility and self-determination (agency) so that in full freedom they are empowered to act in accordance with the moral law and their conscience.

Relational dynamics of abuse. As stated, the conscience develops in a relationship with God, and power is always exercised in relationships with other people, even within institutions. Similarly, abuse occurs within the context of a relationship, and this relationship typically has specific patterns or characteristics related to the context and the people in it. Before elaborating more on perpetrator dynamics and grooming tactics, it is important to understand how power can be used to create particular abusive relationship dynamics and the subsequent impact on the victim and community's conscience.

The World Health Organization's (WHO) definition of child abuse provides a helpful framework for understanding how abuse occurs:

> all forms of physical and/or emotional ill-treatment, sexual abuse, neglect or negligent treatment or commercial or other exploitation, resulting in actual or potential harm to the child's health, survival, development or dignity in the context of a relationship of responsibility, trust or power. (2006, p. 9)

This definition recognizes the use of power to cause a vulnerable person harm; we can also broaden this definition to include vulnerable adults and abuse that occurs in relationships with a wide power differential, such as priests and adult parishioners.

Abuse develops over time within the context of a relationship, through the use of grooming tactics. Grooming begins with the perpetrator's decision to approach a minor or a vulnerable adult with the goal of using his or her power and influence to get to know the victim, build trust, and slowly overstep the boundaries of appropriate relationships for their own selfish gain. Anna Deodato, in her book *I Would Like to Rise Again from My Wounds: Consecrated*

---

[3] It has been translated from the Italian version: "La coscienza è dunque l'organo per l'eterna esigenza del bene. . . . La coscienza è per l'uomo come una finestra aperta sull'eternità."

Women and Sexual Abuse (2016, pp. 21-22), describes three forms of grooming: physical, psychological, and communal. Physical grooming involves the perpetrator physically touching the victim, at first in an acceptable, nonsexual way, so as to nurture trust and familiarity with the victim. As trust develops, the perpetrator intensifies the physical touch until it leads to sexual contact. Psychological grooming occurs when the perpetrator provides excessive attention and care to the victim, showing empathy and understanding to create a sense of dependence. Communal grooming occurs when the perpetrator projects an overall positive image of himself to the community to ensure that if the abuse is discovered, the community is prone to disbelieve the victim. This can be especially potent when the perpetrator is charismatic and has a measure of spiritual authority.

In the case of clergy abuse, perpetrators often misuse Scripture to draw in the victim and excuse their abusive behavior and initiating the dynamics that lead to spiritual abuse. When perpetrators have spiritual authority, victims see them as authoritative interpreters of the sacred text. This position of power is exploited to manipulate victims' understanding of Scripture, leading them to believe that it is according to the sacred text itself that the abuse occurs and that it is the will of God. In spiritual abuse, doctrine and Scriptures are also used to silence victims and isolate them from the rest of the community so that the perpetrator goes unpunished and the abuse continues. When leaders use this borrowed power to manipulate and exploit others, they invade the healthy relationship that the person has with God, who is the source of power. This has a severe impact on the conscience of the victim.

Impact of abuse on conscience: Is God still speaking? As the perpetrator uses his spiritual authority to manipulate the victim, he makes her question her judgment and "normalize" what is abnormal. The victim finds herself accepting what she would otherwise never accept. This manipulation of conscience makes the victim completely dependent on the perpetrator. The perpetrator not only subjugates victims in the name of God but also assumes the authoritative position of God himself. If, as previously mentioned, the conscience is the place where the person is free to relate to God, discern right from wrong, and decide responsibly, then abuse of power by church ministries or trustworthy church people is a severe violation of this "sanctuary." The integrity of the conscience can be lost. We might wonder: Is God still speaking since those people are replacing God's voice?

A significant aspect of a survivor's healing from the abuse of power is a process toward regaining confidence in the distinction between the voice of God and the voice of the perpetrator, reestablishing the integrity of the conscience, and recovering a healthy relationship with the divinity.

The impact of abuse on agency. Grooming and abuse affect not only the victim's ability to discern the voice and character of God but also their sense of agency or confidence in their ability to use their power to impact their circumstances and act to improve the social structure. In the case of manipulation of conscience, the victim's responsibility, agency, and self-determination are violated with possibly extreme effects on their awareness and ability to relate with other people in their community, make responsible and free decisions, and build relationships that promote their own and their community's well-being. Survivors of abuse may experience a feeling of helplessness and worthlessness, evidence of the stolen confidence in their God-given power. This feeling of powerlessness can restrict their ability to exercise agency and also impact the way they relate and connect with God, others, and themselves. The consequences on faith and trust toward God and the church are evident, even looking at the church abuse history of the past few decades.

All this might be a great loss to the community. The Scripture says that "if one part of the body suffers, all the other parts suffer with it" (1 Corinthians 12:26 NLV). So, if a communitarian commitment to the empowerment of victims is lacking, the whole community ends up suffering. One important aspect of safeguarding is empowering the survivor to exercise their power and influence on the social structure to move toward personal healing and contribute to the community's healing and development. This is not to say that survivors are ready or obligated to serve in the church as they heal from abuse; rather, the goal is to empower survivors with renewed hope for thriving in their mission for themselves and within their community.

The impact of abuse on communities: The abusive system. Abuse is a complex phenomenon that involves not only the victim and the perpetrator but also all the people, conditions, contexts, and experiences that might contribute to an environment which fosters and enables the abuse. All families, institutions, and organizations have complex relational dynamics and social norms that function as a *system*. These systems can contribute either to a culture of health that protects and empowers the vulnerable or a culture of exploitation that enables the use of power to manipulate the vulnerable for selfish gain. Even though leaders can have a large effect on the culture of a system, all participants play a role and therefore have some measure of power and influence over the culture. For all members of a system, the challenge is to contribute to cultivating a culture of safeguarding by committing themselves to the common good.

When abuse occurs, it is not only the perpetrator and the abused who are involved; the whole community is affected in some way, potentially to the point of being considered *secondary victims*. Environments that are conducive to the abuse of power are characterized by fear of excommunication, forced silence by the perpetrator, institutional protection of perpetrators, emphasis on blind obedience, fear of being judged as an enemy of the church or God, and rigid adherence to rules. In religious institutions where abuse happens, the system often leverages its divine message to institute a culture of silence regarding reporting and accountability. Taking advantage of the faith and trust of the members, the abusive system cultivates an exaggerated sense of belonging, which leads to the idealization of the institution and severe consequences for contradicting its message. Speaking against the institution is conflated with speaking against God. Abuse impacts the conscience not only of the victim but also of the whole community.

When we consider the abuse crisis in the Catholic church, we must recognize the ongoing abuse of minors and vulnerable people that is still occurring *and* the institutional trust crisis that resulted from a historical lack of action and accountability (Rinaldi & Zollner, 2022). Over the years, the church has not faced the abuse crisis transparently and truthfully, resulting in various consequences. These consequences are magnified in the Catholic church given the scope and duration of the abuse crisis; however, there are similar effects within other denominations and religious institutions. Religious systems that refuse accountability have the following characteristics:

1. Confusion between the church as an institution and the church as the people of God. This is both the cause and effect of the abuse crisis. A distorted belief system that gives higher dignity to religious leaders than lay people creates a culture in which perpetrators have unhindered access to vulnerable populations and victims are silenced by systemic coverups, all in the name of preserving the good name of the church.

2. Impunity of perpetrators and religious leaders. The abusive religious system protects the perpetrators at the expense of the victims by using their power to protect themselves and the institution and sacrificing the truth and victims' safety. The victims and the people of God have paid and continue to pay the costs of religious leaders' refusal to hold one another accountable.

3. Repeated attempts of the religious leadership to defend the institution in the media. Various media agencies have publicly exposed abuse crises. In response, many members of the church have contributed to demonizing these channels with the sole aim of defending the religious institution so that it is not at the center of "media earthquakes." This has contributed to polarization within the public. There are those who remain blindly faithful to the institution and its doctrine, disregarding the suffering experienced by the victims. On the other hand, many people have left the church feeling disillusioned by its teaching and betrayed by its leaders.

Though there is a history of severe abuses of power by religious leaders, we can also feel hopeful about the work some religious institutions are doing to raise awareness among the people. Over the past decade, we have seen significant advances in the church's consciousness of the dangers of absolute authority, the horrific consequences of abuse, and effective policies for preventing abuse. There is still much work to do, which is why we must raise up safeguarders—as professional figures—who are committed to protecting the vulnerable and preventing abuses.

SAFEGUARDING: A WAY FOR PREVENTION

Safeguarding is a call to care for others and the good and healthy culture of our institutions. It should be seen as common responsibility to contribute to the common good in the systems in which we live and work. Safeguarding not only is understood as the protection of vulnerable people from potential abuse but also implies the creation of systems where personal and institutional relations work in the opposite direction of abusive systems—cultivating good. Therefore, if abusive systems have thrived in silence, coverups, and deceit, safeguarding is instead committed to preventing abuses, communicating with transparency, developing healthy relationships, uncovering taboos, and revealing the truth. In order to effectively accomplish this, safeguarders must be trained on the risk factors and consequences of abuse, use their power for the good of the vulnerable ones, and recognize that every person within a system has a responsibility to contribute to a culture of goodness and safety. Safeguarding in these areas requires the assumption of responsibility by every person, not only the people directly involved in abuse but the whole community, so that anyone who may hold a position of vulnerability is valued and protected. It is a matter of being committed to contributing to systems and communities in which the principles, rules, and practices inspired by safeguarding are introduced in everyday life—protecting vulnerable people, healing from past trauma, and preventing future abuses. The path is long and requires a lifelong commitment.

PERSONAL REFLECTION

1. Identify a few of your relationships in which there is a significant power differential. In the relationships in which you are the more powerful, where do you feel tempted to use your power for your own gain? How can you steward your power more faithfully?

2. In relationships in which you are less powerful, how do you feel when the other's power is used for their own gain? How do you feel when their power is used for your good?

3. Where have you seen power and authority misused in the church, workplace, or family contexts? Where have you seen power and authority used to serve the more vulnerable?

GROUP DISCUSSION

1. Describe the relationship and distinction between power and authority.

2. Consider the discussion on power and conscience. How can abuse from spiritual leadership impact the victim's experience of their relationship with God?

3. How can safeguarders empower abuse survivors to regain agency?

REFERENCES

Boudon, R. (1991). Azione sociale. In *Enciclopedia delle scienze sociali*. Rome: Istituto della Enciclopedia Italiana. www.treccani.it/enciclopedia/azione-sociale_(Enciclopedia-delle-scienze-sociali)

Cabrera Martín, Y. (2020), Algunos factores macrosistémicos que pueden influir en la victimización sexual de los niños. In R. Meana Peón & C. Martínez García (Eds.), *Abuso y sociedad contemporánea. Reflexionaes multidisciplinares* (pp. 133-71). Aranzadi.

D'Ambrosio, R. (2021). *Il potere. Uno spazio inquieto*. Castelvecchi.

Deodato, A. (2016). *Vorrei risorgere dalle mie ferite. Donne consacrate e abusi sessuali*. EDB.

Figueroa, R., & Tombs, T. (2022). Spiritual abuse: A case study of the servant of God's plan. *The Canonist: Journal of the Canon Law Society of Australia and New Zealand, 13*(2), 243-63.

Finkelhor, D. (1995). The victimization of children: A developmental perspective. *American Journal of Orthopsychiatry, 65*(2), 177-93.

Guardini, R. (1933). *La coscienza*. Morcelliana.

Guardini, R. (1951). *La fine dell'epoca moderna. Il potere*. Morcelliana.

Guardini, R., (1987). *Accettare se stessi*. Brescia: Morcelliana.

Langberg, D. (2020). *Redeeming power. Understanding authority and abuse in the church*. Brazos Press.

López Quintás, A. (1987). *El secuestro del lenguaje. Tácticas de manipulación del hombre*. Asociación para el progreso de las ciencias humanas.

Mounier, E. (2003). *Anarchia e personalismo*. Ecumenica.

Oakley, L., & Humphreys, J. (2018). *Escaping the maze of spiritual abuse: Creating healthy Christian cultures*. SPCK.

Pacheco Romero, J. (2019). Cuidado y protección de niñas, niños y adolescentes. *Revista CLAR*, n. 2, 18-23.

Plato, *La Repubblica*, libro IV, 41c.

Plato, *Sofista* 247e.

Pope Francis (2023). *Apostolic Letter, Motu Proprio, Vos Estis Lux Mundi*. https://www.vatican.va/content/francesco/en/motu_proprio/documents/20230325-motu-proprio-vos-estis-lux-mundi-aggiornato.html

Pope Pius XII (1952). *Radiomessaggio in occasione della giornata della famiglia*. www.vatican.va/content/pius-xii/it/speeches/1952/documents/hf_p-xii_spe_19520323_la-culla.html

Rinaldi, A., & Zollner, H., SJ. (2022). The abuse crisis. In G. Bellido (Ed.). *A church in dialogue: The art and science of church communication* (pp. 213-28). Santa Croce Editions.

Weber, M. (2004). *Il lavoro intellettuale come professione. Due saggi*. Einaudi.

WHO & International Society for Prevention of Child Abuse and Neglect (2006). *Preventing child maltreatment: A guide to taking action and generating evidence*. www.who.int/publications/i/item/preventing-child-maltreatment-a-guide-to-taking-action-and-generating-evidence

SECTION II

ABUSE SYSTEMS, DYNAMICS, AND ORIGINS

THE FOLLOWING FOUR CHAPTERS PROVIDE SPECIFIC examples of how power and coercion can lead to abusive actions. These chapters are a collection of different lenses from expert authors and meant to enhance the reader's understanding of safeguarding from multiple angles. While we believe that specific examples provide practical ways to conceptualize the knowledge learned thus far, there is also the potential that readers will consider these as the only issues the church must face. As we emphasized in chapter one, we encourage you to lean in and consider the various applications of these topics in your church community and your personal lives.

Chapter three highlights the breadth of clergy-child sexual abuse in the Catholic church and the historic use of cover-up. However, assuming that this issue only exists in the Catholic church and not across Protestant denominations would be far from accurate. Although Protestant ministries such as Mars Hill, Chi Alpha, and RZIM have had public scandals, and the celebrity status of many Protestant leaders has stimulated an environment ripe for abuse of power, there is still little research in this area (Graham, 2021; Kyle, 2023; Welch, 2016; Witt et al., 2022).

Chapter four explores abuse from a systems perspective. The chapter provides details on the increased risk of abuse within closed systems and the role of attachment within traumatic situations. The two main areas of focus in this systems chapter are sexual abuse within family systems and clergy sexual abuse within ministry systems, and the provided examples illustrate the impact of sexual abuse on families and church communities. Ideally, the reader will recognize how other forms of abuse such as physical, emotional, and spiritual can all occur in these settings and result in similar devastation.

Chapter five covers the characteristics and dynamics of perpetrators. This information is useful in identifying risk factors, conceptualizing perpetrating behaviors, and highlighting the risk of reoffending. While the chapter primarily focuses on adults who commit sexual abuse against children, some of the same traits are evident in adults who engage in various forms of abuse with both minors and adults.

Chapter six explores the topic of sexual morality and how evangelical purity culture used some harmful and manipulative methods to control behaviors in young people in order to achieve abstinence. The principles concerning sexual scripts are important for people of all ages to consider their own sexual scripts and how those impact their beliefs and actions around sexuality. The information is also imperative for education and training programs in families and ministry settings to consider how to share biblical truths using a noncoercive approach. While the emphasis of the chapter is on sexual scripts related to evangelical purity culture, it is valuable to recognize potential distortions in biblical sexuality in various cultural groups and denominations. Additionally, sexual morality and biblical sexual scripts are important throughout the lifespan, not only in singleness.

The goal of dedicating these chapters primarily to the topic of sexual abuse among ministry leaders is not necessarily to tear down clerical systems but to preserve the church. We must not allow abuse of power to run rampant at the hands of those commissioned to represent God and his character. Abuse extends beyond a discussion of sinfulness. We have all sinned, and no one leader is perfect or without weaknesses. However, clergy sexual abuse represents patterns of exploitation, lack of sincere repentance, shunning of meaningful accountability, and a sense of entitlement to a position of leadership. We encourage you to read these chapters with the perspective that coercion and abuse of power could manifest in a variety of ways in any family, ministry, or societal setting.

REFERENCES

Graham, R. (Feb. 11, 2021). Ravi Zacharias, influential evangelist, is accused of sexual abuse in scathing report. *New York Times.* www.nytimes.com/2021/02/11/us/ravi-zacharias-sexual-abuse.html

Kyle, M. (Oct. 16, 2023). More charges added against sex offender linked to ex-Baylor Chi Alpha minister's arrest. *Waco-Tribune-Herald.* https://wacotrib.com/news/local/crime-courts/daniel-savala-sexual-assault-charge-chris-hundl-chi-alpha-baylor-university-sam-houston-state/article_6d5e43d4-6c42-11ee-b1c7-973dd2ef363e.html

Welch, C. (Feb. 4, 2016). The rise and fall of Mars Hill Church. *The Seattle Times.* www.seattletimes.com/seattle-news/the-rise-and-fall-of-mars-hill-church

Witt, A., Brähler, E., Plener, P. L., & Fegert, J. M. (2022). Different contexts of sexual abuse with a special focus on the context of Christian institutions: Results from the general population in Germany. *Journal of Interpersonal Violence, 37*(5-6), NP3130-NP3151. https://doi.org/10.1177/0886260519888540

3

CHILD SEXUAL ABUSE IN THE CATHOLIC CHURCH

UNDERSTANDING THE NATURE OF THE ABUSE CRISIS

DR. KAREN J. TERRY

THOUGH CHILD SEXUAL ABUSE within the Catholic church is not a new phenomenon, the scale of the sexual abuse crisis in the United States was exposed to the public in 2002. It was at this time that the case of John Geoghan in Boston was headline news. Geoghan was accused of abusing more than 130 children across six parishes over three decades. He was eventually defrocked and convicted of one count of indecent child assault, and while serving his prison sentence was murdered by a fellow inmate. Though his case was extreme, it was the catalyst for an ensuing media frenzy that led survivors to come forward in record numbers to report their cases of sexual abuse. The *Boston Globe*, *New York Times*, and *LA Times* together published more than two thousand articles in that year alone on the sexual abuse crisis in the church (Terry, 2008). The *Boston Globe* even published a special Spotlight series highlighting the extent of the sexual abuse crisis and the insufficient responses to the abuse by the church leaders (Carroll et al., 2002). As Catholic communities, survivors' groups, and the general public were seeking to understand how such a crisis could occur, the church was grappling with the need for more information about the crisis itself. As such, the church commissioned two studies to address these issues: one on the nature and scope of the crisis and a second on the causes and context of it. Scholars from John Jay College were selected to conduct this research, and subsequently published multiple reports (John Jay College, 2004, 2006; Terry et al., 2011) and articles (Criminal Justice & Behavior, 2008) on the topic.

In the years since these publications, further investigations have been published about the sexual abuse crisis nationally and in other countries. In the United States, the Center for the Applied Research of the Apostolate (CARA) has collected information from dioceses annually about the allegations of sexual abuse. Additionally, several states have initiated grand jury reports or investigations to better understand what happened in specific jurisdictions. Globally, many countries have commissioned extensive investigations to conceptualize what happened and how the church has responded to sexual abuse allegations. Reports from Canada, the United Kingdom, Ireland, Belgium, the Netherlands, Australia, Germany, Poland, France, and New Zealand show similar patterns of behavior to the United States regarding sexual abuse within the Catholic community. These reports also make many recommendations about how the church can better respond to survivors.

This chapter summarizes what is currently known about the sexual abuse crisis in the Catholic church in the United States and other countries. The focus is twofold: to explain what is known about the nature of the sexual abuse crisis and to outline the steps the church has taken to prevent and respond to the abuse. Though the church's response to the sexual abuse of minors has shifted significantly over the last twenty years, diocesan leaders must continue to study the shortcomings of their responses and work to create safe environments for the most vulnerable individuals within the community.

THE JOHN JAY STUDIES: A COMPREHENSIVE EVALUATION OF THE ABUSE CRISIS

In June 2002, at the height of reporting about sexual abuse in the church, the US Conference of Catholic Bishops (USCCB) created the *Charter for the Protection of Young People* (hereafter the *Charter*). The primary goal of the *Charter* was to identify ways to better understand and address the problem of child sexual abuse by Catholic priests. As part of this goal, the bishops agreed to support two studies and commissioned scholars from John Jay College to conduct this research. The mandate of the first study was to help understand the nature and scope of the sexual abuse crisis, focusing specifically on the characteristics and extent of sexual abuse, the characteristics of abusers and victims, and the financial impact on the Catholic church. This became known as the *Nature and Scope* study and was the first comprehensive study of child sexual abuse in the Catholic church worldwide. The 2006 report addressed issues in more detail, including the estimation of the overall problem and patterns of sexual abuse in the church, duration of abusive behavior, priests with one allegation compared to priests with multiple allegations, and the institutional response to the sexual abuse problem. The second study noted in the *Charter,* known as the *Causes and Context,* provided an in-depth account of how and why the church was experiencing the sexual abuse crisis (Terry et al., 2011).

The *Nature and Scope* study provided an important overview of the extent of the crisis (John Jay College, 2004). Data showed that, as of 2002, approximately four percent of priests in ministry had allegations of sexual abuse against nearly 11,000 minors. The majority of those sexually abused were male (81 percent) and between 11 to 14 years of age. Two-thirds of the sexual abusers were diocesan priests, often with a lengthy duration of abusive behavior. Fifty-five percent of the abusive priests had a single known allegation of sexual abuse, and just over three percent had ten or more victims. Three percent of abusive priests were responsible for approximately 26 percent of all the known abuse. The peak of the abuse crisis was in the 1970s and early 1980s, at which point there was a steep decline in known cases of abuse. Many survivors waited years, often decades, to report their abuse. Although recent reports of abuse continue to show that the abuse incidents peaked in the 1970s and 1980s, there are still cases of abuse that occur each year.

While the *Nature and Scope* data provided an overview of *what* happened, the *Causes and Context* study analyzed factors that could help explain *why* it happened. Findings showed that the sexual abuse crisis was a complex phenomenon that developed through a combination of factors, including the individual characteristics of the abusers, the situational factors that provided opportunities for the abuse, and the organizational structure and culture of the church (Terry et al., 2011).

To help understand the sexual abuse from an individual perspective, the researchers evaluated psychological data of priests with allegations of sexual abuse compared to those without allegations of sexual abuse. The data showed that priests with allegations of sexual abuse did not differ significantly from non-abusers in IQ or personality and mood disorders. Additionally, less than five percent were diagnosed pedophiles (individuals with a strong sexual attraction to prepubescent children). In fact, 80 percent of child sexual abusers had also had sexual relationships with adults at some point. While there was much speculation about the sexual identity of abusive priests, given the high percentage of male victims, the data showed that homosexual orientation alone was not a significant predictor of the sexual abuse of minors. Rather, the priests who abused had substantially higher access to boys than girls (e.g., as altar boys, on recreational trips, etc.). The priests who were at the highest risk to sexually abuse were those that lacked close social bonds and exhibited a delayed psychosexual development.

Societal and organizational factors also played a role in the sexual abuse crisis. The *Nature and Scope* data indicated an increase in sexual abuse cases from the 1960s to 1970s, which coincided with changing social and cultural norms. Additionally, the post-war expansion of seminaries did not provide prospective priests with an adequate understanding of human formation, and those with high individual risk factors were, therefore, unprepared for the challenges they faced. The structure of the church, whereby priests often lived alone in parishes with little oversight, created opportunities for sexual abuse to occur. Plus, priests experienced unique levels of power, trust, and reverence in society, and abusive priests often took advantage of that status to exploit the youths to whom they had access. This reverent status is one factor that led to the reluctance of victims to report that sexual abuse occurred.

When victims did report sexual abuse, the response from the church was often inadequate, lacked transparency, and failed to address the harm caused to the victims (Terry et al., 2011). The response of the church to allegations of sexual abuse was not static, however, and in fact evolved over time. A critical year of change was 1985, when the high-profile case of Gilbert Gauthe gained widespread attention. The public was shocked to learn that Gauthe, a priest in the diocese of Lafayette at the time, admitted to sexually abusing thirty-seven children and was sentenced to ten years in prison. The high-profile nature of the Gauthe case led to the first spike in reports of sexual abuse by priests. Only 840 cases of sexual abuse had been reported to dioceses before 1985, even though much of the abuse that is now known had already occurred. In cases reported before 1985, the main focus of diocesan leaders was to help the priests, frequently neglecting any care for the victims. They would send abusers for spiritual or psychological treatment and then often return them to ministry, even though such treatment was not shown to be effective at reducing sexually abusive behaviors. For example, 35 percent of priests with allegations of abuse between 1950 and 1979 were reprimanded and returned to ministry (John Jay College, 2004). However, by 2000, most diocesan leaders knew better than to return sexually abusive priests to ministry, with only four percent taking such an action. Alternatively, the percentage of priests given administrative leave and not returned to ministry increased every decade from the 1950s to 2000s.

Because of the church's lack of response on an institutional level to victims, advocates outside of the church began to work together to try to understand the problem of sexual abuse and respond to the needs of sexual abuse survivors. In the 1980s, as the church was just beginning to assess its own response strategies to sexual abuse, survivors started forming organizations such as the Survivors' Network of those Abused by Priests (SNAP) and Voice of the Faithful (VOTF), but there was still little observable shift in the response to sexual abuse in the church until the next crisis occurred in 1993. At that time, James Porter was arrested for the sexual abuse of more than two dozen children (though he later admitted to sexually abusing more than 100), and the publicity around his shocking case led to the second spike in reporting of abuse. This case also led to renewed discussions among the bishops on how to respond when allegations of sexual abuse were made against priests. They formed an ad hoc committee on sexual abuse and in 1994 released the first of three volumes on restoring trust (Bishops Ad Hoc Committee, 1994), which identified Five Principles (p. 4):

1. Respond promptly to all allegations of abuse where there is reasonable belief that abuse has occurred.

2. If such an allegation is supported by sufficient evidence, relieve the alleged offender promptly of his ministerial duties and refer him for appropriate medical evaluation and intervention.

3. Comply with the obligations of civil law regarding reporting of the incident and cooperating with the investigation.

4. Reach out to the victims and their families and communicate sincere commitment to their spiritual and emotional well-being.

5. Within the confines of respect for privacy of the individuals involved, deal as openly as possible with the members of the community.

Unfortunately, despite the good intentions of the ad hoc committee, diocesan leaders did not implement the five principles consistently and evenly across dioceses, and by 2002, few bishops even knew what the five principles were. Even after the publication of *Restoring Trust*, diocesan leaders continued to primarily focus on priests instead of victims and failed to meet with victims directly. They rarely followed up on reports of sexual abuse and continued to return some priests to ministry after they completed treatment. Leaders continued to handle most cases of sexual abuse through internal mechanisms except for the most severe cases of serial sexual abusers. A few leaders, including cardinals, stated under oath that they had no knowledge of sexual abuse within their dioceses even though cases had been reported to them by that time.

After the storm of reports in 2002 and the affirmation of the *Charter*, meaningful change finally began to happen. Dioceses have now implemented safe environment training and education for the community, and they have external audits to ensure dioceses are complying with these requirements. They have victim advocates and lay review boards, and some have implemented restorative processes for survivors. Most dioceses in the United States have released to the public the names of all credibly accused priests, and leaders in the highest positions of power are now being held accountable for their inadequate responses to sexual abuse decades earlier. Since 2019, two cardinals have been removed from office by laicization (Theodore McCarrick) or resignation (Donald Wuerl) because of allegations of sexual abuse against them or their inadequate responses to sexual abuse, respectively. Despite these unprecedented actions against church leaders, the church must continue to work on changing the culture so that all diocesan leaders respond to sexual abuse reports immediately, fully, and transparently.

THE SEXUAL ABUSE CRISIS TODAY: WHAT IS NOW KNOWN IN THE UNITED STATES AND GLOBALLY

Though the John Jay studies are valuable for providing the initial information about the sexual abuse crisis in the United States, much more information has emerged both in the United States and globally since the publication of the *Nature and Scope* and *Causes and Context* studies. In the United States, the Center for the Applied Research of the Apostolate (CARA) has continued to collect information from dioceses annually about the allegations of sexual abuse (Secretariat of Child and Youth Protection, 2023). Several states have initiated grand jury investigations (e.g., Pennsylvania and Colorado) or investigations through the attorney general's office (e.g., Illinois, Florida, Missouri). Regarding the nature and scope of the problem of sexual abuse in the church, the findings from CARA and the state investigations are consistent with what was found in the *Nature and Scope* study concerning the distribution of sexual abuse events over time, the gender and age of victims, and the number of known victims per offender. In other words, the incidence of sexual abuse rises in the 1960s, peaks in the 1970s and early 1980s, and then experiences a sharp decline. The priests accused of abuse are primarily diocesan and serve as parish priests, and the victims of abuse were predominantly males between the ages of 11 and 14.

Throughout the early 2000s, the sexual abuse of children by Catholic priests was almost exclusively viewed as a US problem. This is despite the fact that similar patterns of sexual abuse were evident in Canadian Catholic dioceses prior to this time (Kenny, 2012), though the Canadian crisis garnered far less media attention. By 2010, however, the reports began to emerge about sexual abuse by Catholic priests in South America, Europe, and Australasia. To date, commissions, research, and investigations have led to extensive reports on sexual abuse in Canada, the United Kingdom, Ireland, Belgium, the Netherlands, Austria, Australia, Germany, Poland, France, New Zealand, and even the Vatican. These studies and commissions have led to similar findings about the nature of sexual abuse incidents and organizational responses to the sexual abuse, as well as recommendations for abuse prevention.

All of these studies, reports, and commissions have varying methodologies and time frames. Not all provide data on the percentage of abusive priests in their respective study time periods. However, findings that have been published show similarities regarding the scope of the problem, the distribution of events over time, the delay in disclosure of reporting sexual abuse, the gender and age of victims, the characteristics of abusers, and the situations in which the sexual abuse occurred.[1]

---

[1] The one outlier in regard to number of estimated victims is the Sauvé report in France. Using a different methodology, they estimated that 330,000 individuals have been sexually victimized by members of the church. When looking at the number of alleged sexual abusers, it means they estimate each priest abused more than 100 victims on average.

Perhaps most importantly, all of these reports address the church's response to abuse and the organizational factors that put children at risk of being sexually abused. Every report notes that the church has not responded adequately to individual victims or the sexual abuse crisis generally. Many reports stated that the culture and power dynamics of the Catholic church, as well as the lack of oversight of parish priests, leads to an increased risk of child sexual abuse. Diocesan leaders have much discretion in how they respond to any given situation within the diocese, and their power to make nearly unilateral decisions was rarely questioned. Because of these factors, diocesan leaders have been able to cover up sexual abuse and transfer accused priests to different parishes and dioceses without disclosing the allegations against them. In many cases, diocesan leaders failed to initiate canon law proceedings, and even when such proceedings did occur, the outcome took years to implement. Combined with that are the situational factors that created opportunities for sexual abuse, such as the fact that priests had been able to spend time alone with youths.

In addressing the church's inadequate response to sexual abuse, the reports have identified several factors of particular concern. The reports note that the church tended to respond to allegations of sexual abuse internally rather than through civil authorities. In many cases this involved sending the priest for treatment and then reinstating him, as was done in the United States. Many of the reports argued that they did so to protect the church's reputation and assets. Whatever the response was from diocesan leaders, it lacked transparency to the victims and the community generally. Most importantly, the focus was almost always on the sexually abusive priest, with little attention ever paid to the harm caused to the victims.

RECOMMENDATIONS FOR REFORM

Reports from the United States and around the world have issued a variety of recommendations on how to prevent sexual abuse and respond appropriately when abuse has been reported. As shown in table 1, these recommendations focus on three areas: the individuals, the situations in which sexual abuse occurs, and the organization (Harris & Terry, 2019).

Table 1. Report recommendations on preventing and responding to sexual abuse

Domain	Areas of research focus	Practical applications
Perpetrator and victim characteristics	Case profiles and risk factors; typology development	Screening, individual-level risk management
Incident dynamics: situational factors, abuse precursors	Offending pathways (e.g., grooming, trajectories); incident circumstances and dynamics (e.g., locations, interaction opportunities, locations, and dynamics)	Situational awareness training (staff, parents, volunteers); modifications of physical environment; policies to mitigate "high risk" victimization situations and opportunities for offending
Organizational structure: policies, resources, mechanisms of accountability	Parameters of institutional safeguarding policies and systems; factors affecting understanding of and adherence to such policies among key constituencies; likelihood and predictors of reporting	Organizational checks and balances; systems of reporting and accountability; policies ensuring swift response and intervention for cases of alleged abuse; "whistleblower" protections
Organizational culture: norms, values, leadership, power dynamics, trust of constituents	Stakeholder knowledge, attitudes, and beliefs about CSA and its perpetration; cognitive barriers to reporting	Shared culture of youth safety and child protection across all key constituencies, including those inside and outside the organizations

Source: Adapted from Harris & Terry (2019, p. 641)

The top row in table 1 refers to the individual factors that are associated with sexual abuse, and the second row focuses on situational factors that allowed for sexual abuse to occur. Most dioceses have implemented safeguarding policies addressing these issues through the use of strategies such as background checks and two-deep leadership policies (e.g., adults are not allowed to be alone with a youth). The more challenging factors are the organizational domains in the bottom two rows, which are related to the structural and cultural changes that the church can take to further protect children from sexual abuse in the future. The fact that recent reports are making the same recommendations as those released twenty years earlier shows that changes in these areas are not yet fully accepted or realized, and they must be in order for survivors, and the church itself, to begin to heal.

CONCLUSION

Child sexual abuse is a widespread phenomenon, and it is particularly prevalent in institutions where adults interact with, mentor, or nurture children and adolescents. Sparked by several high-profile cases, such as that of John Geoghan, media outlets began reporting on the topic regularly. At the time, questions about the sexual abuse crisis centered around two key issues: How could a priest commit such acts, and how could an organization knowingly allow the sexual abuse to occur? As Catholic communities, survivors' groups, and the general public sought answers to these questions, so did the church. This led to the commission of two studies in the United States to better understand these issues, and in the subsequent twenty years many other scholars, commissions, and investigators have released reports worldwide.

The findings in the myriad reports are remarkably consistent. They show that the organizational culture of the church has historically provided opportunities for sexual abuse to occur, and there were many barriers to identifying, responding to, and reporting sexual abuse. Not only were there low levels of reporting abuse, but when it was reported, many of the leaders did what they could to protect the organization from outsiders or from ruining the reputation of their organization for what they perceived to be a single bad apple. In fact, in most cases, the diocesan leaders attempted to help the accused priest by sending him to treatment, though these treatments were often inadequate. But unfortunately, almost no attention was given to the sexual abuse victims.

Since the affirmation of the *Charter* in 2002, the church has taken many steps to create and implement safeguarding policies to protect children and improve responses to survivors. However, institutional cultures are difficult to change. For example, the idea of the five principles was sound, but the lack of consistent implementation of these policies allowed for sexual abuse to continue. It was only after the scandal was fully realized a decade later that the bishops as a body made significant efforts to change their culture and focus on the protection of children from harm. For real change to happen, welfare of children must be top priority. This means not focusing on protecting the organization from lawsuits but focusing on the best interest of the children and their health. Instituting sexual abuse prevention programs that train staff is essential to curtail organizational behaviors that enable sexual abuse to happen. That training must be about more than just procedures; it must reflect an organizational culture in which everyone expects sexual abuse to be reported, investigated, and acted upon in order to protect children from known perpetrators (Boyle, 2014).

Accountability of the organizational leaders and transparency of their actions is critical for change to happen. We must do more than simply enact policies; the full implementation of the policies, supported by leaders of the organization and with buy-in from the constituents, signifies that there is a change in the culture—that the organization as a whole deems sexual violence unacceptable. As O'Hare (2004, para. 6) states, these policies and procedures will only be effective if "bishops maintain a commitment to meaningful reform and vigilant enforcement that outlasts the immediate crisis and becomes ingrained in the character of the church itself."

PERSONAL REFLECTION

1. What thoughts, feelings, and physical sensations did you experience as you read about the Catholic abuse crisis, the number of victims, and the efforts to cover up? Were there any aspects of the chapter that were particularly distressing?

2. How does knowledge of widespread abuse and cover-up in religious institutions impact your experience of your faith?

3. How does knowledge of widespread abuse and cover-up in religious institutions impact your experience of the church?

GROUP DISCUSSION

1. Identify ways the church exercised complicity. How have they attempted to correct?

2. In what ways could this abuse crisis impact people's relationship with the church? How could your local church support people who have previously felt harmed or betrayed by religious institutions?

3. How could these recommendations be adopted in your local church contexts?

REFERENCES

Bishops Ad Hoc Committee on Sexual Abuse. (1994). *Restoring trust: A pastoral response to sexual abuse* (Vol. 1). National Conference of Catholic Bishops.

Boyle, P. (2014). How youth-serving organizations enable acquaintance molesters. *Journal of Interpersonal Violence, 29*(15): 2839-48.

Carroll, M., Pfeiffer, S., & Rezendes, M. (2002, January 6). Church allowed abuse by priest for years. *Boston Globe.* www.bostonglobe.com/news/special-reports/2002/01/06/church-allowed-abuse-priest-for-years/cSHfGkTIrAT25qKGvBuDNM/story.html

Criminal Justice & Behavior. (2008). *Child sexual abuse in the Catholic church* [Special issue], *35*(5).

Harris, A. J., & Terry, K. J. (2019). Child sexual abuse in organizational settings: A research framework to advance policy and practice. *Sexual Abuse, 31*(6): 635-42.

John Jay College (Principal Investigator and Author). (2004). *The nature and scope of sexual abuse of minors by Catholic priests and deacons in the United States, 1950-2002.* United States Conference of Catholic Bishops.

John Jay College (Principal Investigator and Author). (2006). *The nature and scope of sexual abuse of minors by Catholic priests and deacons in the United States, 1950-2002: Supplementary data analysis.* United States Conference of Catholic Bishops.

Kenny, N. (2012). *Healing the church: Diagnosing and treating the clergy abuse crisis.* Novalis Publishing.

O'Hare, J. A. (2004). Of many things. *America, 190*(12). www.americamagazine.org/issue/480/many-things/many-things

Secretariat of Child and Youth Protection, National Review Board, and USCCB. (2023). *Report on the implementation of the Charter for the Protection of Children and Young People.* US Conference of Catholic Bishops.

Terry, K. J. (2008). Stained glass: The nature and scope of child sexual abuse in the Catholic church. *Criminal Justice & Behavior, 35*(5), 549-69.

Terry, K. J., Smith, M. L., Schuth, K., Kelly, J., Vollman, B., & Massey, C. (2011). *Causes and context of the sexual abuse crisis in the Catholic church.* United States Conference of Catholic Bishops.

4

A SYSTEMS LENS FOR UNDERSTANDING ABUSE

DR. VANESSA KENT AND DR. MARY L. TROY

So we, being many, are one body in Christ, and
every one members of one another.

ROMANS 12:5 KJV

ALL ABUSE HAPPENS within the context of systems. Understanding abuse from a systems lens allows safeguarders to understand the complex religious-socialization factors that contribute to the opportunity for perpetration, the impact of the trauma, and the potential for prevention. Attachment theory may also be helpful in explaining the possible long-range effects of sexual abuse on victims and their families. Understanding the victim's attachment style and the significance of betrayal by an attachment figure and having access to emotionally safe support persons are critical factors in the relational system. Both systems and attachment theories provide insight into known protective factors and effective interventions to reduce the impact of trauma on the victim, the family, and the church community, and to identify procedures to prevent future victimization of our children and vulnerable adults.

Closed systems are at particularly high risks for abuse to occur. These systems have historically functioned as their own judge and jury to abuse allegations with little to no input or accountability from those outside of the system who do not have the same conflicts of interest. Closed systems include large institutions such as the military and religious groups and smaller systems such as families. Closed systems foster a strong sense of belonging, which creates even deeper wounds of betrayal when abuse does occur. There have been several public scandals in the United States concerning abuse in closed systems, such as the Boy Scouts of America and USA Gymnastics (Levenson, 2018; Romo, 2021). Many of these closed systems have elevated the value and prosperity of the organization above the well-being of the individual, which is a significant risk factor for abuse to flourish. It is also contrary to Jesus' example of protecting the individual sheep and not just the well-being of the flock as a whole (Matthew 18:12).

While we focus primarily on the impact of clergy sexual abuse on systems in this chapter, it is important to note that other forms of abuse, including physical, emotional, and verbal, perpetrated by family members and other trusted adults can all cause a ripple effect through family, church, and community systems. Sexual abuse can carry serious repercussions on the psychological, emotional, and neurobiological well-being of the victim that can extend long into adulthood (Amado et al., 2015; Crocetto, 2019). Sexual abuse within a family system has a similar pattern to clergy sexual abuse within the church in that it confuses the roles of family members and betrays the victim's physical, relational, and emotional boundaries. For example, incest interferes with the natural balance within the family system and decreases the ability to maintain a secure attachment to the caregiver. An offending caregiver violates the role of protector and is instead the source of harm, thus distressing and damaging the victim's ability to trust and develop age-appropriate behaviors and relationships (Karakurt & Silver, 2014). Understanding the multiple systems within the church community as well as the importance of strengthening secure attachment relationships with the victim's caregivers are key in mitigating the effects of childhood sexual abuse (Crocetto, 2019).

SEXUAL TRAUMA FROM A SYSTEMS PERSPECTIVE

What is a "systems perspective"? To answer this question, it is important to understand what "system" means. In Bronfenbrenner's ecological systems theory (1979), the individual is shaped and formed by the microsystem (family, friends), the mesosystem (work, school), the exosystem (community, neighborhood), and the macrosystem (government, culture, laws). Environments where people live, work, learn, worship, play, and interact are all independent systems. A church community comprises several systems. Ministries, families, neighborhoods, schools, church leadership, and the global church are a few of the systems that operate with the larger church system. A systems perspective looks at the reciprocal relationship between different parts of that system and how the various systems influence each other (Bronfrenbrenner, 1979). One cannot look at just the sexual trauma that occurred but also must understand how family, school, community, and culture interact within the church community to shape and develop each individual's behaviors and responses to the trauma.

Systemic response in the church: The double bind theory. Research has shown that childhood sexual abuse perpetrated by a member of the clergy or church leadership leads to deep spiritual wounds that often alienate survivors from their church, their faith, and God. For survivors of sexual abuse by clergy and/or church leaders, the physical and psychological trauma is compounded by the spiritual trauma inflicted by their abusers. When abusers are members of the clergy or in positions of church leadership, it is extremely difficult for victims, especially young victims, to differentiate between the human abuser and God. This can result in "transforming the person's beliefs about God or generating emotional experiences of extreme fear or distrust of the divine being and/or the religious community" (Panchuk, 2018, p. 516).

Survivors of childhood sexual abuse that is perpetrated by individuals affiliated with the church may have higher levels of spiritual alienation (Easton et al., 2019; Tobin, 2019). To understand how this occurs, an examination of the double bind theory is helpful. A double bind is a psychological predicament in which a person receives from a single source conflicting messages that allow no appropriate response to be made. The double bind theory consists of four characteristics:

1. Two or more people are involved in a relationship in which one holds physical or psychological power over the other.
2. Conflicting messages are conveyed. The first message (usually verbal) usually threatens punishment for specific behavior. The second message (usually nonverbal) conflicts with the first message and is enforced with punishments or threats to survival.

3. The receiver of the conflicting messages is unable to withdraw from the relationship/environment due to threats, fear, or maturity level.

4. Due to the characteristics of double binding, once established it trends toward self-perpetuation (Visser, 2003, p. 273).

The following scenario is an example of the double bind theory.

Joe is an eleven-year-old male whose family is heavily involved in their church community. Joe's parents volunteer for different ministries, and Joe often helps around the church. Joe has been taught to respect and obey church clergy members and to consider them God's authority here on earth. Disobedience (in Joe's mind) is viewed as a sin against God and could harm his relationship with Jesus. The assistant pastor of the church has been sexually abusing Joe for the past year and has told Joe that they have a special relationship that others would be jealous of or have difficulty understanding. Therefore, Joe shouldn't tell anyone what is happening.

This scenario demonstrates the four characteristics of the double bind theory as follows:

1. Joe has been coerced into an abusive relationship that is damaging—physically, spiritually, and psychologically.

2. Joe is receiving two very different messages. First, he is required to obey the assistant pastor or face spiritual consequences (alienation from God). Second, obeying the assistant pastor leads to physical, psychological, and spiritual pain.

3. Joe is afraid to tell anyone what is happening, as that would be disobeying the assistant pastor and committing a sin. He feels he cannot refuse to be around his abuser, as that would cause people to ask questions about why he doesn't want to be with that person. Therefore, he feels trapped in the situation.

4. Without some type of intervention, the abuse will continue.

Impact of trauma on the family system: The ripple effect. Church-related sexual trauma also negatively impacts families of abuse victims. Feelings of anger, guilt, and grief are profound psychological responses that many families struggle to process.

Betrayal of trust. For many families of abuse victims, betrayal has occurred on two different levels—betrayal by the abuser (individual) and betrayal by the church (institutional). The effects of this betrayal have extreme consequences that often last for decades and can include guilt, denial, family fragmentation, a crisis of faith, and a loss of community.

Guilt. Family members of abuse victims, particularly parents, often feel immense guilt for not protecting the child who has been abused. They feel they failed to see that something was wrong or signs that the abuser was dangerous. Often, the perpetrator was someone the family considered a friend and/or a trustworthy person. Perpetrators use their positions in the church to deliberately ingratiate themselves with the families and communities of their intended victims (Raine & Kent, 2019; Spraitz & Bowen, 2019). Families often blame themselves for allowing the abuse victim to be in proximity to perpetrators, either through sports, activities, or friendships. Helping families understand this component of victim grooming is essential to helping assuage some of the guilt they may feel.

Denial. Some families do not believe a victim when the abuse is disclosed (McGraw et al., 2019; Spraitz & Bowen, 2019). They either deny the abuse happened or refuse to believe the accused perpetrator is capable of such a heinous act. Denial can stem from belief in the absolute authority of the church, friendship with the perpetrator, or an inability to comprehend what has happened to the abuse victim (McGraw et al., 2019; O'Brien, 2020; Spraitz & Bowen, 2019). Families may fracture if some members believe the abuse victim while other members deny the abuse happened. Individuals who are in denial about the abuse may accuse those who believe the victim of rejecting their faith or turning their back on God. Conversely, those who are in denial may be accused of abandoning the abuse victim or caring more about the church (institution) than their own family (O'Brien, 2020). This conflict often leads to family separation and/or alienation from family members.

Crisis of faith. Due to the prevalent belief in many religious denominations that members of the clergy and church leadership are representatives of God on earth, sexual abuse of a child by members of the clergy can have a devastating impact on the faith of both the abuse victim and their family members (O'Brien, 2020; Raine & Kent, 2019). Like the victim of the abuse, family members may have a difficult time separating the perpetrator from God. They may begin to question if God is displeased with them or if they have angered God and are now being punished. Family members may also decide that a God who is loving would not have allowed the abuse to happen and therefore distance themselves from God (O'Brien, 2020; Raine & Kent, 2019).

Loss of community. Victims of church sexual abuse are more likely to have families who are heavily involved in their church community (Hurcombe et al., 2019; Raine & Kent, 2019; Spraitz & Bowen, 2019). Family members often volunteer in various church ministries or programs. Their social lives frequently involve attending church activities with other members of their church community. Children may attend a school and/or participate in sports leagues affiliated with the church. Loss of this community can result in severe psychological distress, isolation, and distancing from God and/or their faith (Hurcombe et al., 2019; Raine & Kent, 2019; Spraitz & Bowen, 2019).

Impact of trauma on the congregation/parishioners: A fragmented body. Church communities are also impacted by church sexual trauma. Researchers have identified common themes in connection with church communities that are affected by child sexual abuse perpetrated by members of the clergy and church leadership, including anger, hurt, and betrayal; the opening of old wounds; and fractured communities (Benkert & Doyle, 2009; Kline et al., 2008).

The sense of betrayal and hurt felt by many members of the church due to the sexual abuse of children by members of the clergy and church leadership is often fueled by intense anger (Kline et al., 2008; McGraw et al., 2019; O'Brien, 2020). The anger is connected with the fact that the church covered up the extent of past abuse cases to protect the institution, moved offenders around without notifying their new congregations of abuse allegations, were more concerned with protecting perpetrators than children, and/or created environments conducive for abuse to occur (Benkert & Doyle, 2009; Kline et al., 2008; McGraw et al., 2019; O'Brien, 2020). Abuse allegations also caused people to recall times when they felt the church rejected them or treated them harshly (e.g., refusal of baptism, marriage, or funeral, or rejection/banishment) (Martyr, 2019; Kline et al., 2008). This added to the anger and sense of betrayal by the church.

Church communities can systemically fracture as the result of abuse. As with families, some church members may deny that the abuse occurred while others may disagree with how the church responds, either to victims or to perpetrators. Others call for new church leadership (Hurcombe et al., 2019; Kline et al., 2008; McGraw et al., 2019; O'Brien, 2020). Parish/congregation membership declines in many denominations after abuse cases become known.

While many of those who leave the church still identify as Christian, they no longer affiliate with their former church congregations (Jones, 2021).

UNDERSTANDING SEXUAL TRAUMA THROUGH AN ATTACHMENT LENS

Attachment is a deep and enduring emotional bond that connects one person to another, across time and space, from the cradle to the grave (Ainsworth, 1978; Bowlby, 1973, 1982). Attachment theory describes the early emotional bonds between a young child and his or her caregiver that continue to influence attachment throughout adulthood. Infants seek close connection (proximity) to their primary caregiver (attachment figure) in times of distress. This is observed when a small child playing about runs to his mother when frightened by a loud clap of thunder. If the caregiver is available and responds to the child's needs, the child will be comforted and develop a sense of security. This activation system is repeated over time so that the child learns that the caregiver is dependable, which creates a secure base or safe haven for the child to explore the environment and engage with others.

Children also develop an internal "sense of self" that tells them they are lovable, understood, and cared for. This positive mental picture of self and others, called *internal working model* (Bowlby, 1973, 1982), helps shape the child's expectations of future experiences with their caregivers and other relationships. Even though older children may not always have their parent present, they can internally recall their caregiver's reassuring voice or touch and be able to self-regulate. These early childhood experiences help to create one of four attachment styles that tend to persist into adulthood (Ainsworth, 1978; Mikulincer et al., 2015). When strong attachment bonds are created, the child is said to have a secure attachment style. Securely attached children communicate their needs when distressed and receive empathy and reassurance from their caregivers. As adults, they are capable of building rewarding close relationships with a romantic partner, family, and friends.

However, when the primary attachment figures are not consistently available or fail to comfort at critical periods of development, the child is unable to find relief from stressful situations and therefore fails to develop a sense of security. Without a secure base to turn to, they may learn to use ineffective means to calm their aroused state of distress and try to make meaning of the experience. The child may develop a negative working model of self that states, "I am not lovable, and my caregiver is unreliable, unsupportive, or abusive," depending on the severity of their experiences. Developmentally, these experiences rewire the brain as to how it will react to stress and sense danger—either by hyperarousal or hypo-arousal. Three insecure attachment styles may develop: anxious, avoidant, and disorganized. Those with an anxious attachment style tend to express distress (high arousal) through behaviors such as crying, clinging, controlling, or an overdependence on others to counter feelings of helplessness. These behaviors help regulate emotions that include sadness, anger, powerlessness, and worthlessness.

On the opposite end of the spectrum, those with a high avoidance attachment style will tend to downregulate emotions (hypo-arousal) by using strategies such as avoidance and dismissive behaviors to maintain emotional distance. They will appear independent, self-reliant, or overly confident and display little emotion except for flares of intense anger. However, underneath they feel distressed, lonely, vulnerable, and weak. This style of relating develops from early experiences with attachment figures who were neglectful or punitive toward the child when expressing needs (Ainsworth et al., 1978; Mukulincer et al., 2008).

The third attachment style, disorganized, is the result of interactions with an inconsistent caregiver who acts caring in one moment and then abusive in another. The child never knows what to expect, leading them to respond in disorganized patterns of anxious and avoidant behaviors (Main & Solomon, 1986). They may move close to the caregiver only to be hurt or rejected, and they avoid relationships that could be helpful. Attachment questionnaires can help identify the risks of relational and psychological concerns and guide the interventions needed to build secure attachments (Karakurt & Silver, 2014; Mikulincer & Shaver, 2008). We will explore attachment styles in more detail in the chapter on children.

Developmental effects of abuse on attachment. Studies have looked at the lifelong effect of child sexual abuse, specifically those occurring in precarious periods of child development (Finkelhor,1990; Finkelhor et al., 2014). Symptoms include increased risk of posttraumatic stress disorder (PTSD) that may include nightmares, intrusive thoughts, anxiety, depression, substance abuse, low self-worth, and poor school performance for children or teens (American Psychiatric Association, 2013). Mental health problems may persist in adulthood with additional issues of lifelong inability to trust others, problems with intimate relationships, sexual and marital distress, and chronic health issues. The risk factors are much greater for developing enduring emotional dysregulation, relational disturbance, and negative self-concept if the sexual abuse occurs during key developmental periods of childhood, is inflicted by a parental figure or trusted adult, or is ongoing for an extended period of time; if there appears to be no way to escape the abuse due to circumstances or threats; and if the victim receives little or no social support from the family, church, or community after disclosing the abuse—or worse, is blamed or not believed (Amado et al., 2015; Jardin et al., 2017).

The prime age for clergy-perpetrated child sexual abuse (CPCSA) is between the ages of 10 and 14 with documented reports of up to 81 percent of the victims being prepubescent boys (Dreßing et al., 2019). The numbers are less clear for CPCSA for females as the media and research teams have focused primarily on the Catholic and Anglican churches (Dreßing et al., 2019; John Jay College, 2004). It is known that females have a higher prevalence of sexual abuse as global estimates indicate 20 to 30 percent are likely to be sexually abused before the age of 18 (Barth et al., 2013; Finkelhor et al., 2014). During the time of emerging sexual curiosity and physical changes, some families forego explaining puberty and/or sex education to their children and leave this exploration period and education to chance or entrust the education to clergy and youth leaders (Fogler et al., 2008). Depending on the child's cognitive stage of development, younger children who see the world more concretely can be "tricked" into believing what a trusted adult (endorsed by their parents) says or does must be okay. Those starting to develop abstract reasoning skills and the ability to hold experiences as both positive and negative may experience a double bind—they see the experience as inappropriate but determine that disclosing would shame parents or community and therefore feel trapped into suffering silently.

Gender may also play a role in the victim's response to the abuse. Male victims tend to underreport, minimize the effects, or express themes of wanting to get revenge on the perpetrator. Feeling their anger is justified, they may act out their anger in aggressive or bullying behaviors (Fogler et al., 2008). Male victims may question their sexual identity and feel embarrassed to talk about their experiences. Female victims may feel abandoned or experience ambivalent feelings toward the abuser, as they may have been made to feel special. They tend to turn their anger inward and may experience depression or thoughts of self-harm. Teens may blame themselves for their participation even though they did not seek out these experiences. Understanding these dynamics is helpful in working with families and recognizing that there may be a myriad of underlying issues below the surface. However, these are generalizations for genders, and each person may experience their own unique reactions to the abuse.

Protective factors of secure attachment. The role of attachment is significant in understanding the risks of child sexual abuse and the impact that it may have on the victim's ability to recover (Ensink et al., 2021; Mikulincer et al., 2015). As caregivers are perhaps the most significant support and influence in a child's overall development, understanding the attachment style to these caregivers lends insight into the child's ability to recover from adverse events. In short, the responses and reactions of the caregiver during times of a child's distress matter (Crocetto, 2019; Ensink et al., 2021). Secure attachments serve as a protective factor in reducing trauma and increasing resiliency. Studies show that children, adolescents, and adults having a secure attachment to their caregiver or significant other believe that they will be supported; therefore, in times of distress, they will seek connection with caring persons, express their painful emotions, receive comfort, and be able to return to a regulated emotional state. Those with secure attachments are less likely to develop long-term or severe symptoms such as PTSD, anxiety, depression, dissociation, somatic symptoms, or personality disorders (Barazzone et al., 2019; Ensink et al., 2021; Jardin, et al., 2017). Contrasting this, children and teens with insecure attachments whose needs have not been met carry a higher risk for abuse and have significantly more PTSD and mental health concerns (Ensink et al., 2021; Karakurt & Silver, 2014). They may have less access to supportive adults and use ineffective methods to calm themselves, especially those who down-regulate their emotions by ignoring feelings and pulling away from others.

Furthermore, families who operate within a secure attachment system (close connections, open communication, established support networks) tend to have more hope, resiliency, and ability to utilize available resources. When a trauma occurs, they can support each other and seek outside help. However, when their support system is the church where the abuse happened, it may shatter the trust in others who are highly esteemed or considered safe and good. This can activate attachment insecurities of the parents as well as the victim. The family may become isolated if ostracized by other church members or leave the church if not supported. This lack of social support and rejection may further traumatize the family. Helping the family members increase their internal and external resources through connections and support services is an important aspect of safeguarding.

God as an attachment figure. God has been described as an attachment figure who is stronger and wiser and serves as a secure base in times of distress (Granqvist & Kirkpatrick, 2008). Psalm 91:2 provides this sentiment: "I will say of the LORD, 'He is my refuge and my fortress, my God, in whom I trust'" (NIV). Some, however, see God through an attachment lens created from human experiences of loss (Counted, 2016). Those with insecure attachment styles may struggle with the tension of trusting someone whom they can neither see nor touch. They fear that they may disappoint God or that he abandoned them when bad things happened. Those with avoidant attachments may feel that they must remain self-reliant and tend to avoid turning to God as their attachment figure when in distress. Finally, some develop a strong attachment to God despite their losses and insecurities, relying on Scripture and prayer to help regulate their emotions when anxious. Psalm 34:18 remind us of his unfailing love and comfort as the Good Shepherd: "The LORD is close to the brokenhearted and saves those who are crushed in spirit" (NIV).

Sacred betrayal. "Where we find trauma, we often find spirituality" (Pargament et al., 2009, p. 398). Research shows that life traumas impact people spiritually as well as psychologically, physically, and socially. Often people find comfort in their faith and seek support from the church when faced with individual or family crises. Many find that their spirituality helps them find hope. This is why CPCSA has been labeled one of the most destructive types of abuse (Benkert & Doyle, 2009) and described as "soul murder" (McPhillips, 2018). When sexual abuse is perpetrated by an attachment figure who has taken a vow to protect and nurture the spiritual well-being of the members as a representative of God, "it is as if God himself has committed the violation" (Pargament et al., 2009, p. 403). Victims may feel betrayed by God who allowed this tragedy to happen, often despite prayers pleading for it to end. They may feel abandoned or punished by God for sins they committed but cannot reconcile out of fear. Their image of a loving, kind Father is replaced by an angry, punitive God who is distant at best or fails to exist at all. The result on the victim and family is a spiraling of negative spiritual effects that can shake their foundational belief system, their spiritual identity, and ultimately their relationship with God. One survivor commented, "I don't think I'll ever step foot in a church again. . . . I lost my religion, faith, and ability to trust adults and institutions" (Matchan, 1992, p. 8).

Further damage that impacts family systems is the failure of church leaders and institutions to protect the victim upon disclosure, and instead, abandoning the victim and family to deal with the aftermath alone. When victims get the courage to finally reveal their secret, the church community may act in disbelief or fail to acknowledge the child's distress or protect the child from further harm (McPhillips, 2018). The church's response may be to protect the accused, hide the egregious acts to protect the institution, or simply fail to come to the rescue of the victim and their family. "Like an earthquake, CPCSA is a desecration that creates spiritual havoc" (Pargament et al., 2009, p. 404). The result is an attachment wound that goes deep into the core of the human soul, disconnecting it from once-loved spiritual traditions and practices, and leaving survivors as "spiritual orphans" (McPhillips, 2018). Loss that can extend into adulthood includes a shattered image of a loving, protective God; loss of a sacred part of themselves as spiritual beings; the capacity to enjoy sexual intimacy; the ability to trust others, especially those who hold positions of authority; and the ability to recognize appropriate physical or emotional boundaries to avoid revictimization (McPhillips, 2018, Pargament et al., 2008). Victims of CPCSA may forgo dreams of becoming ministers or priests due to effects of shame, self-loathing, or mistrust that further erode their spiritual identity.

Healing attachment wounds. The antidote to betrayal, powerlessness, and loss of the sacred is re-creating a safe attachment for the victim and the family. Immediate systemic intervention is important to stabilize and provide a sense of security in the victim's life. This may include finding supportive services in the community (inside and outside of the church system).

Social support may be important in reducing the negative effects of CPCSA (Karkut & Silver, 2014). As described earlier, each family member is part of a system that affects the other parts. The initial tasks for helpers are to connect compassionately with the victim and family and offer supportive resources and damage control. Those with insecure attachment styles can develop an earned secure attachment style through positive relational experiences with helpers as well as a counselor. Several steps are identified below that can be part of the safeguarding efforts (Karakurt & Silver, 2014; Pargament et al., 2008).

1. *Believe the victim.* This can be difficult due to the nature of the offender's reputation and the relationship others have had with him or her. When the victim and the family are well liked and respected, it is difficult to believe that misconduct has occurred, but if the victim or family is unknown or disliked, then the chances of being believed only occur if there are others who come forward or shed light on the accusations. Not being believed creates a secondary injury to the victim and their family. As safeguarders, it is not our job to investigate allegations but to honor the courage required in coming forward and to provide support. There are other systems besides safeguarding (legal, etc.) in place to investigate and provide the accused due process. Allegations of child abuse should be brought before the church publicly while maintaining the privacy and dignity of the victim. This enables members of the church to make an informed decision about their children's safety during investigations into abuse allegations. The congregation cannot help if they do not know the truth and the system remains unhealthy.

2. *Listen to their story repeatedly, without judgment or interruption.* Recognize that the initial story given by the victim is likely the tip of the iceberg, a test to see if they will be believed or supported. The victim also may have suppressed memories of events as a way of surviving the trauma of abuse. They may show little or no reaction due to feeling numb or detached as they disclose horrible stories. The safeguarder may be the first person who is able to listen and respond with empathy, thus creating a new experience for the victim. When this happens, the safeguarder may become a temporary safe attachment figure.

3. *Restore their sense of power.* Allowing the victim to take ownership of their story—who they will share it with and how it will be disclosed to others, including their family—is a way to safeguard their privacy. If the victim wants to share their story with their close community, those members should rally around them in support.

4. *Create safety.* The victim needs to be shielded from the offender so that there is no further abuse, and the offender cannot be allowed to threaten or coerce the victim. The victim may also need to be protected from members of the congregation who blame or accuse them of out of their own pain or loss. In extreme cases, the victim may also need protection

from family members if they are not believed or could face additional fallout from reporting the abuse.

5. *Provide time for mourning.* Allow space for the victim and family to grieve their losses—innocence, identity, faith, dreams, and possibly community. The church system will also need to mourn the loss of a trusted leader, their place in the community, and the disillusionment of righteousness. This may be done both individually and as a group. Too often, sexual misconduct, whether it is child sexual abuse, adultery, or sexual activity between a ministry leader and someone in the congregation, is announced publicly to the church as a vague "moral failure" and immediately followed by a sermon stressing the importance of not discussing the issue, as it would be considered gossip, and focusing on moving forward. This attempt to control the feelings and reactions of the congregants inhibits the grieving process.

6. *Seek justice.* The offender must be held responsible for his or her actions both legally and spiritually. Religious abuse is an exploitation of power due to the power differential and responsibility to do no harm while requiring "blind trust" in their special skills or knowledge (Martyr, 2019; O'Brien, 2020). While some in the church system have marked these similar behaviors as moral failings or indiscretions, it is important to seek justice outside of the church. Cooperation with and following the laws of the local/regional/national civil authorities in regard to child protection is a vital component of preventing further abuse by the offender as well as contributing to the healing of the abused. Victims may also need a guardian-ad-litem or someone to offer support if legal proceedings occur.

7. *Seek spiritual healing when they are ready.* Finally, help the victim and families to rebuild spiritual practices when their faith has been shaken. One victim described worrying constantly about his sins and his need to speak to a priest, but he was too afraid of priests to go to confession or take Communion (Mart, 2004). Some survivors leave the church and their religious practice, but others return over time as they find healing and reconnection to the sacred. Helpers can facilitate healing by creating space for spiritual dialogue to allow victims to talk not only about their physical and emotional hurts but also about their spiritual wounds. It

may require sitting in dark places of the soul and allowing space for the victim to wrestle with God. Lamenting is another way of voicing anger toward God that may be healing. Expression of the full range of tears, rage, and mourning can lead to acceptance, hope, and renewal of faith.

Finally, spiritual resources may be offered to the victim and family. For example, visualization exercises can be a powerful way to reconnect to spirituality. Flaherty (1992) suggests asking a female victim to picture herself sitting in the place of Mary Magdalene, weeping outside the empty tomb of Jesus as a way of representing all the losses she has experienced. She is to imagine Jesus approaching and asking, "Woman, why are you weeping?" (p. 56). The woman is encouraged to feel the presence and support of Jesus in her pain. Using biblical characters such as Tamar, Joseph, and others who experienced unjust suffering at the hand of someone else can be encouraging. Allowing victims to tell their stories with a trusted helper or counselor, give their testimonies to a small group, and practice two-way journaling with God (writing and listening) may put balm on their soul wounds. Although time does not always heal, with the compassion of helpers, victims and their families can have a transformational spiritual experience and develop or regain a secure attachment to God, who will "bestow on them a crown of beauty instead of ashes, the oil of joy instead of mourning, and a garment of praise instead of a spirit of despair" (Isaiah 61:3 NIV).

STRENGTHENING THE SYSTEM: EQUIPPING THE CHURCH FOR TRAUMA RESPONSE

Who is responsible for protecting the vulnerable in our churches? The answer is that all members of the body of Christ (institution, clergy, and members) play a part in protecting those vulnerable to abuse. The church (institutional system) is responsible for developing and implementing policies and procedures that protect the vulnerable. Systemic policies should include the following at a minimum: psychological and background screenings of potential clergy prior to seminary training; procedures for reporting and investigating accusations of abuse that must include authorities outside of the church (e.g., local law enforcement); background checks for all church leaders and volunteers; transparency regarding investigation outcomes; and procedures for caring for the physical, mental, and spiritual well-being of abuse victims.

Within the international, national, and local church systems, policies must mandate clergy responsibilities for creating environments that promote safety and security. Some ways to create these types of environments include implementing required child abuse prevention trainings for anyone working/volunteering with children, and mandating a minimum of two adults always be present when working with children. Offering free seminars on child abuse prevention to all congregation members enables churches to be proactive in preventing abuse and creates an environment where everyone participates in the protection of vulnerable populations.

Developing healthy relational patterns. Sexual predators tend to pick victims from environments that are dysfunctional in some way (Briggs et al., 2021; Easton et al., 2019; O'Brien, 2020; Spraitz & Bowen, 2019). Research has demonstrated that families, communities, and church systems with healthy relational patterns have lower rates of abuse and trauma (Crooks et al., 2019). Healthy relational patterns consist of open communication, honesty and transparency, appropriate affection, and boundaries.

Open communication involves everyone having permission to communicate thoughts, ideas, feelings, and opinions without fear of punishment, censure, or rejection. There are no limitations on topics discussed or questions asked. Open communication creates an atmosphere where individuals feel heard and valued.

While all cultures have different ways to show affection, appropriate affection follows certain parameters. Physical touch should never be required—for example, making children hug relatives when they have indicated they do not wish to. Affection should not involve secrecy. Lastly, individuals are allowed to reject physical or verbal affection without repercussion.

Healthy relational patterns also include boundaries. Boundaries are limits that individuals set for themselves to maintain physical and emotional health. While boundaries are different for everyone, healthy relationships respect others' boundaries and do not try to run over limits others have set in place. Creating and maintaining healthy relational patterns in families, communities, and church systems is a process that takes great effort and willingness of all parties involved but results in safer systems and environments for the most vulnerable in our society.

PERSONAL REFLECTION

1. It can be difficult to read about clergy-perpetrated child abuse. What thoughts, feelings, and physical sensations did you experience as you read about clergy-perpetrated child sexual abuse and its consequences?

2. Several steps were provided for building secure attachment with trauma survivors and their families. Which of these steps feels most challenging and why? Which feels most natural and why?

3. What feels most challenging about developing healthy relational patterns?

GROUP DISCUSSION

1. How does an understanding of abuse from a systems perspective help you to support families and communities impacted by abuse?

2. Explore the role of leadership within the church system in creating a culture that values and prioritizes the safety of individuals. How can leaders and safeguarders foster an environment that encourages accountability and addresses systemic issues contributing to and resulting from abuse?

3. What is the impact of abuse on systems? How does this relate to the previous discussion on complicity from chapter one?

REFERENCES

Ainsworth, M. D. S., Blehar, M. C., Waters, E., & Wall, S. (1978). *Patterns of attachment: A psychological study of the strange situation.* Lawrence Erlbaum Associates.

Amado, B. G., Arce, R., & Herraiz, A. (2015). Psychological injury in victims of child sexual abuse: A meta-analytic review. *Psychosocial Intervention, 24,* 49-62. doi: 10.1016/jpsi.2015.03.002

American Psychiatric Association. (2013). *Diagnostic and statistical manual of mental disorders* (5th ed.). https://doi.org/10.1176/appi.books.9780890425596

Barazzone, N., Santos, I., McGowan, J., & Donaghay-Spire, E. (2019). The links between adult attachment and post-traumatic stress: A systematic review. *Psychology and Psychotherapy: Theory Research, and Practice, 92*(1), 131-47. dol: 10.1111/papt.12181

Barth, J., Bermetz, L., Heim, E., Trelle. S., & Tonia, T. (2013). The current prevalence of child sexual abuse worldwide: A systematic review and meta-analysis. *International Journal of Public Health 58,* 469-83. https://doi.org/10.1007/s00038-012-0426-1

Benkert, M., & Doyle, T. P. (2009). Clericalism, religious duress and its psychological impact on victims of clergy sexual abuse. *Pastoral Psychology, 58*(3), 223-38.

Bowlby, J. (1973). *Attachment and loss: Vol. 2. Separation: Anxiety and anger.* Basic Books.

Bowlby, J. (1982). *Attachment and loss: Vol. 1. Attachment (2nd ed.).* Basic Books.

Briggs, E. C., Amaya-Jackson, L., Putnam, K. T., & Putnam, F. W. (2021). All adverse childhood experiences are not equal: The contribution of synergy to adverse childhood experience scores. *American Psychologist, 76*(2), 243.

Bronfenbrenner, U. (1979). *The ecology of human development: Experiments by nature and design.* Harvard University Press.

Counted, V. (2016). God as an attachment figure: A case study of the God attachment language and God concepts of anxiously attached Christian youths in South Africa. *Journal of Spirituality in Mental Health, 18*(4), 316-46. https://doi.org/10.1080/1934963 7.2016.1176757

Crocetto, J. (2019). The unique contribution of attachment theory in understanding the nonoffending fathers in the care of children who have been sexually abused: A historical lens. *Families in Society: The Journal of Contemporary Social Services, 100*(4), 381-91. doi: 10.1177/1044389419852022

Crooks, C. V., Jaffe, P., Dunlop, C., Kerry, A., & Exner-Cortens, D. (2019). Preventing gender-based violence among adolescents and young adults: Lessons from 25 years of program development and evaluation. *Violence Against Women, 25*(1), 29-55.

Dreßing, H., Dölling, D., Hermann, D., Kruse, A., Schmitt, E., Bannenberg, B., Hoell, A., Voss, E., & Salize, H. J. (2019). Sexual abuse at the hands of catholic clergy: A retrospective cohort study of its extent and health consequences for affected minors (the MHG Study). *Deutsches Ärzteblatt International 116*(22), 389.

Easton, S. D., Leone-Sheehan, D. M., & O'Leary, P. J. (2019). "I will never know the person who I could have become": Perceived changes in self-identity among adult survivors of clergy-perpetrated sexual abuse. *Journal of Interpersonal Violence, 34*(6), 1139-62.

Ensink, K., Fonagy, P., Normandin, L., Rozenberg, A., Marquex, C., Godbout, N., & Borelli. J. L. (2021). Post-traumatic stress disorder in sexually abused children: Secure attachment as a protective factor. *Frontiers in Psychology,12,* 646680. doi:10.3389 /fpsyg.2021.646680

Finkelhor, D. (1990). Early and long-term effects of child sexual abuse: An update. *Professional Psychology: Research and Practice, 21,* 325-30.

Finkelhor, D., Shattuck, A., Turner, H., & Hamby, S. (2014). The lifetime prevalence of child sexual abuse and sexual assault assessed in late adolescence. *Journal of Adolescent Health, 55,* 329-33. doi: 10.1016/j.jadohealth.2013.12.026

Flaherty, S. M. (1992). *Woman, why do you weep? Spirituality for survivors of childhood sexual abuse.* Paulist Press.

Fogler, J. M., Shipher, J. C., Clarke, S., Jensen, J., & Rowe, R. (2008). The impact of clergy-perpetrated sexual abuse: The role of gender, development, and posttraumatic stress. *Journal of Child Sexual Abuse, 17*(3-4), 301-28. doi:10.1080/10538710802329940

Granqvist, P., & Kirkpatrick, L. A. (2008). Attachment and religious representations and behaviour. In J. Cassidy, P. R. Shaver, J. Cassidy, & P. R. Shaver (Eds.), *Handbook of attachment: Theory, research, and clinical applications* (2nd ed., pp. 906-33). Guilford Press.

Hurcombe, R., Darling, A., Mooney, B., Ablett, G., Soares, C., King, S., & Brähler, V. (2019). *Truth Project Thematic Report: Child sexual abuse in the context of religious institutions.* Independent Inquiry Child Sexual Abuse.

Jardin, C., Venta, A., Newlin, E., Ibarra, S., & Sharp, C. (2017). Secure attachment moderates the relationship of sexual trauma with trauma systems among adolescents from an inpatient psychiatric facility. *Journal of Interpersonal Violence. 32,* 1565-85. doi: 10.1177/0886260515589928

John Jay College (Principal Investigator and Author). (2004). *The nature and scope of sexual abuse of minors by Catholic priests and deacons in the United States, 1950-2002.* United States Conference of Catholic Bishops.

Jones, J. M. (2021, March 29). U.S. church membership falls below majority for first time. Gallup. https://news.gallup.com/poll/341963/church-membership-falls-below-majority-first-time.aspx

Karakurt, G., & Silver, K. E. (2014). Therapy for childhood sexual abuse survivors using attachment and family systems theory orientations. *The American journal of family therapy, 42*(1), 79-91.

Kline, P. M., McMackin, R., & Lezotte, E. (2008). The impact of the clergy abuse scandal on parish communities. *Journal of Child Sexual Abuse, 17*(3-4), 290-300.

Levenson, E. (2018, January 24). Larry Nassar sentenced to up to 175 years in prison for decades of sexual abuse. *CNN News.* www.cnn.com/2018/01/24/us/larry-nassar-sentencing/index.html

Main, M., & Solomon, J. (1986). Discovery of an insecure-disorganized/disoriented attachment pattern: Procedures, findings and implication for the classification of behaviour. In T. Berry Brazelton & M. W. Yogman (Eds.), *Affective development in infancy* (pp. 95–124). Ablex Publishing.

Mart, E. G. (2004). Victims of abuse by priests: Some preliminary observations. *Pastoral Psychology, 52*(6), 465-72.

Martyr, P. (2019). Why get over it isn't enough for victims of clerical sexual abuse. *Church Life Journal.* University of Notre Dame.

Matchan, L. (1992, June 8). Ex-priest's accusers tell of the damage. *Boston Globe,* 1, 8.

McGraw, D. M., Ebadi, M., Dalenberg, C., Wu, V., Naish, B., & Nunez, L. (2019). Consequences of abuse by religious authorities: A review. *Traumatology, 25*(4), 242.

McPhillips, K. (2018). Soul murder: Investigating spiritual trauma at the royal commission. *Journal of Australian Studies, 42*(2), 231-42. doi: 10.1080/14443058.2018.148329

Mikulincer, M., & Shaver, P. R. (2008). Adult attachment and affect regulation. In J. Cassidy & P. R. Shaver (Eds.), *Handbook of attachment: Theory, research and clinical application* (2nd ed). Guilford Press.

Mikulincer, M., Shaver, P. R., & Solomon, Z. (2015). An attachment perspective on traumatic and posttraumatic reactions. In M. Safir et al. (Eds.), *Future directions in posttraumatic stress disorder.* doi: 10.1007/978-1-4899-7522-5_4

O'Brien, P. M. (2020). Transparency as a means to rebuild trust within the church: A case study in how Catholic dioceses and eparchies in the United States have responded to the clergy sex abuse crisis. *Church, Communication and Culture, 5*(3), 456-83.

Panchuk, M. (2018). The shattered spiritual self: A philosophical exploration of religious trauma. *Res Philosophica, 95*(3): 505-30.

Pargament, K. I., Murray-Swank, N. A., & Mahoney, A. (2009). Problem and solution: The spiritual dimension of clergy sexual abuse and its impact on survivors. In R. McMackin, T. Keane, & P. Kline (Eds.), *Understanding the impact of clergy sexual abuse* (pp. 200-223). Routledge.

Raine, S., & Kent, S. A. (2019). The grooming of children for sexual abuse in religious settings: Unique characteristics and select case studies. *Aggression and Violent Behavior, 48*, 180-89.

Romo, V. (2021, July 2). Boy Scouts of America reaches historic settlement with sexual abuse survivors. *National Public Radio.* www.npr.org/2021/07/01/1012388865/boy -scouts-of-america-settlement-with-sexual-abuse-survivors-victims

Spraitz, J. D., & Bowen, K. N. (2019). Examination of a nascent taxonomy of priest sexual grooming. *Sexual Abuse, 31*(6), 707-28.

Terry, K. J. (2015). Child sexual abuse within the Catholic church: A review of global perspectives. *International Journal of Comparative and Applied Criminal Justice, 39*(2), 139-54. 10.1080/01924036.2015.1012703

Tobin, T. W. (2019). Religious faith in the unjust meantime: The spiritual violence of clergy sexual abuse. *Feminist Philosophy Quarterly, 5*(2).

Visser, M. (2003). Gregory Bateson on deutero-learning and double bind: A brief conceptual history. *Journal of the History of the Behavioral Sciences, 39*(3), 269-78.

5

PERPETRATOR DYNAMICS

REV. DAVID COOK

THE CHURCH IS COMMISSIONED BY GOD to share the gospel with those who are rebelling against him, calling them to repentance and obedience to Christ. When dealing with perpetrators of abuse, the church has at times interpreted this to mean "quick forgiveness" and "redemption at all costs." The comfort or rehabilitation of the perpetrator has been prioritized over the safety and well-being of the victim and the protection of the vulnerable. This emphasis on redemption for the perpetrator has had dire consequences, as it promotes a lack of accountability that enables the ongoing perpetration of abuse. On the other hand, many perpetrators are Christians and called to be members of the body of Christ. All perpetrators need to hear the gospel, and the church cannot avoid this responsibility. This begs the question, How can the church balance its responsibility to protect the vulnerable *and* walk with the perpetrator through the process of repentance, accountability, and redemption through Christ? To make wise decisions about how to protect the vulnerable, we must (1) recognize how perpetrators of many types of abuse groom themselves and their communities to enable perpetration and (2) have an accurate understanding of the nature of pedophilia and child sexual abuse.

HOW PERPETRATORS OFFEND

Perpetrators of abuse do not typically just select a victim and offend. There are a series of emotional states and grooming behaviors that occur before the abuse takes place that foster an internal tolerance of offending and a communal acceptance and trust of the perpetrator. First, the perpetrators must convince themselves that they will cause minimal harm, or perhaps even some benefit, to the victim. Then, they have to find a way to act out without getting caught. To push through the internal barriers, the perpetrators must groom themselves. To push through the external barriers, the perpetrators must groom the environment and the victim (Whittaker, 2013). The grooming strategies described in this chapter can be present in all types of abuse, including spiritual, physical, and emotional abuse. In addition to exploring general perpetrator dynamics, we will also identify how these strategies manifest specifically in sexual offenders who have preyed on children.

Grooming the self. Before perpetrators offend, they often cultivate complex internal dialogue that justifies the abuse and protects them from the feeling of guilt. For example, the spiritual leader who uses his power to coerce congregants to submit to his authority without question has often built a belief about receiving a specific calling from God that justifies his behavior. He tells himself that his manipulation and verbal abuse are acceptable because how else will he preach the gospel, call others to repentance, and preserve the church. Even those who sexually offend against children often go to great lengths to convince themselves that they are not harming the victim (Dietz, 2020). For example, a study of child sex offenders found that the participants emphasized the perceived benefit to the child (e.g., "Do you think the child benefitted from the experience?"), complicity of the child (e.g., "Do you think the child enjoyed what happened?"), and the responsibility of the child (e.g., "Do you believe the child was responsible for what happened?") to justify sexual offending against children (Hempel et al., 2015). Perpetrators build a persona based on the denial of facts, impact, and responsibility that enables continued offending.

Denial of facts. Denial of facts ranges from simple bald-faced lies despite overwhelming evidence to the contrary to sophisticated and convoluted explanations for why everybody else is misunderstanding or misinterpreting what happened. This is sometimes described as "gaslighting," or the use of "misdirection, denial, lying, and contradiction" to make others question their perception of reality (March et al., 2023, p. 2). For example, in instances of domestic violence, it is not uncommon for perpetrators to deny assaulting the victim, despite clear bruises and wounds.

Denial of impact. Denial of impact is a self-grooming strategy that includes minimizing the consequences of abusive behaviors or dismissing the vulnerability of the victim. For instance, an abusive spiritual leader who is making sexually explicit remarks to a member of his staff may claim that he did not commit any offense because he did not physically touch her and she is an adult and can leave any time she wants. This argument ignores the impact of the power imbalance given that he is both her employer and a spiritual leader. In the case of child sex offenders, the perpetrator may deny the frequency, duration, and intensity of the offenses (Dietz, 2020). Similarly, the impact of the behavior may be minimized by implying that the victim was not harmed, justifying the abuse because the victim was already sexually active, or claiming that the sexual abuse is part of a genuine and committed relationship.

Denial of responsibility. Denial of responsibility is also known as blame shifting (Ward, 2000). Sometimes, blame is shifted to the victim (e.g., "She led me on"). Sometimes, blame is shifted to circumstances or substances (e.g., "If I hadn't forgotten my swimsuit, this never would have happened," "I didn't realize how much I had to drink"). Perpetrators can often use spiritual language to justify their actions and avoid responsibility and meaningful repentance. They might quote Romans 14:13 to claim the victim was "causing them to stumble" into sinful behavior due to their clothing choices, perception of flirtatious behavior, or provoking them to anger.

Grooming the environment. In addition to grooming themselves to enable ongoing abuse with minimal feelings of guilt, perpetrators also employ strategies to groom their environments. These strategies allow perpetrators to build trust with others within their community, increasing their access to the vulnerable and making it more likely that others will disbelieve victims' accusations against them. This illustrates the sinister connection between spiritual abuse and sexual abuse. When a spiritual leader persuades the congregation that he or she is God's chosen leader, commands complete obedience, and punishes anyone who disobeys, they create an environment where they can commit all kinds of abuses without fear of consequences. If this spiritual leader lures a teenage congregant into a sexual relationship, few people are likely to question the appropriateness of the attention he gives her, and she may fear personal and familial consequences if she reports the abuse. When a spiritual leader grooms his environment to create a spiritual pedestal that permits his coercion, lorded authority, and unhealthy seeking of validation from needy or vulnerable congregants, the match is lit. Without the damp blanket of accountability and a foolproof plan to extinguish the flame, the fire can quickly ignite, causing an incredible amount of spiritual, emotional, psychological, and sexual trauma within the church.

Grooming the victim. For a child sex offender capable of grooming an environment managed by competent, educated adults familiar with accountability, discipline, and structure, grooming a child is not difficult. Perpetrators are skilled at identifying and manipulating vulnerable children (Fortune et al., 2015). Manipulation strategies include everything from gift giving to highly restrictive and controlling behaviors to offering affirmation and acceptance. Victims are groomed to keep secrets by being made to feel complicit and responsible or through coercion and threats (Winters et al., 2020). These victim-grooming strategies will be explored in more depth in future chapters, but it is vital that the church recognize that the only safe child sex offender is one without access to children.

CONCEPTUALIZING SEXUAL OFFENDING AGAINST CHILDREN

While there are general grooming strategies utilized by perpetrators of all types of abuse, there are also unique dynamics at play with child sex offenders. Understanding the distinction between pedophilic attraction and behavior, the factors and characteristics that contribute to sexual offending against children, and why risk management strategies are the only safe option for convicted child sex offenders enables the church to protect the vulnerable and minister to the perpetrator.

Pedophilic attraction vs. behavior. According to the *Diagnostic and Statistical Manual of Mental Disorders* (*DSM-5*), pedophilia applies to both attraction *and* behavior (American Psychiatric Association, 2013). However, it is helpful to distinguish between a pedophilic orientation, where the individual experiences persistent and arousing fantasies and urges toward children (akin to any other sexual orientation), and pedophilic *offending* (Seto, 2012). For our purposes, pedophilic *attraction* is defined by persistent and arousing fantasies and urges (a deviant sexual orientation) toward prepubescent, pubescent, and adolescent minors. Pedophilic *offending* is acting on those urges.

Pedophilic attraction causes significant distress when present in adults with well-developed empathy and impulse control. Many people who struggle with pedophilia never prey on children because the internal barriers to acting out are substantial. These individuals know that the behavior is morally wrong and do not want to harm a child. The feelings of attraction alone create significant guilt, shame, and fear of disclosure (Silaghi & Rosu, 2020). While pedophilic attraction is not necessarily curable with psychotherapy, medication, or medical procedures, anyone who acknowledges that they struggle with pedophilic attraction before offending should seek therapeutic treatment to learn how to manage these impulses safely (Çöpür & Çöpür, 2021; Harvard University, 2010; Seto, 2009).

Characteristics. It is a common misconception that it is because children have been sexually abused that they grow up to be sexual abusers (Widom & Massey, 2015). The reality is that the contributing factors to sexual offending against children are complex and multifaceted (Clayton et al., 2018). Rather than looking to etiology, it is more helpful to consider perpetrator characteristics from within three broad profiles: the addict, the stunted child, and the egomaniac. These three profiles each have different grooming and risk mitigation strategies. However, these neat categories are simplistic representations of complex overlapping characteristics. It is not uncommon for perpetrators to have aspects of all three categories (Heffernan & Ward, 2015; Yates, 2013). Understanding these profiles enables the church to establish risk management strategies that are comprehensive enough to address the full range of contributing factors.

The addict. In substance use addiction, the person with the addiction experiences an intense urge to use a substance and seeks opportunities to satisfy the urge. For example, someone with an alcohol addiction may spend his day trying to identify when he can have the next drink. He might attempt to create opportunities to satisfy his urge to drink by hiding a flask in his office desk, rummaging through friends' liquor cabinets at dinner parties, or adding alcohol to his morning coffee. The behavioral life of the addict is built around using. For the perpetrator who functions like an addict, their "substance of choice" is sexual release stimulated by sexual contact with or between children. For this category, grooming takes place quickly and is opportunistic, resulting in many different victims that they do not know well. For example, they might lure a child into a bathroom, behind a building, or into a car. Convicted child molesters in this category have already offended, demonstrating they have poor impulse control skills and limited ability to manage their deviant attraction to children. Their previous sexual gratification reinforces the offending behavior and increases their desire to act out (Jimenez-Arista & Reid, 2023). Fear of disclosure can heighten the affective state of the offender, lead to secrecy, and prompt the offender to an escalating series of acting-out behaviors, similar to someone relapsing on a substance (Howells et al., 2004; Luoma et al., 2007).

The stunted child. Though offenders in this category are adults in their physical ability and intellectual capacity, they have severely stunted emotional development. In these cases, intimacy deficits, defined as a lack of "abilities for communication, emotional expression, respect, and interdependence in romantic relationships," are the drivers for sexually offending behaviors (Martin & Tardif, 2015, p. 378). Perpetrators in this category often have significant attachment deficits and interpersonal immaturity contributing to their drive "to seek relationships with children in order to avoid discomfort in social interactions, reduce social and emotional loneliness, or achieve affection or positive regard" (McPhail et al., 2013, p. 737). These intimate bonds develop over a long period. Children are targeted because of the nature of the predator-child relationship; if a child experiences emotional and social issues, such as poverty or abuse in the home, they are even more vulnerable to being targeted by a perpetrator (Swaminath et al., 2023). These relationships typically form between the child and a trusted adult, such as a scout leader, neighbor, close family friend, uncle, or stepfather.

The danger to the church context is clear—adults in church communities are seen and perceived as trustworthy by children and their unaware adult guardians. Although particularly true in the case of spiritual leaders, it applies to almost any adult in a church community who has become familiar with the child. The church uses words to convey this familial safety, such as *brother, father*, and *church family*. The violation of trust combined with the prolonged, repeated nature of the sexual molestation compounds the psychological trauma for the child (Gómez & Freyd, 2017).

The egomaniac. "Egomaniac" in this context does not necessarily refer to grandiose perceptions of oneself but instead implies that the perpetrator interprets every piece of information as self-referential. For example, a perpetrator in this category may interpret a store clerk's kindness to him as a clear indication that she wants to have sex with him. He may use this interpretation of her actions to justify aggressive sexual advances. Perpetrators in this category are often driven by an "all about me" perspective and include those clinically diagnosed with a personality disorder—most often antisocial, narcissistic, or avoidant type. These personality disorders are notoriously hard to treat and share common characteristics of unpredictable behavior, lack of empathy, risk-taking, and a need for instant gratification (Gilbert & Focquart, 2015). The co-occurring diagnosis of a personality disorder makes this category of perpetrator the most dangerous and most likely to reoffend. It can be difficult to predict grooming and offending behaviors for perpetrators in this category (Cohen et al., 2018).

RESPONSIBILITY TO REPORT

If there is an allegation of child abuse in your church, you *must* report that allegation to local law enforcement and remove the alleged perpetrator from any and all interactions with children. Churches sometimes feel apprehensive to report child abuse allegations, because they believe the abuse was "not that bad" or they want to protect the perpetrator from legal consequences. This is an extraordinarily dangerous perspective, as it places children and vulnerable adults at risk of abuse. Additionally, it is not a helpful perspective for the perpetrator. Scripture is clear that there are consequences for sin, and these consequences are an important step for perpetrators to be drawn to repentance. Perpetrators must face the reality of their actions and walk through the "valley of the shadow of death" if they are to experience true sorrow and repentance over their sin and receive grace and mercy from God (Psalm 23:4 KJV).

CONVICTED CHILD MOLESTER

How does the church respond to a perpetrator who has been convicted through the criminal justice system of sexual offending against children, served their prison sentence, and is reintegrating back into the community? The distinction between perpetrators of other types of abuse and convicted child molesters is important, as the risk management strategies for convicted child molesters require more than just implementing general safe church policies and practices. All the behaviors that are required to keep a child molester safe in a church context need to be documented and agreed on between the church leadership and the child molester prior to him attending the church in any capacity. It must be clearly stated that ongoing church attendance requires mandatory and complete adherence to the safety plan.

While safety plans will need to be adapted based on particular church practices, they follow three basic principles: no unstructured environments with children present, a deliberate and intentional commitment to leave any situation that is unstructured where children unexpectedly are present, and the understanding that at all times and in all circumstances there will be at least one person from the church who is familiar with both the offense history and the safety plan and is willing to hold the child molester accountable. These safety plans must be developed in partnership with law enforcement and treatment providers. A convicted child molester who is genuinely repentant will ask for and insist on this. It keeps him safe from any accusations as well as any temptations. Convicted child molesters are at high risk for reoffending when they make small or incremental violations of the established safety plan and justify these changes to themselves and those responsible for holding them accountable (Ward, 2000). In these instances, intentional efforts to be around children are explained as "accidental," and convoluted explanations are given for why they made certain choices or decisions. It is important to understand the risk of reoffending and the importance of maintaining strict guidelines about their interactions with the community, out of protection for both children and convicted offenders.

Churches should be places of grace where any of us can stand before the throne of God, comforted by his mercy, unafraid of our histories of sin. Churches should also be places of spiritual, emotional, and physical safety and nurture for all people. This creates a problem for church leaders wanting to create space for convicted child molesters in church communities. Leaders have often adopted false redemptive narratives that convicted child molesters can be reformed to the degree that they no longer pose a risk of reoffending. This logic is often applied by the church to any convicted criminal, regardless of the nature of the crime. Here's how this is often played out. Consider an offender who was incarcerated, was released, and completed a rehabilitation program and has lived incident-free within the community for several years. He claims he accepted Jesus and is now "saved." He may have indeed experienced Holy Spirit–empowered transformation and now be a follower of Christ. However, these communities often believe that when an offender expresses repentance and has not yet reoffended, he should be fully reintegrated back into the life of the church without holding firm on boundaries to protect children and vulnerable persons should he experience a relapse. They say, "All have sinned and fall short of the glory of God" (Romans 3:23); who has the right to deny the work of Christ and restrict this new creation from the fellowship of the church?

Some statistics on recidivism, or the act of reoffending, highlight why this approach is problematic with convicted child molesters. The Office of Sex Offender Sentencing, Monitoring, Apprehending, Registering, and Tracking reports the recidivism rate of convicted child molesters in the United States is 5.1 percent after three years, 23 percent after fifteen years, and 52 percent after twenty-five years (United States Department of Justice, 2015). It is worth noting that these figures are not general recidivism rates for any crime but specifically for sexual crimes against children. Even more problematic is that these figures represent reconviction rates, not offenses, so the likelihood of reoffending is potentially much higher. Although these statistics are from the United States, sex offender recidivism rates are comparable between North America, Britain, and Europe (Craig et al., 2008).

For convicted child molesters trying to reintegrate into church communities, grooming of the environment often begins with offenders being helpful and contributing in very safe ways. They may become one of the most reliable and capable volunteers in the church. The offender earns trust with his diligence in service, which is easily misapplied to his ability to regulate offending impulses. Church leaders become more relaxed about enforcing the established safety plan. Convicted child molesters have proven they are masters at the art of manipulation, and they will utilize this skill to groom their communities to allow them continued access to children.

Understanding the nature of sexual offending against children and the reality of recidivism helps us to provide both safety for the child and grace to the child molester. It is obviously dangerous to children to ignore strong risk management strategies with convicted child molesters; however, it is also dangerous to the child molester. It is not gracious or loving to put the convicted child molester in the position to likely relapse. The most loving responses from the church toward children *and* convicted child molesters are long-term risk management strategies that prevent child molesters from having access to children in perpetuity.

WHERE IS THE GRACE?

Church attendance at a healthy church is a positive experience for a child molester. Churches are among the few places where offenders can be accepted despite their brokenness. People who have committed sex crimes are exposed to their community through a public sex offender registry, community notification, and an ankle bracelet used for GPS tracking (Lussier et al., 2020). Housing and employment options are limited because landlords and employers do not want their premises associated with sex offenders through community notification programs. Child molesters are the unclean of our culture. Acceptance is akin to the healing touch given by Jesus to the lepers of his day who were forced to live on the margins of the cities (Luke 5:12-15). It changes everything.

However, no one knows whether an offender will try to reoffend. Not the probation officer, the parole officer, the treatment provider, the pastor, the elders, friends, family, or the offender himself knows if or when that time will come. Motivation to offend depends on the offender's level of supervision; feelings of shame, guilt, and remorse for previous offenses; recognition of victim impact; and empathy for the victim. Maintaining barriers to prevent offending depends on managing impulsiveness and difficult emotions (Howells et al., 2004). Motivation to offend and the capacity to maintain barriers waxes and wanes.

Grace does not deny brokenness. Grace comes around brokenness and shares in the burden-bearing that comes with being broken. When a church embraces the offender in a way in which neither the church nor the offender is in denial of the risk, everybody wins. Grace abounds. When a church asks an offender to leave because he is not following his safety plan, the offender is warned that they are at dangerous risk of reoffending. Everybody wins. Grace abounds. When a church is timid about establishing or enforcing a safety plan or over-spiritualizing the recovery of the offender, they are enabling denial, compromising the child molester's ability to adhere to his relapse prevention plan, and putting children at risk. Everybody loses—the child, the church, and the offender.

PERSONAL REFLECTION

1. Learning about perpetrator dynamics and grooming strategies can be distressing. What thoughts, feelings, and physical sensations did you experience as you read about perpetrator dynamics and pedophilia?

2. Consider the concept of grooming of self and environment within the context of abuse. Reflect on instances where grooming dynamics may have been present in your own experiences or observations.

3. Where have you seen churches or institutions prioritize "grace" and "forgiveness" over accountability and safety for victims?

GROUP DISCUSSION

1. How can understanding perpetrator dynamics and traits contribute to early intervention and abuse prevention?

2. Explore the impact of grooming on the church community. How might the church unintentionally enable or overlook signs of grooming behaviors? What steps can be taken to increase awareness and prevention?

3. Consider the relationship between accountability and grace. Explore how holding perpetrators accountable is consistent with the gospel message on grace, forgiveness, and the consequences of sin.

REFERENCES

Adam Walsh Child Protection and Safety Act 120 Stat. § 587. (2006).

American Psychiatric Association. (2013). *Diagnostic and Statistical Manual of Mental Disorders* (5th Ed.). Washington, DC.

Civil Commitment of a Sexually Dangerous Person Act 18 U.S. Code § 4248. (2006). www.govinfo.gov/link/plaw/109/public/248

Clayton, E., Jones, C., Brown, J., & Taylor, J. (2018). The aetiology of child sexual abuse: A critical review of the empirical evidence. *Child Abuse Review, 27*(3), 181-97. https://doi.org/10.1002/car.2517

Cohen, L. J., Ndukwe, N., Siegried, R., Kopeykina, I., Yaseen, Z., & Galynker, I. (2018). Attraction versus action in pedophilic desire: The role of personality traits and childhood experience. *Journal of Psychiatric Practice 24*(6), 374-87.

Çöpür, M., & Çöpür, S. (2021). Chemical castration as an evolving concept: Is it a possible solution for sexual offences? *The Journal of Forensic Psychiatry & Psychology, 32*(2), 326-351. https://doi.org/10.1080/14789949.2020.1849359

Craig, L. A., Browne, K. D., Stringer, I., & Hogue, T. E. (2008). Sexual reconviction rates in the United Kingdom and actuarial risk estimates. *Child Abuse & Neglect, 32*(1), 121-38. https://doi.org/10.1016/j.chiabu.2007.09.002

Delcea, C. (2020). Sexual offenders—psychological approaches. *Proceedings of the International Conference on Legal Medicine from Cluj* (3rd Ed., Vol. 2, pp. 9-20).

Dietz, P. (2020). Denial and minimization among sex offenders. *Behavioral Sciences & the Law, 38*(6), 571-85.

Fortune, C., Bourke, P., & Ward, T. (2015). Expertise and child sex offenders. *Aggression and Violent Behavior, 20*, 33-41. https://doi.org/10.1016/j.avb.2014.12.005

Gilbert, F., & Focquaert, F. (2015). Rethinking responsibility in offenders with acquired paedophilia: Punishment or treatment? *International Journal of Law and Psychiatry*, 38, 51-60. https://doi.org/10.1016/j.ijlp.2015.01.007

Gómez, J., & Freyd, J. (2017). High betrayal child sexual abuse and hallucinations: A test of an indirect effect of dissociation. *Journal of Child Sexual Abuse*, 26(5), 507-18. https://doi.org/10.1080/10538712.2017.1310776

Harvard University (2010). Pessimism about pedophilia. In *Harvard Mental Health Letter*. Harvard Health Publications Group.

Heffernan, R., & Ward, T. (2015). The conceptualization of dynamic risk factors in child sex offenders: An agency model. *Aggression and Violent Behavior, 24,* 250-60. https://doi.org/10.1016/j.avb.2015.07.001

Hempel, I. S., Buck, N. M. L., Van Vugt, E. S., & Van Marle, H. J. C. (2015). Interpreting child sexual abuse: Empathy and offense-supportive cognitions among child sex offenders. *Journal of Child Sexual Abuse*, 24(4), 354-68. https://doi.org/10.1080/10538712.2015.1014614

Howells, K., Day, A., & Wright, S. (2004). Affect, emotions and sex offending. *Psychology, Crime & Law*, 10(2), 179-95. https://doi.org/10.1080/10683160310001609988

Jimenez-Arista, L. E., & Reid, D. B. (2023). Realization, self-view, and disclosure of pedophilia: A content analysis of online posts. *Sexual Abuse, 35*(2), 214-40. https://doi.org/10.1177/10790632221099256

Kafka, M. (1996). Therapy for sexual impulsivity: The paraphilias and paraphilia-related disorders. *Psychiatric Times*, 13(6), 1-6.

Krueger, R. B., & Kaplan, M. S. (2016). Non-contact paraphilic sexual offenses. In A. Phenix & Harry M. Hoberman (Eds.), *Sexual offending: Predisposing antecedents, assessments and management* (pp. 79-102). Springer. https://doi.org/10.1007/978-1-4939-2416-5_6

Lee, A. F., Li, N.-C., Lamade, R., Schuler, A., & Prentky, R. A. (2012). Predicting hands-on child sexual offenses among possessors of Internet child pornography. *Psychology, Public Policy, and Law*, 18(4), 644-72. https://doi.org/10.1037/a0027517

Levenson, J. S., & Macgowan, M. J. (2004). Engagement, denial, and treatment progress among sex offenders in group therapy. *Sexual Abuse*, 16(1), 49-63. https://doi.org/10.1177/107906320401600104

Luoma, J. B., Twohig, M. P., Waltz, T., Hayes, S. C., Roget, N., Padilla, M., & Fisher, G. (2007). An investigation of stigma in individuals receiving treatment for substance abuse. *Addictive Behaviors, 32*(7), 1331-46. https://doi.org/10.1016/j.addbeh.2006.09.008

Lussier, P., McCuish, E. C., & Cale, J. (2020). A scarlet letter in the digital age: Sex offender registration and public notification. In *Understanding sexual offending* (pp. 313-56). Springer International Publishing. https://doi.org/10.1007/978-3-030-53301-4_9

March, E., Kay, C. S., Dinić, B. M., Wagstaff, D., Grabovac, B., & Jonason, P. K. (2023, June 23). "It's all in your head": Personality traits and gaslighting tactics in intimate relationships. *Journal of Family Violence*. https://doi.org/10.1007/s10896-023-00582-y

Martin, G. M., & Tardif, M. (2015). Examining sex offenders' intimacy deficits: Their nature and their influence on sexually abusive behaviours. *Journal of Sexual Aggression*, 21(2), 158-78. https://doi.org/10.1080/13552600.2013.849768

McPhail, I. V., Hermann, C. A., & Nunes, K. L. (2013). Emotional congruence with children and sexual offending against children: A meta-analytic review. *Journal of Consulting & Clinical Psychology, 81*(4), 737-49. https://doi.org/10.1037/a0033248

Petrunik, M., & Deutschmann, L. (2008). The exclusion–inclusion spectrum in state and community response to sex offenders in Anglo-American and European jurisdictions. *International Journal of Offender Therapy and Comparative Criminology, 52*(5), 499-519. https://doi.org/10.1177/0306624X07308108

Seto, M. C. (2009). Pedophilia. *Annual Review of Clinical Psychology, 5*(1), 391-407. https://doi.org/10.1146/annurev.clinpsy.032408.153618

Seto, M. C. (2012). Is pedophilia a sexual orientation? *Archives of Sexual Behavior, 41*(1), 231-36. https://doi.org/10.1007/s10508-011-9882-6

Silaghi, A. R., & Rosu, Ş. (2020). Forensic evaluations of sexual offenders. *International Journal of Advanced Studies in Sexology, 2*(2), 101-8. https://doi.org/10.46388/ijass.2020.13.28

Stinson, J. D., Robbins, S. B., & Crow, C. W. (2011). Self-regulatory deficits as predictors of sexual, aggressive, and self-harm behaviors in a psychiatric sex offender population. *Criminal Justice and Behavior, 38*(9), 885-95.

Swaminath, S., Simons, R., & Hatwan, M. (2023). Understanding pedophilia: A theoretical framework on the development of sexual penchants. *Journal of Child Sexual Abuse, 32*(6), 732-48. https://doi.org/10.1080/10538712.2023.2236602

United States Department of Justice. (2015). Sex Offender Management Assessment and Planning Initiative Research Brief. Office of Justice Programs. Washington DC: National Institute of Justice.

Ward, T., (2000). Sexual offenders' cognitive distortions as implicit theories. *Aggression and Violent Behavior, 5*(5): 491-507. https://doi.org/10.1016/S1359-1789(98)00036-6

Whittaker, S. D. (2013). *S.O.T.P: Sex offender workbook.* Createspace Independent Publishing Platform.

Widom, C. S., & Massey, C. (2015). A prospective examination of whether childhood sexual abuse predicts subsequent sexual offending. *JAMA pediatrics, 169(1),* e143357. https://doi.org/10.1001/jamapediatrics.2014.3357

Winters, G. M., Jeglic, E. L., & Kaylor, L. E. (2020). Validation of the sexual grooming model of child sexual abusers. *Journal of Child Sexual Abuse, 29*(7), 855-75. https://doi.org/10.1080/10538712.2020.1801935

Yates, P. M. (2013). Treatment of sexual offenders: Research, best practices, and emerging models. *International Journal of Behavioral Consultation & Therapy, 8*(3/4), 89-95.

6

SEXUAL MORALITY AND SEXUAL SCRIPTS

DR. KRISTI CRONAN

MORALITY IS A concept that most Christians agree is needed for a healthy life. In general terms, it is defined as the ability to engage in consistent decision making that results in good behavior which benefits society, self, relationships, and God. Morality is what directs our steps as we navigate complex situations and make personal decisions about how to respond. Simple examples of morality in action include deciding to tell the truth at work after an error has been made, returning a lost item that we found, or helping a child who has lost their caregiver be reunited with them. The list could go on and on because the truth is that morality is a foundational principle that exists within Christianity and even in the secular culture in which we live. As Christians, we seek to develop moral maturity based on biblical principles that inform our decision making so we can honor God to the best of our ability in the fallen world. Developing this understanding of biblical principles can be quite complex, though, because different Christian traditions often teach different moral certainties, specifically related to sexual morality.

FORMATION OF SEXUAL MORALITY BELIEFS IN CHRISTIANITY

Regardless of denominational affiliation or geographic location, most Christians would agree that the Bible calls us to avoid sexual immorality (1 Corinthians 6:18; 1 Thessalonians 4:3-5).[1] However, conversations that seek to illuminate what that tangibly means may vary based on the sources a person

---

[1]Scripture quotations, unless otherwise noted, are from the ESV.

draws on for Christian moral knowledge. For instance, Catholics honor that there is a natural law which is a source of reason that guides morality. Roman Catholics may also adhere to this tradition while honoring that the Magisterium is the respected and preferred translator of Scriptures. Conversely, Protestants' beliefs related to sexual morality are likely to prioritize the importance of individuals' interaction with Scripture without reliance on a hierarchy of leadership to be the voice of these truths. Progressive Protestants may even pair biblical truths found in Scripture with experiences to inform their definitions of morality. Because of these foundational differences that can exist within the Christian faith, there often are disputes about the application and absoluteness of moral norms like sexual morality (Kohlhaas, 2017). This chapter will illuminate both the commonalities and variations that can occur throughout various Christian subcultures regarding sexual morality because understanding these foundations is essential to discern how churches interpret and respond to sexual abuse.

Biblical sexual morality, in its simplest and most widely accepted form, is likely to be described as abstaining from sexual intercourse outside of marriage. When people get married, they become "one flesh" (Genesis 2:24; Matthew 19:4-6). This union is often depicted as both a functional partnership as well as the physical joining of bodies through intercourse (1 Corinthians 6:13-18). Biblical sexuality may honor that intercourse is used not only to procreate (Genesis 1:28) but also for intimacy (Song of Solomon 1:13; 2:3), for companionship (Song of Solomon 3:1), and for physical pleasure (Song of Solomon 1:2). More importantly, though, biblical sexuality is meant to be symbolic of Christ and the church (Ephesians 5:31-33). For some Christians, this means that their view on biblical sexuality is founded on a commitment to celibacy for the duration of their lives. For others, this means that they engage in sex only within the confines and mutual consent that exists in marriage.

Because most Christians view sexual morality as a sacred metaphor for Christ and the church, it is often accepted that it must be closely guarded and protected from any distortions that would misrepresent its true purpose. These distortions extend a great deal past simply not having sex outside marriage, though. Sexual morality often includes avoiding incest, bestiality, fornication, and prostitution, and protecting children (Leviticus 18; Matthew 18:10). As a result, this is typically how sexual morality is discussed and portrayed by religious leaders at a foundational level within Christian communities. Even still, there are cultural variations regarding biblical sexuality and sexual morality that exist within Christianity.

Take, for example, Julie's story. She grew up in a conservative Protestant home and was taught that sexual intercourse and any other sexual behaviors were intended to be enjoyed in the confines of marriage with her future husband. Diligent to maintain her sexual ethics, she prioritized a goal to avoid all sexual behavior until marriage. When she met her boyfriend, Jared, he shared that he was a devout Christian and that he was also committed to remaining sexually abstinent. However, as their relationship progressed, it became apparent that what he defined as sexually abstinent was different than what Julie would describe. For instance, Jared was perplexed why they could not French kiss or talk about their future sexual lives together, and Julie was distressed at the expectation that they should. This was incredibly confusing for the couple, especially as they navigated the complexities of the reality that Jared had already engaged in sexual encounters that would not meet Julie's threshold for sexual abstinence. Julie went to her religious leaders for support in the matter as she worked to discern how to make healthy sexual decisions for herself. Her leaders affirmed that Jared was not raised with the same, proper sexual standards, and this led Julie to question if Jared was even a practicing Christian at all. Jared was then hurt that she questioned his commitment to Christ.

While this story is fictitious, it is a simple representation of the differences that can exist across the Christian faith regarding sexual decision making. Within different Christian faith traditions, you will hear a myriad of Scripture interpretations that lead religious leaders to expand on what they believe sexual morality pertains to in addition to the call to sexual abstinence outside of marriage. Research has shown that Christians are likely to vocalize their views on sexual morality as a means to differentiate themselves from secular culture. These differences are often expressed as criticisms of different views of sexual morality that exist in secular culture and even within more liberal Christian cultures (Beekers & Schrijvers, 2020). As a result, it is important to understand what variations may exist in diverse Christian sexual ethics discussions.

The most conservative Christian traditions may adhere to principles like avoiding lustful thoughts and masturbation. They may suggest that people only engage in penial-vaginal intercourse for the purposes of procreation within marriage as well. Other cultural variations may include prohibiting the use of contraception or refraining from engaging in same-sex attraction or behaviors. Additionally, some Christians also recommend that sexual morality means avoiding dialogue that references sexual content and encouraging women to be sexually submissive to their husbands. As a result, the vast dialogue related to sexual morality in Christianity can be varied by geographic cultures and denominational differences. With these differences in mind, it is no shock that research has shown that there is a mixed consensus about what constitutes sexual morality among Christians (Kohlhaas, 2017). It is also important to consider that while Christianity affirms various moral guidelines regarding sexuality, there is also a significant weight placed on forgiveness, grace, and redemption for immoral behaviors. It is common for Christians to believe that God can transform, heal, and restore people who struggle with sexual immorality.

SEXUAL SCRIPTS WITHIN CHRISTIANITY

Although more research is needed to understand whether or not the varied perspectives related to biblical sexual morality play a role in identifying and responding to sexual abuse within the Christian church, there are ample research foundations that explore the sexual scripts that Christianity promotes, which may shed light on how the church identifies and responds to sexual abuse. Sexual scripts are cognitive constructs that direct sexual and romantic decision making, and they help a person make sense of sexual responsibilities and experiences both in their own lives and in the lives of others (Jones & Hostler, 2001). Frequently, sexual scripts are passed down within cultures through religious teachings, media, and family dialogue during childhood, and then they are subsequently reinforced throughout our experiences in adulthood. Examples of potentially harmful sexual scripts include: it is appropriate for men to have a strong sex drive but not women; victims of sexual crimes have lost their virginity and are no longer "pure"; any sexual act within marriage is acceptable even if it makes one spouse feel uncomfortable; and wives should be available to meet their husband's sexual needs at any time. These cultural scripts become internalized and are used to create a set of rules for interpersonal interactions and to make meaning of future experiences. Internal scripts are ultimately what establishes our perspectives about how to behave, respond, and interpret various situations and experiences (Wiederman, 2015).

Culture plays a significant role in sexual script development, and therefore it is imperative to explore how Christian culture contributes to sexual script formation. First, it is common for Christians to avoid discussing sexual topics and instead focus on secondary constructs, like gender roles. This lack of specific focus on sexual topics means that some Christians have limited sexual awareness and understanding of themselves as sexual beings. This can lead to immature spiritual formation because Scriptures associated with sexual morality may be inadvertently deprioritized or misinterpreted. These factors make individuals more susceptible to becoming perpetrators of sexual abuse, especially those in power within high-stress Christian leadership positions (Terry, 2015).

Within Christianity, sexual scripts are heavily influenced by the sexual morality teachings promoted within the local church. These sexual scripts provide a roadmap for people to follow to be sexually moral, and they play a vital role in sexual identity development. Much of this research associated with these sexual scripts is rooted in a subdivision of Christian sexual ethics that provides insights related to sexual abstinence. In the United States, these scripts around sexual abstinence are most commonly referred to as "purity culture," but similar teachings and methods are present in Christian experiences throughout the world across Catholicism and Protestantism (Ortiz, 2019; Stanley, 2020). Purity culture aims to promote sexual abstinence until heterosexual marriage by creating specific sexual script narratives. It is important to note that the goal of biblical sexual abstinence is strongly rooted in Scripture, and therefore it is often highly valued across different domains of Christian culture. While this is a biblical goal that many Christians rightfully aspire to, research highlights potential limitations and concerns with certain teaching methods utilized by purity culture. To be clear, we are not stating that purity is the issue of concern; instead, we want to highlight the harmful methods utilized by some groups attempting to enforce purity. To help understand this differentiation, consider how parents can utilize different methods to motivate their children to develop healthy hygiene habits. One parent may have a conversation with their child about why they need to brush their teeth; explain about cavities; supply them with a toothbrush, toothpaste, and floss; and model what appropriate brushing and frequency look like. This method provides the child with a sense of connection, meaning, and opportunity to be a good steward of their health because they understand they are worthy and deserving of self-care. Conversely, another parent may elect to simply say "brush your teeth because I said so" with no other explicit conversation and solely rely on punishments to demand compliance, perhaps even telling the child that their teeth will fall out overnight if they forget to brush. While the child may somewhat brush their teeth for a time, the child is unlikely to develop long-term healthy oral hygiene because the driving force for the habit is to avoid punishment and negative outcomes, not to honor their body in a meaningful way.

Now, let's apply the same concepts to sexual abstinence discussions within purity culture. Similar to the previous example, Christian leaders can have the best of intentions to promote sexual abstinence, but their approach may or may not be effective and healthy. For instance, purity culture's teaching methods have been proven to use sexual scripts related to shame, gender roles, and manipulation to coerce and pressure nonmarital sexual abstinence (Blyth, 2021; Ortiz, 2019). A common example of this is how purity culture utilizes a metaphor that compares women to chewed up gum that no longer has purpose in the event she kisses a man before marriage. This metaphor essentially teaches women that their value diminishes as a result of any sexual mistakes that are made. Ultimately, these types of experiences within purity culture diminish a young woman's self-worth and distort messages related to grace and redemption found throughout the Bible.

The first way purity culture markets the sexual script of biblical sexual morality is by educating Christians on the rewards of their sexual abstinence (Ortiz, 2019). Some Christian traditions promote the idea that remaining sexually abstinent until heterosexual marriage will result in an idealistic quality of life, marriage, sexual satisfaction, and relationship with God. This can create unrealistic expectations for newlyweds in the event they experience sexual engagement difficulties. This disrupts marital satisfaction, creates shame in wondering if they did something wrong to deserve this problem, and may impact their relationship with God because they perceive that he did not grant the marital bliss that was promised within purity culture.

Next, Christianity often reinforces the sexual script that unpleasant emotional experiences, like guilt and shame, will follow a person should they elect to engage in sexual activity outside of the confines of a heterosexual, monogamous marriage (Ortiz, 2019). Second Corinthians 7:10 provides a helpful distinction for this context. It states, "Godly grief produces a repentance that leads to salvation without regret, whereas worldly grief produces death." Essentially, pastors should aim to present the truth that if we live outside of God's design and experience the feeling of (godly) guilt, we are motivated to move toward God in repentance knowing we can be redeemed. If pastors instead promote a guilt without hope for redemption, people are prone to hide in shame. Furthermore, Christian leaders should apply caution using shame-based teaching that implies the person, as opposed to the behavior, is bad and disgraceful, as such teaching is associated with an increased likelihood that the recipient will adopt shame-based core beliefs that will repeat throughout their lifespan (Sedgwick & Frank, 1995). This habituation of shame-based responses leads to sadness, fear, rumination, anger, unworthiness, rejection, isolation, and hypersexuality (Gilliland et al., 2011; Lichtenberg, 2011). It also causes victims of sexual abuse to remain silent and incorrectly accept responsibility for the abuse they were victim to.

Finally, Christian leaders are likely to affect the sexual scripts of Christians by conceptualizing that conservative, westernized gender role beliefs are associated with sexual morality and sexual safety (Ortiz, 2019). When presented in a healthy framework, these gender roles create synchronicity where men lead humbly, modeling Christlike sacrifice and care for their wives with the goal of promoting their flourishing. Wives are valued as equal members of the partnerships who honor their husbands' strengths as well as their own gifts and exercise their voices to promote goodness. In contrast, these gender roles become unhealthy when men are the unquestioned authority as they manage their communities, and women are required to be submissive to their directives despite personal harm (Ortiz, 2019; Schleicher & Gilbert, 2005). Research shows that these types of gender role beliefs have the potential to create power imbalances and social inequity where both genders are negatively impacted due to their influence on sexual script development (Jones & Hostler, 2001). For example, males may feel pressured not to report when they have been victimized by abuse due to scripts dictating expectations to be "tough and macho," and females may not recognize abuse due to scripts requiring them to be "submissive" to the desires of others.

CHRISTIAN SEXUAL SCRIPTS AND ABUSE RECOGNITION

As people work to internalize these culturally informed sexual scripts, it is common for there to be a host of different opinions about what is acceptable, where boundaries lie, and who is responsible if those boundaries are crossed. These discrepancies can contribute to sexual abuse because they lead to consent confusion and victim blaming among men and women alike. Currently, statistics show that one in five women will experience completed or attempted rape in their lifetime and 43.6 percent of women have experienced sexual violence (Owens et al., 2020). Because female sexual assault is this prevalent, it has desensitized people so significantly that they struggle to label it correctly (Hlavka, 2014). This contributes to the narrative of rape myths. An example of a rape myth that is prominent within both secular and Christian communities is assuming that a victim is lying about past sexual abuse because many years have passed since the sexual trauma occurred. In reality, it is common for sexual abuse survivors to carry this burden in isolation for many years. Research has shown that rape myth acceptance is more common in populations with increased religiosity; however, different subcultures within Christianity may not struggle with rape myth acceptance as much as others (Burt, 1980; Barnett, 2018). For instance, in some fundamentalist Christian communities, a woman may be blamed for her sexual assault if it was deemed that she tempted her male perpetrator by dressing provocatively or entertaining his sexual innuendos (Owens et al., 2020).

Christian sexual scripts also create other openings for confusion in recognizing abuse. Many Christian sexual scripts are also correlated with domestic violence myth acceptance, which is the tendency to possess prejudicial, stereotyped, or false beliefs about domestic violence victims (Ortiz et al., 2023). Domestic violence can include physical violence, emotional abuse, sexual assault, stalking, or threats. Research has shown that Christian leaders and their associated sexual scripts play an integral role in the decision-making process of abused Christians as they discern whether to remain in an abusive environment or to leave, specifically as it relates to married women and their children (Wang et al., 2009). Imagine a pastor who is providing pastoral counseling to a church member who has previously shared that domestic violence occurs at home. At the onset of the appointment, the pastor notices that the member has severe abrasions on her face, neck, and arms. Although the pastor inquires about her safety, she frantically denies that she and her husband had any recent altercations. In this event, some pastors' sexual scripts lead them to direct the woman to try to fortify her marriage while other pastors have a sexual script that would allow them to support the women in the event she chose to leave the abusive marriage. Church leaders are encouraged to be intentional and cautious as they work to support a victim through domestic violence by not using Scriptures about divorce to coerce a person to stay in an abusive relationship.

Christian sexual scripts also influence the way victims and perpetrators of sexual abuse are viewed. Directly stated, sexual scripts provide a framework for us to understand all sexual encounters, and this extends into how we identify and interpret sexual abuse. Because sexual scripts present within the Christian community are associated with traditional gender role beliefs, women are not perceived as sexually driven. This often causes sexual abuse from female perpetrators to go unnoticed (Denov, 2003). In a similar fashion, sexual scripts within Christianity frequently instill the belief that religious leaders are sexually moral, and therefore it can easily be assumed that they are not as likely to commit sexual abuse. Unfortunately, though, the grim reality is that sexual abusers are often leaders throughout Christianity and other religions (Rashid & Barron, 2019). Christian leaders and helpers must reflect on their beliefs about their own sexuality so they can steward their authority in a way that honors, rather than exploits, others. By protecting their communities in this way, we are not only reducing sexual abuse encounters, we are supporting healthy sexual script development and reducing traumatic sexualization as well.

HELPFUL ACTION STEPS TO CONSIDER

In an effort to protect vulnerable populations from sexual abuse within the church, Catholics and Protestants alike have clarified and expanded their opinions on what constitutes sexual morality by issuing statements regarding abuse, thereby setting precedents that will impact the sexual scripts of their communities. These trends have been evaluated in research to discern the updated teachings related to sexual morality in the Christian church (Kleiven, 2018). Christian churches most often link the terminology "sexual abuse" to childhood sexual abuse, and sexual abuse of nonvulnerable populations is more likely to be referred to as "sexual misconduct" (Kleiven, 2018). Furthermore, this analysis revealed that churches likely categorize and conceptualize sexual abuse in distinct ways.

Many churches have taken steps in the right direction toward addressing sexual abuse through updated policies and procedures. In these public documents, churches have sought to describe sexual misconduct more clearly. Leaders and congregants are encouraged to avoid specific behaviors deemed immoral or abusive. These documents communicate the dos and don'ts of Christian sexual morality described earlier, and they extend the dialogue into more culturally informed protections for minors, women, and other vulnerable populations. Next, it is common for churches to define harassment and recommend that we honor the subjective experiences of victims of sexual harassment and abuse to learn how to protect our communities better. Additionally, churches are likely to utilize ethical and cultural policies to measure appropriate and inappropriate behavior by providing examples of each. For instance, many churches would affirm that sexual morality extends to the avoidance of specific behaviors like patting buttocks, groping breasts, or touching genitals. Some policies may also indicate that sexual topics should be discussed in the presence of a third party and avoid flirtatiousness or crudeness. These church statements go as far as labeling sexual misconduct as morally reprehensible. Finally, it is now more common for churches to highlight that sexual morality extends to honoring and respecting the power differentials that exists between religious leaders and their communities (Kleiven, 2018).

While these institutional steps to better define sexual morality have been initiated to protect victims of abuse in the church, more work still needs to be done at the micro level to safeguard religious communities. Individual church leaders and helpers should educate themselves on their institution's policies and create policies if they are absent. These documents should outline the expectations related to what constitutes sexual morality, abuse, sexual misconduct, and sexual harassment, and the steps that leaders will take to protect victims in the event abuse occurs. There should be direct commentary regarding how abusers' crimes and misconduct will not be hidden from the community, and specific attention and intentionality are needed to protect the anonymity of victims. These documents should be discussed with staff and provided to the church so that a unified narrative is endorsed.

This tangible step not only increases the church's awareness of abuse, it also begins the restorative work of adjusting any maladaptive, or unhealthy, sexual scripts that are present within Christian communities. Because sexual scripts have the power to influence our ability to recognize sexual abuse and how we interpret it, this step is crucial for safeguarding our communities from abuse. As a result, church leaders and helpers should engage in deep personal reflection to uproot any biases or unhealthy sexual scripts they possess that could unintentionally harm the communities they serve. For some, an initial exploration of these constructs may produce significant personal reactions. In this event, Christian leaders would benefit from exploring their sexual scripts within the safety of a therapeutic relationship with a Christian professional counselor.

Finally, when Christian leaders couple clarification of institutional policies regarding sexual abuse and personal sexual script processing with trauma and abuse education, it means that they can lead from an intentional and informed place of restoration that is aligned with God's perfect love for us. As a result, Christian leaders and helpers should prioritize learning about patterns of sexual abuse and sexual misconduct so they are prepared to identify potential perpetrators and respond as the hands and feet of Christ to those in need. Additionally, these efforts protect future victims of abuse by identifying perpetrators and holding them accountable for their sexual misconduct. This ensures that everyone from the most vulnerable to the strongest members of our community are protected to the best of our abilities from abuse in the church.

PERSONAL REFLECTION

1. What were you (implicitly or explicitly) taught about your own sexuality by your family? By your church? By your community as a whole?

2. How have you seen people teach good principles with questionable methods? How have you seen this play out with regard to sexual scripts?

3. How can an understanding of your own sexual development equip you for the work of safeguarding?

GROUP DISCUSSION

1. How do distorted sexual scripts enable or perpetuate abuse?

2. How can safeguarders contribute to the development of healthy sexual scripts within their faith communities?

3. How can some of the messages related to "purity culture" impact trauma survivors' perception of their self-worth and experience of shame?

REFERENCES

Barnett, M. D., Sligar, K. B., & Wang, C. D. C. (2018). Religious affiliation, religiosity, gender, and rape myth acceptance: Feminist theory and rape culture. *Journal of Interpersonal Violence, 33*(8), 1219–35. https://doi.org/10.1177/0886260516665110

Beekers, D., & Schrijvers, L. S. (2020). Religion, sexual ethics and the politics of belonging: Young Muslims and Christians in the Netherlands. *Social Compass, 67*(1), 137-56. https://doi.org/10.1177/0037768620901664

Blyth, C. (2021). Rape culture, purity culture, and coercive control in teen girl Bibles. Routledge.

Burt, M. R. (1980). Cultural myths and supports for rape. *Journal of Personality and Social Psychology, 38*(2), 217-30. https://doi.org/10.1037/0022-3514.38.2.217

Denov, M. S. (2003). The myth of innocence: Sexual scripts and the recognition of child sexual abuse by female perpetrators. *The Journal of Sex Research, 40*(3), 303-14. https://doi.org/10.1080/00224490309552195

Gilliland, R., South, M., Carpenter, B. N., & Hardy, S. A. (2011). The roles of shame and guilt in hypersexual behavior. *Sexual Addiction & Compulsivity, 18*, 12-29. http://doi.org/10.1080/ 10720162.2011.551182

Hlavka, H. R. (2014). Normalizing sexual violence: Young women account for harassment and abuse. *Gender and Society, 28*(3), 337-58. https://doi.org/10.1177/0891243214526468

Jones, S. L., & Hostler, H. R. (2001). Sexual script theory: An integrative exploration of the possibilities and limits of sexual self-definition. *Journal of Psychology and Theology, 30*(2), 120-30.

Kleiven, T. (2018). Sexual misconduct in the church: What is it about? *Pastoral Psychology, 67*(3), 277-89. https://doi.org/10.1007/s11089-018-0807-3

Kohlhaas, J. (2017). Christian sexual ethics: The ongoing conversation(s). *Religious Studies Review, 43*(2), 101-8. https://doi.org/10.1111/rsr.12897

Lichtenberg, J. D. (2011). *Sensuality and sexuality across the divide of shame* (Vol. 25). Taylor & Francis.

Navarro, J. C., & Tewksbury, R. (2018). Deconstructing the associations of religiosity, Christian denominations, and non-religions to rape myth acceptance among university students. *Deviant Behavior, 39*(1), 80-93. https://doi.org/10.1080/01639625.2016 .1260386

Noll, J. G. (2021). Child sexual abuse as a unique risk factor for the development of psychopathology: The compounded convergence of mechanisms. *Annual Review of Clinical Psychology, 17*(1), 439-64. https://doi.org/10.1146/annurev-clinpsy-081219-112621

Ortiz, A. M. (2019). *Developing a measure of purity culture: Sexual messages in evangelical Christian culture* [Doctoral dissertation, Biola University].

Ortiz, A. M., Sunu, B. C., Hall, M. E. L., Anderson, T. L., & Wang, D. C. (2023). Purity culture: Measurement and relationship to domestic violence myth acceptance. *Journal of Psychology and Theology, (51)*4, 537-56. https://doi.org/10.1177/00916471231182734

Owens, B. C., Hall, M. E., & Anderson, T. L. (2020). The relationship between purity culture and rape myth acceptance. *Journal of Psychology and Theology, 49*(4), 405-18. https://doi.org/10. 1177/0091647120974992

Rashid, F., & Barron, I. (2019). Why the focus of clerical child sexual abuse has largely remained on the Catholic church amongst other non-Catholic Christian denominations and religions. *Journal of Child Sexual Abuse, 28*(5), 564-85. https://doi.org/10.1080/10538712.2018.1563261

Schleicher, S. S., & Gilbert, L. A. (2005). Heterosexual dating discourses among college students: Is there still a double standard? *Journal of College Student Psychotherapy, 19*(3), 7-23. https://doi.org/10.1300/J035v19n03_03

Sedgwick, E. K., & Frank, A. (1995). Shame in the cybernetic fold: Reading Silvan Tomkins. *Critical Inquiry, 21*(2), 496-522. https://doi.org/10.1086/448761

Stanley, O. (2020). A personal encounter with purity culture: Evangelical Christian schooling in Aotearoa/New Zealand. *Women's Studies Journal, 34*(1), 116-29.

Terry, K. J. (2015). Child sexual abuse within the Catholic Church: A review of global perspectives. *International Journal of Comparative and Applied Criminal Justice, 39*(2), 139-54. https://doi.org/10.1080/01924036.2015.1012703

Tomlinson, J. M., Aron, A., Carmichael, C. L., Reis, H. T., & Holmes, J. G. (2014). The costs of being put on a pedestal: Effects of feeling over-idealized. *Journal of Social and Personal Relationships, 31*(3), 384-409. doi: 10.1177/0265407513498656

Wang, M.-C., Horne, S. G., Levitt, H. M., & Klesges, L. M. (2009). Christian women in IPV relationships: An exploratory study of religious factors. *The Journal of Psychology and Christianity, 28*(3), 224.

Wiederman, M. W. (2015). Sexual script theory: Past, present, and future. In J. D. DeLamater & R. F. Plante (Eds.), *Handbook of the sociology of sexualities* (pp. 7-22). Springer International Publishing. https://doi.org/10.1007/978-3-319-17341-2_2

SECTION III

IMPACT OF ABUSE

7

IMPACT OF TRAUMA

DR. KAITLYN CALLAIS STAFFORD

LIAM SITS QUIETLY as his family eats dinner. His wife passes the bread to their younger son as his daughter makes silly faces across the table. The noise in the room has escalated, and though the noise consists of giggles and common arguments among siblings about the dessert choice for the evening, Liam can't help but notice that his chest feels tight. He starts to feel pressure in his head, a buzzing, and the feeling that something just isn't right. He notices the green peas on the table. His son jokingly throws a few at their daughter, and without hesitation, Liam yells loudly and uncharacteristically, "STOP IT! GO TO YOUR ROOM NOW!" Liam's wife is puzzled because it was just a few peas, and the kids were playing. Liam is staring at the green peas and vaguely hears his wife, but his mind floods with images of that night when he was eight. He had chicken, potatoes, and green peas . . . and screaming, the screams of his mother return to his ears as if he were eight again; her face, bruised and wounded from his stepfather's angry wrath are all he can see. Peas. Wounded flesh. Mom crying. *Why didn't I do something?* His body floods with rage. His ears are hot. His heart and mind are racing, his pupils dilated. "Honey, it's okay. It was just a joke, and the kids were playing," his wife says softly to Liam. *But nothing feels okay to Liam at this moment.*

The vignette of Liam is a snapshot of how quickly and deeply a person who has experienced trauma can be transported physiologically, cognitively, and emotionally out of the present moment. As with Liam, the impact of trauma on a person, and consequently their families, is pervasive. As you read the following chapter, you will learn how trauma and abuse can disrupt a person's life. It is essential to note that humans are remarkably resilient, and research shows that resilience and even growth are possible despite enduring abuse, neglect, violence, terror, and other traumatic experiences (Bonanno, 2004; Tedeschi & Calhoun, 1996). As helpers, it is vital to remember the truth that healing can occur despite a history of horrific trauma: "For with God nothing will be impossible" (Luke 1:37 NKJV). Though healing and recovery can seem impossible for survivors, helpers must keep a perspective of relentless hope and faith and believe that healing *is* possible.

VARIATION IN TRAUMA CIRCUMSTANCES

The various responses to trauma have been documented for quite some time now. Books like the *Diagnostic and Statistical Manual* (*DSM-5-TR*) (American Psychiatric Association, 2022) and the *International Statistical Classification of Diseases and Related Health Problems* (*ICD-11*) (World Health Organization, 2021) provide helpers with an overview of the types of symptoms or reactions commonly occurring when a person has experienced one or multiple traumatic experiences. This chapter will describe the various symptoms and responses that are well documented.

As helpers, it is essential to remember that although there are common reactions and responses to trauma, every survivor is unique. A person's response to trauma may at times overlap with common reactions mentioned in this chapter, or the impact of trauma may differ from some of the information that follows based on the person's gender, age, cultural background, or the type of trauma they experienced. It is important to note that *when* a person experienced a traumatic event (i.e., their developmental stage of life) and *how* a person experienced a traumatic event (e.g., one time or repeatedly, at the hands of a trusted person, the intensity of the event) will affect the frequency, severity, and disruptive nature of a person's symptoms or reactions. Additionally, if a person experienced a traumatic event alone or in isolation (e.g., physical abuse, sexual assault) versus with a group (e.g., natural disaster or war), this will also influence how a person responds and copes with the traumatic event. Human-induced, interpersonal traumas like sexual assault or physical violence will also affect survivors differently than non-human-induced traumas such as natural disasters, medical trauma, or accidental traumas like car accidents. Even so, by reading this chapter, you will hopefully leave with a deeper understanding of what the people you are helping experience daily and how complex and disruptive trauma can be for individuals, families, and communities.

TRAUMA SYMPTOMS

Trauma involves an event, a person's reactions both during and immediately after the event, and the long-term effects of the traumatic event on a person. When a person experiences a traumatic event, the body responds in various ways with one primal goal: to help the person stay alive. Fight, flight, freeze, and fawn are survival responses that have been observed in trauma survivors. It is important to note that we do not consciously choose which response to use; rather, our brains determine whether physically attacking, running away, making ourselves as invisible as possible, or befriending the aggressor poses the highest likelihood of self-preservation.

While fight, flight, freeze, and fawn are immediate brain and body reactions during the trauma, they can also become survival *strategies* in the aftermath of trauma (Contreras, 2024).

In addition to survival responses, survivors may also experience symptoms of posttraumatic stress, including intrusions, hyperarousal and hypervigilance, negative mood and thoughts, avoidance, and dissociation (American Psychiatric Association, 2022; Herman, 2022). Long-term exposure to abuse and/or neglect is highly correlated with adverse health, medical, mental health, financial, educational, and occupational outcomes (Felitti et al., 1998). We will explore these reactions, symptoms, and experiences throughout the chapter.

Fight or flight. One of our primal stress and survival reactions is to fight or flee when we are faced with danger. Fighting is the act of defending ourselves against danger. Fleeing, or flight, is the act of leaving or attempting to leave the danger. Both fight and flight involve a person attempting to move or act. However, fighting or fleeing is not synonymous with everyday movements or physical activities like going for a run or attending a boxing or martial arts class. During a state of fight or flight, the brain and body are primarily focused on staying alive, so the nervous system, heart, and brain operate in different capacities to focus only on survival. While fighting or fleeing are short-term survival mechanisms, trauma survivors can experience fight or flight responses in the immediate and long-term aftermath of trauma in the form of hyperarousal and hypervigilance symptoms, which will be explored later in the chapter. Additionally, our awareness is heightened in a fight-or-flight state, and often, sights, smells, sounds, sensations, and tastes get paired with the fight-or-flight, elevated nervous system state (e.g., racing heart, dilated pupils, higher blood pressure). For trauma survivors, this means that the slightest sensory reminder of the traumatic event can evoke the fight-or-flight response when danger is not actually present.

Freeze. People could also experience a freeze response during a traumatic event. When a person experiences a freeze response, they are acutely aware of their surroundings, including threats, but are *temporarily* immobile (Kozlowska et al., 2015). A sexual abuse survivor I worked with described this well, stating, "I saw him coming. I knew he was dangerous. My heart started beating fast as he turned the corner toward me, but I was stuck. I could not move. If I had just moved, if I hadn't just stayed there, he wouldn't have assaulted me. I'd be free from all of this pain." This survivor's experience highlights the freeze response. Though it's a common biological and physiological reaction to danger, it can leave survivors later feeling guilty, as if they are to blame for the trauma.

Tonic immobility, a type of freeze response, is the body's attempt to psychologically escape and detach from danger when it cannot physically escape using other responses like fight or flight (Kozlowska et al., 2015). It is especially common in trauma survivors who experienced sexual abuse and assault (Moller et al., 2017). I have worked with many sexual assault survivors over the years who, when recounting their trauma, have shared that they felt "frozen in their body" when the assault occurred. They were physically present, experiencing horrific danger and threat, yet their bodies felt paralyzed, unable to fight, run, or even scream. In a tonic immobility response, their body physically shuts down and they experience loss of vocal or physical movement yet retain the memory of the experience (Morabito & Schmidt, 2023). However, when and how the survivor recalls the trauma memory or responds to the traumatic experience is complicated because a tonic immobility response means that a survivor's nervous system is both accelerating and stopping at the same time during the event (Levine, 2015). As a result, they experience various and often unpredictable reactions in the aftermath of trauma, from what might seem to be bizarre behavior, such as a catatonic stare, to inconsistencies in how they report details of the event(s), to a significantly delayed expression of traumatic distress symptoms. A tonic immobility response is an adaptive survival response when fight or flight are not available during the assault. However, research shows that when the body defaults to this response for survival in the short term, it may mean that the survivor is more likely to experience adverse traumatic stress outcomes in the long term (Moller et al., 2017; Morabito & Schmidt, 2023).

Fawn. Fawning is a response that is unique to humans (Walker, 2021). Whereas fight, flight, and freeze are found in other animal species, fawning is often, though not always, a response that a survivor experiences when they are chronically exposed to an abusive perpetrator. Fawning is a person's attempt to appease one's perpetrator by forfeiting one's personal needs to prevent the trauma from occurring or lessen the severity of the attack (Contreras, 2024). I recall a female client I worked with many years ago who experienced a horrific group sexual assault. Despite her desperate desire to fight or flee, she recalled that she willingly took substances offered to her by the perpetrators and laughed at their jokes (despite being utterly terrified). She had hoped her attempts to appease the perpetrators would lessen the severity of the attacks to come. It should be noted that this reaction at the time was not a slow, conscious decision but rather an innate response to the horror that was unfolding before her. In the short term, fawn reactions are a survival mechanism. However, ongoing minimization of personal needs to appease others results in increased risk of retraumatization, poor boundaries in relationships, insecurity, and being overly dependent on others (Owca, 2020).

Intrusions. A hallmark reaction trauma survivors experience is that despite being in the present moment and going about their daily lives, past trauma can suddenly feel as if it is happening again without notice. This occurrence is known as reexperiencing, or intrusions (American Psychiatric Association, 2022; Herman, 2022), which is seen in the vignette with Liam that you read earlier in the chapter. All at once, seemingly out of nowhere, Liam experienced intrusive memories of witnessing domestic violence from childhood. In addition to images and memories flooding the brain, intrusions can be experienced as physiological reactions in which the body feels as if it needs to escape, flee, or hide from danger despite no actual danger being present. As mentioned previously, when a person experiences a traumatic event, images, smells, physical sensations, tastes, and sounds that were occurring at the time of the traumatic event(s) become cognitively associated with the event, and at any given moment, even many years later, the exposure to a similar smell, sound, taste, visual, or physical sensation can trigger the traumatic memory without a person even knowing consciously that this is happening (Foa et al., 2007). For children, intrusions may be expressed through play or reenacting the trauma with their dolls or toys (American Psychiatric Association, 2022). For Liam, the sight of green peas and the loud noise at the dinner table were enough to alert his brain that danger was nearby. Though there was no real threat, Liam's body, mind, emotions, and brain felt that danger was inevitable and already happening.

Distressing dreams and nightmares are also common intrusive symptoms of trauma survivors (American Psychiatric Association, 2022). For example, when working with US military persons who had served in the Iraq and Afghanistan wars, many presented with similar nightmares. They would tell me that in their dreams they were in the middle of a firefight, and suddenly, their gun would not fire, or their gun would turn into some other inanimate object like a stick or an apple. They would be stuck in the middle of terror, rendered helpless without their weapon to defend themselves. Other people experienced less specific, recurring situations in their dreams and awoke with terror and fright that something was terribly wrong because of something they just dreamt about but could not recall the details.

Hyperarousal and hypervigilance. Trauma survivors often experience hyperarousal and hypervigilance. For many trauma survivors, this means they struggle to concentrate, focus, or sleep and are always on edge and wary of danger or threats. Many trauma survivors that I work with in my clinical practice have trouble completing tasks at work or home, because they cannot focus and are exhausted at the end of the day. They have used all their mental energy trying to execute work, academic, or relational tasks like preparing meals for their family or doing homework with their children. It is also common for sleep patterns and cycles to be disrupted, which makes concentration even more difficult. They find themselves on alert or on edge, easily startled or irritated. For most trauma survivors, harmful symptoms or reactions compound, making other common reactions worse, creating a vicious cycle.

When a person experiences a state of hyperarousal, their nervous system is experiencing marked physiological changes and distress. They cannot access the part of their brains that helps them make good decisions, feel positive emotions, or feel connected to their loved ones (Porges, 2007; van der Kolk, 2014). For children, hyperarousal may manifest as temper tantrums or acting out aggressively (American Psychiatric Association, 2022.) When a person is in hyperarousal, their heart rate is faster, their blood pressure is higher, their pupils are dilated, and their bodies are in a state where everything around them appears dangerous. Furthermore, their thoughts are chaotic, rigid, and disorganized. In Liam's case, you can see that he began to experience hyperarousal. His body flooded with rage. His ears were hot. His heart was racing. His pupils dilated. His mind raced. While in a state of hyperarousal, he unfortunately yelled and reacted impulsively by lashing out at his son. When survivors are experiencing hyperarousal, it is difficult for them to react calmly and evaluate potential consequences, which can often lead to them acting impulsively and later regretting their outbursts.

Changes in mood and beliefs. Changes in mood and beliefs or thoughts are also common trauma reactions. When a person experiences a traumatic event, something unthinkable has occurred. It is hard for our brains to make sense of unjust situations that cause distress and suffering. Trauma survivors experience emotional overwhelm and profound cognitive changes in systems of meaning that can often lead to inescapable hopelessness and cynicism and changes in how they view the perpetrator, ranging from vindictiveness to idealization (Herman, 2022). Though there are a variety of ways in which survivors' beliefs change, research shows five common belief areas that are negatively affected by trauma: safety and vulnerability, trust, power and control, intimacy, esteem and defectiveness, and responsibility for themselves, others, and the world (Resick et al., 2017; Shapiro, 2012). Our thoughts and emotions heavily influence each other, and negative thought patterns that emerge because of trauma have been known to contribute to the continuation and maintenance of traumatic stress symptoms (Dillon et al., 2020; Ehlers & Clark, 2000; Foa et al., 1999; LoSavio et al., 2017). These changes in survivors' beliefs impact their feelings, often leading to prolonged states of fear, guilt, shame, anger, and sorrow and a lack of positive emotional experiences like joy or fulfillment. Trauma survivors who experienced abuse or neglect in their early developmental years start in early life to have more rigid and hopeless views of the world and themselves, and later traumatic events confirm their negative beliefs, often making treatment more complex and their symptoms more challenging (Herman, 2022).

In Liam's case, notice that he had the thought, *Why didn't I do something?* Liam's brain cannot make sense of the horror he witnessed as a child, and now, as an adult, he feels pervasive guilt and shame because, though he was a child with limited power and control at the time of the event, he could not do anything to stop the violence in his home. If we continue learning about Liam's history and experiences, we will find that many beliefs have been altered because of his exposure to physical violence, likely leading to changed mood states that cause him difficulty and discomfort in his daily life. For example, Liam demonstrates feelings of frustration that are incongruent with the situation. Upon further investigation, we will likely uncover that Liam believes the world is primarily dangerous or unsafe (safety) and that things must always be controlled to maintain safety or peace (power/control).

Safety and vulnerability. When a person experiences trauma, their sense of internal and external safety is shattered. Before the trauma, survivors may have previously believed that the world was safe, that they had some ability to protect themselves from danger, or that other people generally had goodwill and were harmless. Post-trauma survivors may now accept as true that *the world is entirely dangerous.* There may be a constant internal experience that *nothing and no one is safe* or that *it is not safe to share their feelings with others and be vulnerable.* Additionally, because trauma symptoms can be so fear inducing, survivors may start to feel and believe that *they are not safe with themselves.* When a person does not feel safe, they may develop phobias or compulsions, withdraw from others, constantly worry about future abuse, or experience relentless anxiety or panic; or they may be on edge or on guard, perceiving nonthreatening interpersonal interactions as dangerous or as something they must protect themselves from. In fact, for many trauma survivors, the search for safety and the defense against danger is a constant internal battle. Heading to the market for groceries might seem like a routine activity, but for a trauma survivor, the noise, people, and vulnerability to physical danger from being out in such a public place may feel overwhelming. Alternatively, it could be that the slightest shift in a bystander's stance at the train station (which may or may not actually be threatening) triggers a defensive threat response causing them to act out in anger to protect themselves and others. Safeguarders should never forget how a trauma survivor's sense of safety may be compromised and that they should always intervene in a manner that promotes security and not threat.

Trust. Trauma survivors may struggle to trust themselves, their friends, local communities, faith groups, or even close loved ones, family, and God. Many of the clients I work with verbalize that they cannot trust *themselves,* which leads to indecisiveness and self-doubt. Other clients find themselves isolated and profoundly doubtful or suspicious when forming relationships with others. Many clients tell me, "What is the point in trying to make friends? People will just let me down in the end." This outlook on trust means that trauma survivors may struggle to rely on others for their relational needs and may develop an overly independent demeanor.

Trauma survivors often lose trust in God and ask the question, *God, why did you let this happen to me? Where were you?* We even see this example in the Bible with Jesus, fully God and fully human. In his last words before dying on the cross, he says, "'*Eli, Eli, lema sabachthani*?' (which means 'My God, my God, why have you forsaken me?'"; Matthew 27:46 NIV). In his suffering and depths of pain, Jesus felt abandoned by God, which is how many trauma survivors feel. It can be comforting to know we have a High Priest who is able to sympathize with our weaknesses (Hebrews 4:15).

Esteem and defectiveness. The way that people view themselves and others also changes after trauma. Survivors may notice negative beliefs about who they are and how they look or act (e.g., *I am disgusting. I am ugly. I am worthless*). Trauma survivors experience alterations in their view of themselves that are often marked by chronic shame and an absence of self-worth (Herman, 2022). I recall a former client, early on in her healing journey from sexual trauma, who shared with me that she did not deserve what she wanted in life, like a family or a husband, because she was unlovable and shameful. This pervasive shame led to years of her forming relationships with partners who were emotionally unavailable and abusive and treated her horribly, which only confirmed her negative beliefs about herself that she would never have the family or partner she desired.

Survivors may also have negative beliefs about others and begin to view certain types of people or groups of people in an overly negative manner (e.g., *All men are horrible*). I have often seen this manifest with my clients in the form of skepticism of specific cultural groups. For example, I once had a client who was physically assaulted by someone of a different race than her, and she began to believe that all people of that race were evil. This irrational belief led her to avoid anyone of that race and express hate for people she had never met or only briefly interacted with, which was problematic. Suspicion, recurring anger, general bitterness toward other people in the world, and even antisocial behaviors can occur because of shifts in the esteem beliefs of others (Resick et al., 2017).

Power and control. Additionally, abuse, violence, and terror render a person helpless and powerless, leading to various reactions regarding a person's sense of power and control. On the one hand, people may believe they have no control over anything, resulting in inactive participation at home, work, school, or relationships, just letting life happen to them. On the other hand, a person may believe they need to take control of everything in their life and find themselves trying to control, analyze, and perfect every detail of their lives and relationships.

Intimacy. Our beliefs about intimacy and bonding form during our formative childhood years (Bowlby, 1988). Trauma survivors experience alterations in the way they view and experience intimacy. Many clients I have worked with believe that getting close or opening up to someone is risky. They struggle to feel connected to themselves or others. Sometimes, survivors fear rejection and abandonment to the degree that they seek intimacy at all costs (e.g., *I would rather be in an unhealthy relationship than be alone*). For many years, I worked in substance use programs. I saw many clients who were trauma survivors struggling to self-soothe or calm themselves when alone, which often led to their substance use or seeking sex, food, gambling, or even self-harm to regulate their discomfort. Attachment to substances, food, or the like is a form of artificial connection and attachment. Unfortunately, these behaviors only create more problems for the trauma survivor, leaving them feeling empty, numb, and alone—without real intimacy with themselves or others.

Religious and spiritual intimacy. As you have read, trauma profoundly changes how survivors see themselves, others, and the world—which includes disruption to how a person relates to or feels bonded to God (Proctor et al., 2019). For survivors who experienced trauma during their formative developmental years, they may see and relate to God with rigid views or project traits of their perpetrator(s) onto God. For example, I recall a client I worked with for many years who saw God as a vindictive, unjust, judgmental presence in his life. The attributes he ascribed to God mimicked the attributes of his biological father, who physically abused him throughout his childhood. Additionally, the concepts of faith, hope, and love (1 Corinthians 13:13) are common religious and spiritual principles that require a person to exhibit a level of trust and vulnerability that is often difficult for trauma survivors to fully believe. How does one have faith and hope in the unforeseen or a loving, good God when their experiences have validated the opposite: that bad things happen to good people and that evil people exist in this world?

Responsibility. Liam experienced self-blame when he thought, *Why didn't I do something?* Trauma survivors often feel a sense of responsibility for traumatic events that occurred to them, even though they were the victims and not the perpetrators. It is common for trauma survivors to believe, *It was my fault,* or *I could have done more to prevent or stop it.* You may be wondering why someone who was a victim of something horrible believes they were to blame. The answer is a complex weave of neuroscience and cognitive theory. However, the gist of it is that in order to integrate an experience that does not fit onto our cognitive schema, or belief system, our brains either need to change our beliefs or change the memory itself to try to integrate it. Attributing the event to something that was our own fault might feel safer to our subconscious minds so that we can perceive control over similar events happening again. It might also feel safer than realizing that not everyone is safe or can be trusted, especially if we believed that the world and others were generally good and trustworthy before experiencing trauma. This is particularly true if the perpetrator was a trusted adult such as a family member, coach, teacher, or clergy.

The consequences of self-blame and responsibility for events they did not cause include persistent feelings of guilt and shame. The feeling of shame can lead to extreme difficulties in their interpersonal relationships, perfectionist tendencies, substance use, compulsive behaviors, or risky and illegal behaviors (Covert et al., 2005; Dearing et al., 2005; Stuewig et al., 2015). Even though guilt is our emotional moral compass and tends to be correlated with people making positive changes in their lives (Dearing et al., 2005), most trauma survivors did not do anything wrong or cause abuse, neglect, or violence. Therefore, there is nothing for them to correct. This lack of being able to change anything behaviorally because there is nothing they could have done differently can lead to pervasive, unwarranted feelings of guilt, shame, hopelessness, and powerlessness.

As you can see, trauma can lead to profound shifts in how a person thinks about themselves, others, and the world. Remember that our thoughts change after a traumatic event because the unthinkable has happened, so to adjust to life after something unexpected and improbable happens, our brain attempts to modify our thoughts to keep us safe and prevent further trauma from happening. Unfortunately, these changes in our thoughts and beliefs, though intended by our brains for good, leave many trauma survivors trapped in an endless cycle of doubt, fear, internal chaos, shame, guilt, confusion, depression, hopelessness, and turmoil. These intense emotional shifts profoundly impact how trauma survivors can show up and be present in the world, leading to a range of behaviors—isolation, self-destruction, substance use, violence, and even suicidal ideation.

Avoidance. Avoiding certain people, events, or situations is another common trauma reaction (American Psychiatric Association, 2022). For example, often, my clients come to my office desperate for help—they know that they have been deeply impacted by something from their past (they lost everything in a house fire, were in a terrible near-death vehicle accident, or were sexually abused by someone close to them throughout their childhood). Despite their desperation to heal from these terrible events, when it comes time for us to talk about the awful things that happened to them, they start to move the conversation in a different direction or share that they are not ready to share the details or impact of the event(s). Some of my clients will share that since the trauma occurred, they cannot attend certain events, like a football game or their child's choir concert, or complete basic tasks like going to the grocery store because their anxiety and distress become unbearable before or during these outings.

Survivors also attempt to escape or avoid the emotions, memories, images, or thoughts related to past traumatic experiences. Sometimes, the aftermath of traumatic experiences and its impression on a person are so great that they will go to desperate lengths to prevent, numb, or avoid the feelings associated with the trauma by using substances, sex, gambling, self-harm, compulsive eating, and more. Avoiding people and intimate relationships by isolating themselves is also common. Avoidance is how a person copes with the internal and external haunting that trauma brings about. Unfortunately, avoidance also keeps a person stuck and unable to heal from the cycle of symptoms that trauma exposure has caused (Foa et al., 2007). A note of caution: safeguarders should never push survivors to face the trauma memories. Some survivors will need professional mental health workers who are specifically trained to provide safety and stabilization to help survivors decrease their avoidance and confront the trauma memories. Avoidance is a way the brain attempts to keep the person emotionally safe, and exposure to the trauma memories without someone competent in this regulation can cause retraumatization.

Dissociation. Another common reaction that trauma survivors experience is dissociation. Dissociation is a highly disruptive experience in which a person has difficulty integrating "consciousness, memory, identity, emotion, perception, body representation, motor control, and behavior" (American Psychiatric Association, 2022, p. 329). When a person experiences dissociation, they feel an extreme disconnection from themselves, their reality, and others. When reviewing Liam's vignette, for example, despite physically being in the present, Liam's mind and orientation to his family were temporarily lost. Liam was reliving the past for a few brief moments—disconnected and detached. Dissociation occurs on a spectrum from everyday experiences (daydreaming, driving home and realizing you "spaced out" the whole ride, etc.) to more severe cases involving significant memory gaps and amnesia. A flashback can be dissociating—the survivor's mind and body are experiencing a traumatic event as if it were happening in the present without *any* awareness of their present or current surroundings. I have witnessed this in my office when a client begins to share details of what happened to them, and suddenly, they are no longer making eye contact but seem to be staring right through me—they are lost in the memory, in the past, right in front of me. I have heard many accounts from clients' loved ones that they had found their partner under a table hiding, aggressively fighting nothing in the living room, or screaming when no one was nearby because they were experiencing a flashback. Unfortunately, dissociation can be misinterpreted as "demonic possession" and some well-meaning Christians have tried to cast out the demons from a trauma survivor, causing significantly more harm and trauma. If someone is experiencing dissociative or other odd behaviors, first find out if there is past trauma that needs compassionate care as opposed to forceful rebuke.

Some people experience disconnection from themselves and the world as if they are looking down on themselves, much like they are watching a movie unfold in the audience. Despite being the main character, they experience no emotions or connection to themselves or the other "characters." Dissociation can sometimes be so extreme that trauma survivors experience amnesia or periods of time in their present lives where they go hours or days and have no memory or awareness of what has elapsed. I have worked with clients over the years who have come into my office terrified that they were at work, completing their tasks as usual, and then, hours later, they found themselves at home or at a restaurant without any recollection of how they got there. There are various levels and layers to dissociation, and this trauma reaction can be particularly confusing and distressing for trauma survivors.

LONG-TERM IMPACTS

Adverse health outcomes, medical issues, and physical problems are also consequences of trauma (Felitti et al., 1998; Herman, 2022). A critical study in the United States from 1995 to 1997 provided vital information on the impact of adverse childhood experiences (ACEs), or child traumas, on long-term behaviors, physical health, and mental health (Felitti et al., 2008). The childhood events screened for in the original study included emotional, physical, and sexual abuse; household challenges like domestic violence, substance use, or mental illness in the home; parental divorce or separation; household member incarceration; and emotional or physical neglect (Felitti et al., 1998). The study found that childhood adverse events drastically increased in a dose-response curve (meaning that the risk increased as the number of adverse events someone experienced in childhood increased) the risk of long-term health and behavioral issues, including traumatic brain injury, broken bones, burns, depression, anxiety, suicide, PTSD, unintended pregnancy, pregnancy complications, fetal death, human immunodeficiency virus (HIV), sexually transmitted diseases (STDs), cancer, diabetes, substance use, unsafe sex, less education, and income (Felitti et al., 1998; Centers for Disease Control and Prevention, 2021).

Trauma professionals often discuss the effect of trauma on a person's body. One of the bestselling books on trauma, *The Body Keeps the Score* (van der Kolk, 2014), highlights how trauma impacts biological and neurological processes leading to the body storing and holding the aftermath of trauma. For example, trauma exposure and posttraumatic stress disorder have been linked to digestive issues like irritable bowel syndrome (IBS) (Kearney et al., 2022), increased inflammation (Sumner et al., 2020), and migraine headaches (Minen et al., 2016). Adding that acute inflammation is the wounded body's way of healing from an injury (attempt to prevent wound bleeding out) and protecting against infection (Verhamme & Hoylaerts, 2009). If the immune system continues to detect danger, it will lead to chronic inflammation, the cause of many diseases. Many of my clients over the years have experienced chronic pain, frequent migraines, stomach issues, sleep problems, and invasive physical pain. We cannot underestimate the impact of trauma on the body.

I worked for many years with a man who came to see me in his sixties. He had many health issues, including heart problems, neurological function, frequent headaches, difficulty sleeping, and difficulty eating to the point of malnutrition due to pervasive nausea and gut issues. This client grew up in the foster care system from the time he was a baby, never having a stable home, witnessing physical violence, and experiencing emotional and physical neglect. He had posttraumatic stress disorder and all the previously noted trauma-related symptoms of intrusions, hyperarousal, negative mood and beliefs, dissociation, and so on; yet the impact of trauma on his physical health always struck me. Not only did he have to endure a childhood riddled with abuse and neglect, but he spent most of his adult life paying for the consequences in the form of physical and mental health issues. His life illustrates the cumulative effect of childhood trauma on a person's health, career, and relationships.

THE IMPACT OF TRAUMA ON COMMUNITIES

When trauma happens to a community (e.g., war or natural disasters), for the most part, people feel more comfortable talking about their collective experiences, which can foster the healing process. *Community resilience* is a term often used to refer to groups that experience a mass disaster, exhibit resilience, and recover collectively (Norris et al., 2008; Stebnicki, 2017). I recall a distinct memory of being in the post office a year after my hometown of Denham Springs, Louisiana, tragically flooded in 2016 from what the locals call the no-name storm. The conversation was buzzing: "How's your house coming along? How much water did you get in your home? Where did you guys stay after the flood?" Similar conversations still happen today among communities on the anniversary of events like Hurricane Katrina or the 9/11 terrorist attacks. Communities can reflect, remember, openly grieve, and collectively hope for the future—together.

This ability to collectively heal after mass community trauma is much different than when individuals experience trauma alone, as there is more isolation and shame, and it becomes taboo to talk about their experiences. In fact, "shame derives its power from being unspeakable" (Brown, 2012, p. 67). To counter this sense of isolation and shame, community support and response are vital. As you have read about the various responses to trauma throughout this chapter, it is also possible that communities, like church congregations, experience some similar reactions when learning that a person in power or a trusted authority figure has been the perpetrator of abuse or assault.

Congregations and affected groups may feel shocked, betrayed, confused about who is trustworthy, ashamed, or guilty that they trusted individuals in power, and confused about how to help those impacted by the abuse. These are all normal responses. However, church and community resilience is possible and can be fostered with healthy dialogues that allow for both the good and bad—the grief that something awful happened and the hope that, as a community, we can support those directly impacted by the abuse and build systems to prevent further abuse and trauma.

CONCLUSION

Just like Liam, many people are going about their daily lives, experiencing reminders that trigger episodes of panic and distress. Sometimes, we can see the effects of trauma in others through verbal outbursts, aggression, or temper tantrums. At other times, people suffer silently, experiencing disconnection, depression, and isolation because of their pasts. These trauma symptoms are not a sign of weakness or a lack of faith but a result of the horrors of abuse and the way the brain and body attempt to adjust to it. "When contextual variables are considered, symptoms can be reframed as survival strategies" (Corey, 2017, p. 344). Trauma changes the way we see ourselves, others, and the world. It can lead to highly challenging inner experiences like intrusions, hyperarousal, hypervigilance, nightmares, depression, or dissociation, and to difficult external experiences like trouble connecting to others, conflict in relationships, health and medical problems, and occupational and financial issues. Understanding the vast and complex ways that trauma, abuse, neglect, and violence impact individuals and communities helps provide us with a pathway to intercede and intervene with compassion, understanding, and competence.

PERSONAL REFLECTION

1. Think of a recently distressing experience that felt upsetting but not overwhelming (e.g., a small car accident that felt scary but no one was seriously injured). Reflect on your thoughts, feelings, and physical sensations during the event. Reflect on your thoughts, feelings, and physical sensations in the hours following the events.

2. Reflect on your own experiences of trauma or harm. How have these experiences shaped your beliefs about yourself, others, and the world?

Are there any areas you think you may benefit from additional support from a pastor, doctor, counselor, or friend?

3. How does this understanding of trauma impact how you engage with trauma survivors?

GROUP DISCUSSION

1. How might the trauma responses discussed in this chapter show up in someone at a church event? How could they be misinterpreted by the church community?

2. How can trauma influence a survivor's belief system and worldview? What does it look like to accompany a trauma survivor as they wrestle through this belief system?

3. How can friends, family, and community supports come alongside a survivor as they manage the impact of trauma?

REFERENCES

American Psychiatric Association. (2022). *Diagnostic and statistical manual of mental disorders* (5th ed.). https://doi.org/10.1176/appi.books.9780890425787

Bonanno, G. A. (2004). Loss, trauma, and human resilience: Have we underestimated the human capacity to thrive after extremely aversive events? *American Psychologist, 59*(1), 20-28. http://dx.doi.org/10.1037/0003- 066X.59.1.20.

Bowlby, J. (1988). *A secure base: Clinical applications of attachment theory*. Routledge.

Brown, B. (2012). *Daring greatly: How the courage to be vulnerable transforms the way we live, love, parent, and lead*. Avery.

Centers for Disease Control and Prevention (CDC). (2021, April 6). *CDC-Kaiser ACE study*. https://www.cdc.gov/violenceprevention/aces/about.html

Contreras, A. (2024). *Traumatization and its aftermath*. Routledge.

Corey, G. (2017). *Theory and practice of counseling and psychotherapy* (10th Ed.). Cengage Learning.

Covert, M. V., Tangney, J. P., Maddux, J. E., & Heleno, N. M. (2005). Shame-proneness, guilt-proneness, and interpersonal problem solving: A social cognitive analysis. *Journal of Social and Clinical Psychology, 22*(1). https://doi.org/10.1521/jscp.22.1.1.22765

Dearing, R. L., Stuewig, J., & Tangney, J. P. (2005). On the importance of distinguishing shame from guilt: Relations to problematic alcohol and drug use. *Addictive Behaviors, 30*(7), 1392-1404. https://doi.10.1016/j.addbeh.2005.02.002

Dillon, K. H., Hale, W. J., LoSavio, S. T., Wachen, J. S., Pruiksma, K. E., Yarvis, J. S., Mintz, J., Litz, B. T., Peterson, A. L., & Resick, P. A. (2020). Weekly changes in blame and PTSD among active-duty military personnel receiving Cognitive Processing Therapy.

Behavior Therapy, 51, 386-400. https://cptforptsd.com/wp-content/uploads/2020/10/Dillon_BETH_2020.pdf.

Dougherty, G. W. (2010). *From crisis to recovery: Strategic planning for response, resilience, and recovery.* Rocky Mountain Region Disaster Mental Health Institute.

Ehlers, A., & Clark, D. M. (2000). A cognitive model of posttraumatic stress disorder. *Behaviour Research and Therapy, 38,* 319-45. https://doi.org/10.1016/s0005 - 7967(99)00123-0

Felitti, V. J., Anda, R. F., Nordenberg, D., Edwards, V., Koss, M. P., & Marks, J. S. (1998). Relationship of childhood abuse and household dysfunction to many of the leading causes of death in adults: The adverse childhood experiences (ACE) study. *American Journal of Preventive Medicine, 14*(2), 245-58. https://doi.org/10.1016/S0749-3797(98)00017-8

Foa, E. B., Ehlers, A., Clark, D. M., Tolin, D. F., & Orsillo, S. M. (1999). The Posttraumatic Cognitions Inventory (PTCI): Development and validation. *Psychological Assessment, 11,* 303-14. https://doi.org/10.1037/1040.3590.11.3.303

Foa, E., Hembree, E., & Rothbaum, B. O. (2007). *Prolonged exposure therapy for PTSD: Emotional processing of traumatic experiences, therapist guide.* Oxford University Press.

Hawkins, R. L., & Maurer, K. (2011). "You fix my community, you have fixed my life": The disruption and rebuilding of ontological security in New Orleans. *Disasters, 35*(1), 143-59. https://doi:10.1111.j.0361.3666.2010.01197.x

Herman, J. (2022). *Trauma and recovery: The aftermath of violence—from domestic abuse to political terror.* Basic Books.

Kearney, D. J., Kamp, K. J., Storms, M., & Simpson, T. L. (2022). Prevalence of gastrointestinal symptoms and irritable bowel syndrome among individuals with symptomatic posttraumatic stress disorder. *Journal of Clinical Gastroenterology, 56*(7), 592-96. https://doi.org/10.1097/MCG.0000000000001670

Kozlowska, K., Walker, P., McLean, L., & Carrive, P. (2015). Fear and the defense cascade: Clinical implications and management. *Harvard Review of Psychiatry, 23*(4), 263-87. https://doi.org//10.1097/HRP.0000000000000065

Levine, P. (2015). *Trauma and memory: Brain and body in the search for the living past.* North Atlantic Books.

LoSavio, S. T., Dillon, K. H., & Resick, P. A. (2017). Cognitive factors in the development, maintenance, and treatment of posttraumatic stress disorder. *Current Opinion in Psychology, 14,* 18-22. https://doi.org/10.1016/j.copsyc.2016.09.006

Minen, M.T., Begasse De Dhaem, O., Kroon Van Diest, A., Powers, C., Schwedt, T. J., Lipton, R., & Silbersweig, D. (2016). Migraine and its psychiatric comorbidities. *Neural Neurosurg Psychiatry, 87,* 741-49. http://doi.org/10.1136/jnnp-2015-312233

Moller, A., Sondergaard, H. P., & Helstrom, L. (2017). Tonic immobility during sexual assault—a common reaction predicting post-traumatic stress disorder and severe depression. *Acta Obstetricia et Gynecologica Scandinavica, 96,* 932-38. https://doi.org/10.1111/aogs.13174

Morabito, D. M., & Schmidt, N. B. (2023). Efficacy of a brief web-based tonic immobility psychoeducation intervention among trauma-exposed adults: A randomized clinical trial. *Journal of Traumatic Stress, 36,* 896-906. https://doi.org/10.1002/jts.22955

Norris, F. H., Stevens, S. P., Pfefferbaum, B., Wyche, K. F., & Pfefferbaum, R. L. (2008). Community resilience as a metaphor, theory, set of capacities, and strategy for disaster readiness. *American Journal of Psychology, 41*, 127-50.

Owca, J. (2020). *The association between a psychotherapist's theoretical orientation and perception of complex trauma and repressed anger in the fawn response*. [Doctoral dissertation, The Chicago School of Professional Psychology].

Porges, S. (2007). The polyvagal perspective. *Biological Psychology, 74*(2), 116-43.

Proctor, M., Cleary, M., Kornhaber, R., & McLean, L. (2019). Christians with chronic complex trauma and relationally focused spiritual difficulties: A conversational model perspective. *Journal of Spirituality in Mental Health, 21*(2), 77-110. https://doi.org/10.1080 /19349637.2018.1460228

Resick, P. A., Monson, C. M., & Chard, K. M. (2017). *Cognitive processing therapy for PTSD: A comprehensive manual*. Guilford Press.

Ritchie, E. C., Watson, P. J., & Friedman, M. J. (2006). *Interventions following mass violence and disasters: Strategies for mental health practice*. Guilford Press.

Shapiro, F. (2012). *Getting past your past: Take control of your life with self-help techniques from EMDR therapy*. Rodale Books.

Stebnicki, M. A. (2017). *Disaster mental health counseling: Responding to trauma in a multicultural context*. Springer.

Stuewig, J., Tangney, J. P., Kendall, S., Folk, J. B., Meyer, C. R., & Dearing, R. L. (2015). Children's proneness to shame and guilt predict risky and illegal behavior in young adulthood. *Child Psychiatry Human Development, 26*, 217-27. https://doi.org.10.1007/ s10578.014.0467.1.

Sumner, J. A., Nishimi, K. M., Koenen, K. C., Roberts, A. L., & Kubzansky, L. D. (2020). Posttraumatic stress disorder and inflammation: Untangling issues of bidirectionality. *Biological Psychiatry, 87*(10), 885-97. https://doi.org/10.1016/j.biopsych.2019.11.005

Tedeschi, R. G., & Calhoun, L. G. (1996). The posttraumatic growth inventory: Measuring the positive legacy of trauma. *Journal of Traumatic Stress, 9*, 455-71.

van der Kolk, B. (2014). *The body keeps the score: Brain, mind, and body in the healing of trauma*. Viking Penguin

Verhamme, P., & Hoylaerts, M. F. (2009). Hemostasis and inflammation: Two of a kind? *Thrombosis Journal, 7*(15). https://doi.org/10.1186/1477-9560-7-15

Walker, P. (2021). *Complex PTSD: From surviving to thriving*. Azure Coyote.

World Health Organization (2021). *International statistical classification of diseases and related health problems* (11th Ed.). https://icd.who.int/

8

TRAUMA SURVIVORS AND RISK OF REVICTIMIZATION

TAYLOR PATTERSON

When Sarah arrived at your church, you could tell she was hurting. You would glance at her during worship services and see her staring off in the distance, seemingly in another world. Other times, you saw her standing in a corner shaking and sobbing, having difficulty catching her breath. This confused you, but you care about her and want to be a kind and supportive presence. When you saw her crying and shaking, you tried to comfort her by putting your arms around her. This seemed only to make it worse. One afternoon after church, you invited Sarah out to lunch. During this lunch, she told you she sometimes has trouble going to church because she feels so overwhelmed. Again, you felt a little confused. You have experienced this local church as a blessing, and you believe God has called all believers to meaningful involvement with the local body of believers. You tell her that there are many kind people in the church and that it is good she is being obedient to God and going to church even when it is hard. She got very quiet, but you were hopeful that maybe you got through to her. The following week, you look for Sarah and cannot find her; you are starting to feel weary.

When you hear there is concern about your friend and deacon in the church, John, making inappropriate sexual advances toward Sarah, you're not sure what to believe. John is a well-respected member of the church's leadership team. From your perspective, he's been nothing but kind and helpful to Sarah. He's offered to drive her to and from church services, made house calls to check on her, and met with her regularly for pastoral counseling. In the past, you have wondered if John is maybe a little too involved in Sarah's life, but you attributed that to his compassionate care for church members. You think Sarah has maybe just misunderstood John's faithful care for her as romantic attention. You remember how intensely she responded to you putting your arm around her to comfort her; maybe she misread John's kindness. You think it would be helpful to get John and Sarah in a room together to clarify their relationship so they can be reconciled for the benefit of the church, which also protects the reputation of this church you love.

Sarah's story depicts just one of the ways some survivors of abuse may display emotions and interact with others. As you have read in previous chapters, trauma responses vary greatly. Some survivors may remain on the fringes of church participation, maybe attending a weekly worship service every now and then, while others might dive into church involvement and are faithful volunteers, attendees, or leaders. Some survivors may engage in risky sexual behaviors or struggle with active substance use disorders, while others are model citizens and intent on following every rule. Research shows that survivors of interpersonal violence are much more likely to experience future abuse or assault, and this risk increases with the severity of their posttraumatic stress symptoms (Jaffe et al., 2019)

In this chapter, we'll discuss the ways in which a history of trauma can lead to increased vulnerability to being targeted by perpetrators. We are not suggesting that survivors of abuse are at fault for the choices and actions of their abusers; rather, we will emphasize the strategy of perpetrators and how they take advantage of survivors' attempts at managing their trauma. Second Peter describes perpetrators as having "eyes full of adultery, insatiable for sin. They entice unsteady souls. . . . For, speaking loud boasts of folly, they entice by sensual passions of the flesh those who are barely escaping from those who live in error" (2 Peter 2:14, 18-19).[1] Scripture highlights the wickedness and strategy of those who harm the vulnerable and the responsibility of the church to protect; it does not fault the vulnerability of those who have been wounded.

This is not to say that all the ways survivors of abuse attempt to manage their trauma are helpful or condoned by Scripture. However, the Bible is clear that sin borne out of harm, especially harm done in childhood, heaps judgment on the perpetrator of abuse. Jesus says in Matthew 18:5-6, "Whoever receives one

---

[1]Scripture quotations in this chapter, unless otherwise noted, are from the ESV.

such child in my name receives me, but whoever causes one of these little ones who believe in me to sin, it would be better for him to have a great millstone fastened around his neck and to be drowned in the depth of the sea." As we learned in the previous chapters on the impact of trauma, when a child is physically, sexually, or emotionally abused, they are wounded in such a way that creates a vulnerability to behaviors that can be enduring through adulthood, such as substance use disorders, impulsivity, angry outbursts, and risky sexual behaviors. Although these behaviors are not considered healthy ways to manage emotions, understanding them as attempts to self-regulate and numb extreme pain helps us to have compassion for survivors. Tragically, this difficulty regulating emotions has been used by perpetrators and their communities to justify additional instances of abuse. As a church, we need to rightly name the vulnerability of survivors of abuse and make meaningful efforts to support, heal, and protect those who are likely to be targets of perpetrators.

RISK OF REVICTIMIZATION

In section four, we will examine how children, older adults, and people with disabilities are at increased risk for victimization. These vulnerabilities are sometimes easier to understand as there are external cues that draw us in to protect. When we see the smallness and innocence of children, we may find ourselves compelled to guard and defend. Similarly, older adults and people with disabilities sometimes have increased physical needs that highlight their dependence and show a lack of physical strength; we may find it easier to understand how they did not successfully "fight back" or "resist" if they were the target of an assault. It can be much more challenging to identify the increased risk of victimization for adult survivors of abuse, especially if they are adults with the apparent cognitive and physical ability to resist. Attachment deficits, disruptions in emotional regulation, and distortions in relation to one's body and sexuality all increase vulnerability to the strategies of perpetrators. We will now explore how these three challenges can impact individuals and their interactions.

Attachment deficits. As discussed in an earlier chapter on the impact of trauma on families and communities, attachment theory proposes that our relationship with our caregivers in infancy and early childhood establishes a framework or lens that impacts how we relate to others and regulate our emotions throughout the lifespan (Bowlby, 1988). This theory has been further validated by our growing understanding of the brain, how it develops, and how it changes over the course of our lives (Siegel et al., 2021). Research has shown that we learn what is safe and what is dangerous in our relationships with others through our early childhood experiences and use it as a template to help protect us in the future.

Thousands of years before we had modern neural imaging, the Bible revealed God's design for the formative impact of caregiver/child relationships. The book of Proverbs presents the axiom, "Train up a child in the way he should go; even when he is old he will not depart from it" (Proverbs 22:6). This verse is often used to describe the impact of faithful parenting; it is an encouragement to parents that their consistent love and care for their children and persistence in teaching them to walk with God matters. Anyone who has spent time with children sees that they are prone to repeat what they are exposed to. If a parent models faithful love and obedience to God, it follows that a child will be more likely to learn the goodness of God and the joy of life with him. Similarly, God has designed the family system to help us to experientially know what it is like to feel safe, loved, and protected. This felt sense of safety developed in early childhood translates to the way we engage in adult relationships and the way we relate to God. When parenting functions as God has designed it, children grow into adults who can display empathy, connect with others without losing their sense of self, build emotional intimacy with safe and trustworthy people, and instinctually trust that God is good and can be relied upon (Li et al., 2021).

What happens when children experience abuse in relationships that were designed by God to communicate safety? Let's return to the story of Sarah to better understand how family-of-origin dynamics can translate into adult behaviors and make one vulnerable to revictimization.

Sarah grew up in a Christian home with her mom, dad, and five brothers. On the outside, they seemed to be the perfect, God-fearing family. Her mom homeschooled all six children until they reached middle school, and her dad was an elder in the church who was well regarded by the entire congregation. Both parents taught her about the life, death, and resurrection of Jesus and encouraged her to live a faithful life obedient to God. However, behind closed doors, Sarah's dad was regularly molesting her. Sarah was confused; this didn't feel right, but her dad told her this was how fathers cared for their daughters. When Sarah asked her mom about it, she

got angry and called her a "seductress" for enticing her dad and trying to ruin their
happy family. Sarah felt alone and helpless; where could she go?

As she got older, the abuse progressed to almost daily rape. Every Sunday she
would hear church members praise her dad and tell her how lucky she was to have
such godly parents. When her dad told her, "This is what God wants for little girls,"
she didn't question it. According to the church community, he spoke for God. When
Sarah entered the sixth grade, she began attending public school. She loved her
English teacher, Mrs. Jenson. Mrs. Jenson was kind, funny, and encouraging, and
attended their local church. Sarah felt safe with Mrs. Jenson, and one day told her
about the abuse she was suffering by her father. Sarah was hopeful that maybe Mrs.
Jenson could do something to make the abuse stop. After Sarah disclosed her expe-
rience, Mrs. Jenson put her arm around her and said, "I know this must be hard,
but your dad is doing great things for God. God has called you to forgive him and
protect the local church. I will talk to your parents to try to help you, but do not
share this with anyone else and slander your father and God's name." Sarah im-
mediately regretted daring to hope that she would be protected.

Rather than helping her cultivate a felt sense of God's protective and reliable
care for her, Sarah's family of origin taught her to expect abuse. She learned
that her needs would not be reliably met and that longing for connection with
others will only cause her harm. When she told her mom and Mrs. Jenson
about the sexual abuse, she learned she would be punished if she spoke up,
almost guaranteeing her continued silence. Her dad's actions reinforced that
abuse is inevitable, she is powerless to stop it, and God has forsaken her. Over
the years, Sarah will hear repeatedly that God will never leave or forsake her,
but her experiential knowledge will tell her something very different.

As an adult, Sarah has a cognitive understanding of sexual assault and predatory behavior, but her experience tells her that abuse is normal and that she
doesn't have a voice in her own protection. When John, the deacon at the
church, begins making comments about her body that make her uncomfortable, Sarah is unsurprised and tells no one. John's behavior continues to
escalate until he is regularly assaulting Sarah. Abuse and attachment deficits
in people's families of origin can distort their view of healthy relationships,
making them more susceptible to grooming tactics and less likely to report
instances of assault.

Emotion regulation disruption. A history of trauma not only leaves scars
on survivors' relationship templates, but it can also significantly disrupt their

ability to regulate their emotions. Recent research on neurobiology has provided a more robust view of emotions and how they are experienced physiologically. Emotions are whole-body experiences that result from complex interactions between our brain and nervous system (Siegel, 2015). For example, when I feel defensive, my face gets warm, and I feel a distinct sensation in my chest—almost like a rocket ship propelling forward out of my chest. I do not simply have the thought, *I feel defensive*. Instead, I experience a pronounced shift in my body that communicates perception of a threat. As we explored in the previous chapter, trauma can create an emotional pendulum swing between intense anxiety (hyperarousal) and severe emotional disconnect or "numbing" behaviors (hypoarousal). Survivors often adopt protective strategies for managing these significant emotional swings that are somewhat effective in the short term but have significant long-term consequences (Crittenden & Heller, 2017).

To better understand this, consider the defense system of a well-protected castle. When under attack, the castle warning bell sounds, initiating a comprehensive response from the guards. They pull the drawbridge up and prepare the cannons to fire. If the enemy can penetrate the castle's defenses and successfully take over, the attack gets seared in the memory of the guards for months or years after the fact. What did they do wrong? How can they prevent this from happening again? Even when the enemy is gone and there is no present danger, the warning bell may continue to sound at the slightest hint of danger. The drawbridge remains closed, preventing anyone, even friendly neighbors, from entering the castle. The cannons may fire indiscriminately, depleting the castle's resources and wounding friends who try to approach the castle. Though it is peacetime, the castle functions as if it is still under attack.

This is often how PTSD presents itself. A trauma survivor's "alarm bell," or amygdala, sounds frequently in response to seemingly irrelevant stimuli, eliciting a whole-system defensive response. For example, due to her trauma and abuse, Sarah is always scanning her environment for potential relational threats. Something as simple as the familiar smell of her dad's cologne can "pull up the drawbridge" and "ignite the cannons." She may have difficulty sleeping because her perpetually alert nervous system won't let her body relax. Her chest is tight; her stomach is upset; her constant "on edge" feeling is exhausting. To manage this, Sarah finds herself indulging in anything that will, even just temporarily, calm her nervous system. She drinks heavily, shops impulsively, and regularly binge eats. When she "ignites the cannons," she lashes out at her friends in angry outbursts. The social consequences of these overreactions to environmental cues can be incredibly painful and isolating. Friends and church leaders are frustrated and impatient with Sarah's outbursts or lack of progress in addiction recovery. This isolation makes her a prime target of perpetrators. If she summons the courage to report John's abuse, her church community may not trust her, making John unlikely to be caught or punished for his transgressions. Perpetrators are predatory, wolves in sheep's clothing (Matthew 7:15). They skillfully gain the respect and trust of the community and then seek out vulnerable children or adults who are unlikely to report, and if they do, are unlikely to be believed.

Cognitive distortions. Sexual abuse doesn't only impact a person's emotion regulation strategies; it also harms the way the survivors perceive their bodies and sexuality. God created men and women in his image (Genesis 1:27); this truth has many implications for how humans relate to God and each other. Because we are made in the image of God, we are bestowed inherent dignity, honor, and protection, simply for existing. This is reinforced throughout Scripture as God provides boundaries around how we interact with each other and care for our bodies, protecting the dignity of those made in his image. God prohibits gluttony or overindulgence to establish standards around how we nourish our bodies and trust in God's daily provision (Proverbs 23:20-21). God's law forbids murder, communicating the value of each and every human life and condemning the negligent or selfish harming of another person (Exodus 20:13; Romans 13:9). The sabbath sets a pattern of work and rest that honors our bodies' limits and glorifies God as the one who sustains (Exodus 20:8-11). Our bodies were designed to be protected, cherished, and cared for, honoring the God who created them.

Sexual abuse is a grievous sin against those made in the image of God, as it exploits bodies that are created to be protected and cherished. God created human beings with sexual desires and bodies that experience pleasure. He ordained sex to be experienced in a relationship between husband and wife that mirrors God's covenant relationship with his church (Ephesians 5:22-33). This establishes an incredibly high view of our sexuality and communicates the significant honor and vulnerability of the sexual act. Sex, as God designed it, occurs in a safe, trusting relationship between two consenting adults who honor, respect, and cherish one another. Sexual abuse, especially of children, steals that which is sacred for selfish gain, leaving a terrible scar on the victim and potentially altering the course of their life.

When a person experiences sexual abuse, their perception of their body's value and the design for their sexuality may become severely distorted. Through repeated instances of sexual abuse over the course of her life, Sarah learned that her body was for the predatory use of men. This was reinforced when her perpetrators attributed her abuse to the sovereign will of God and when those she bravely confided in did nothing to protect her. As she enters adulthood, this distortion in her perception of her body and sexuality may manifest in how she dresses, how she touches others and expects to be touched, and her belief about her God-given right to be protected. Perpetrators "entice unsteady souls . . . those who are barely escaping from those who live in error" (2 Peter 2:14, 18); wolves lure a vulnerable sheep and pounce.

UNDERSTANDING THE TRAUMA SURVIVOR

Part of what makes trauma survivors at risk of revictimization is the treatment they receive from communities that do not yet understand the impact of trauma. If we want to serve and protect trauma survivors well, we must effectively apply our understanding of trauma responses to our conceptualizations of survivors' choices and reactions. The topics addressed below do not pertain to every trauma survivor, but these are frequently asked questions about how to understand aspects of their experience that may be informed by their abuse history. Rightly interpreting the behavior of trauma survivors enables us to provide compassionate support that protects them from the predatory strategies of perpetrators.

Why didn't they say no, scream, or fight back during the assault? In previous chapters, we have explored the fight, flight, or freeze response that is common in situations our nervous system perceives to be dangerous. Within a split second of perceiving danger, our brain assesses the present risk and makes a calculation of what response seems most likely to give the least harmful outcome. Sometimes, in this risk calculation, our nervous system determines it is in such grave danger that freezing in order to "get it over with" seems to be the safest decision. Many factors impact this split-second calculation, and it is often a mystery to the trauma survivor why this was their adrenaline-driven response. This freeze response, also called tonic immobility, is almost twice as prevalent in survivors of sexual abuse as compared to survivors of other types of traumas (Kalaf et al., 2017).

In addition to tonic immobility, survivors of sexual abuse employ avoidance and compliance strategies to reduce the severity or frequency of the abuse, particularly when it is ongoing and feels inevitable (Katz et al., 2021). In a qualitative study examining the experiences of adult survivors of child sexual abuse, participants reported believing physical resistance to the abuse would only intensify the harm done to them. Instead, they described avoidance tactics aimed at postponing or decreasing the frequency of the abuse, such as clinging to a non-abusive parent, wearing multiple layers of clothing, or pretending to be asleep when approached by the perpetrator. When avoidance strategies did not work, many participants practiced "compliance" to reduce the harm done to them. For example, one participant reported offering her perpetrator oral sex to avoid painful vaginal penetration (Katz & Nicolet, 2022). Though these attempts at reducing the severity of abuse are as much a survival instinct as fighting or running away, survivors often experience significant shame regarding their response. Doubting survivors' stories because they did not "fight back" reinforces the fear that they are responsible for their abuse and intensifies their experience of shame.

I worked with one trauma survivor who was sexually assaulted while on a date with a man. During the assault, her brain reminded her of a movie she had recently watched in which a woman was being assaulted and tried to escape. In the movie, the perpetrator kills the woman while trying to catch her. At this moment, this trauma survivor's brain assessed the present threat and determined it was better to be sexually assaulted than to be killed. After the fact, she felt significant shame about not fighting back. But the reality is, it is quite possible her brain made the most resourceful decision possible in a moment of terrible harm in response to the feeling of being trapped.

When a trauma survivor makes an allegation of abuse against someone in the church, it may be tempting to discredit them based on a perception of their compliance with the abuse. If Sarah from our case study willingly rode in a vehicle with John despite alleged experiences of assault, you might be tempted to think she was also consenting to his sexual advances. However, understanding trauma responses lets us reinterpret Sarah's compliance as evidence of her potential feelings of powerlessness to prevent the abuse or attempts at reducing the severity of the abuse.

Why does the trauma survivor forget details? Our memories do not work like a camera—objectively taking note and storing all details of an experience. Rather, our brain is a complex organ that filters our present experiences through the lens of our past experiences and our current needs (Goodman et al., 2019). For example, if you are going to watch your son play a baseball game, you might vividly remember watching him strike out while at bat. You saw the disappointment on his face before he hung his head in shame. Your parental instincts were telling you this was important data that you must be highly attuned to. A week later, you may still remember these details. However, a parent of the shortstop on the opposing team watched the same strikeout but may have completely disregarded and filtered it out because they were highly attuned to their own son's interaction with his coach.

This understanding of memory storage helps us conceptualize the ways in which our mind is designed by God to serve us well. When the amygdala perceives danger, it releases adrenaline and cortisol that help ignite the survival response and direct all the brain and body's resources toward what will most promote survival (Hakamata et al., 2022). This process is a gift from God to help us navigate life in a sometimes dangerous, fallen world. When a person perceives their life may be in danger, an accurate chronology of events may not be the most important detail the mind holds onto, while the expression on the perpetrator's face is highly important. Similar to the fight, flight, freeze response, these attention and memory storage decisions happen in a split second, often mysterious to the survivor.

One key aspect of PTSD is the presence of intrusive memories or sensory experiences that arise involuntarily in response to a stimulus or "trigger." These intrusive memories, or flashbacks, are often vivid and make the survivor feel as if the event is happening all over again. It is common for these memories to be fragmented and difficult to retrieve voluntarily, or without the triggering stimulus, which limits survivors' ability to tell their stories in a coherent or chronological manner (Brewin et al., 2010). This is one reason why survivors may give seemingly conflicting or insufficient reports of their abuse to leaders or law enforcement. These gaps in memory are often distressing to survivors who want to have a clear understanding of what happened to their bodies.

I worked with a trauma survivor who experienced almost daily sexual abuse for several years, perpetrated by the administrator of her Christian school. Our creaky office door brought back vivid memories of the sound of the door creaking shut and the lock turning before her perpetrator approached her each day. On the other hand, she had difficulty remembering details like the duration of the abuse or when and how it started. She could not recall friends and teachers' names, birthday parties, school dances, and high school graduation. The frequency and intensity of the abuse amplified her sensory memory and dulled her autobiographical memory.

Again, this natural trauma response may prompt people to disbelieve survivors' allegations of abuse. A person might hear a survivor disclose her experiences of abuse and be prone to feel suspicious of her fragmented storytelling. On the contrary, this fragmented memory is evidence for rather than against a potential trauma history. The more trauma survivors are supported by their community, the less likely they are to be targeted by perpetrators.

Why didn't they report sooner or at all? Approximately 69 percent of sexual assaults in the United States go unreported (RAINN, 2020). Research reveals a number of reasons abuse survivors delay or avoid reporting their experience, including fear of not being believed, feelings of shame, fears of future harm if they report, and the belief that they must protect the perpetrator from consequences (Lemaigre et al., 2017; McElvaney et al., 2022; Stiller & Hellmann, 2017). Child victims typically first disclose abuse to a parent, usually their mother. Even in the context of safe and attuned parent/ child interactions, children often delay reporting out of confusion about the nature of the abuse, protection of their family, or feeling ashamed or responsible for the abuse. The average time it takes someone to report childhood sexual abuse is eighteen years (Solberg et al., 2021). This delay in reporting is exacerbated when there is additional physical or emotional abuse in the home, as the child is uncertain if they will be supported (Tashjian et al., 2016). As we have discussed, perpetrators target victims who are vulnerable and unlikely to report, putting children who have experienced abuse in their homes at increased risk for revictimization. The targeting and grooming process builds a relationship with the child that makes them feel chosen and special, creating a dynamic in which the child wants to please the perpetrator. This power imbalance increases victims' perception of their complicity in the abuse and decreases the likelihood they will report the abuse (Caprioli & Crenshaw, 2017).

For adult victims, there is a common misconception that sexual assault most often occurs in a dark alley by a stranger wielding a weapon who overpowers the victim. In reality, most sexual assaults are perpetrated by someone known to the victim (Wegner, 2014). This misconception impacts victims' own perception of their abuse and the perception of those to whom they report. When victims believe sexual assault typically occurs by an overtly violent stranger, they are less likely to report their experience to law enforcement (Lathan et al., 2023).

Victims also feel confused about how to categorize their experience of abuse when they notice their body responds to sexual stimulation by perpetrators. Some victims experience sexual arousal during their assault, often prompting them to feel betrayed by their bodies and decreasing the likelihood of reporting the abuse (Bunderson, 2020). This is exacerbated in male survivors of sexual abuse, as they often feel ashamed about experiencing an erection and uncertain if their experience "counts" as abuse. A study examining the experience of male survivors of child sexual abuse found men to be hesitant to report their abuse out of fear they would be perceived as gay in the case of male perpetrators (Attrash-Najjar et al., 2023). Survivors who experienced abuse in the context of school or religious institutions described the abuse as a normalized aspect of their daily lives and expressed feeling "trapped" due to the power imbalance between themselves and their perpetrators (Attrash-Najjar et al., 2023, p. 9). Considering the number of factors aimed at silencing victims, it's a miracle of courage and bravery that any instance of sexual abuse is reported.

What does this mean for safeguarders? Research is clear that safe, attuned, and supportive relationships encourage prompt disclosure (Lemaigre et al., 2017; Tashjian et al., 2016). In their engagement with the relationship between survivors' experience of shame and their likelihood to report abuse, McElvaney and colleagues (2022) write,

> Being understood and having someone to talk to outside the family where they did not have to be worried about the reactions of others helped them to express themselves, which in turn helped them make sense of what had happened and who was responsible for the abuse. (p. 6)

As a safeguarder, you provide an opportunity for survivors to experience meaningful connection that drives out shame, emboldening them to advocate for justice and heal from abuse. As we have said before, perpetrators target victims who are unlikely to report and, if they do report, are unlikely to be believed. Cultivating an environment in which trauma survivors are cared for and abuse allegations are taken seriously by the whole community discourages predatory behavior and prevents future abuse.

Why do they self-harm or abuse substances? To understand the relationship between trauma and self-harm or addiction, we have to revisit the concept of emotion regulation. We have established that trauma can both intensify survivors' emotional experiences and stunt their ability to identify and regulate emotions (Siegel, 2015). For some survivors, self-harm turns their emotional pain into a more tangible form of physical pain (Gurung, 2018). Addiction to substances (alcohol, smoking, methamphetamines, etc.) or behaviors (pornography, gambling, video games, etc.) helps survivors manage overwhelming emotions (Estévez et al., 2017). For example, a person who has not experienced trauma and has advanced emotion regulation skills may experience mild anxiety at an upcoming performance review with his boss. He may notice a slightly tense feeling in his chest the morning of the evaluation and choose to go for a run around his neighborhood to settle his nerves. When he enters his boss's office, he still feels apprehensive about the outcome but has confidence that he can manage either good or bad news.

Now, replace him with a man who experienced ongoing child sexual abuse perpetrated by his pastor. He spent years in childhood disconnecting from his physical and emotional experience in an attempt to manage horrific abuse. At the time, this was a helpful, adaptive response to significant, seemingly unavoidable pain. However, in adulthood, this dissociative response keeps him disconnected from helpful emotional cues. As he anticipates being alone in a room with another man in a position of authority, he experiences heightened anxiety. Unlike the non-traumatized man, his disconnection from his physiological experience keeps him from identifying and responding to the anxiety. Instead, he knows he feels overwhelmed but cannot effectively attune to and regulate this experience. He goes out for a drink with friends the night before the performance review and discovers he *loves* the calming effects of alcohol. He does not stop drinking until he blacks out and can finally go to sleep.

For trauma survivors, self-harm and addiction are often attempts at finding peace amid torment. While these efforts at emotion regulation can cause significant long-term damage, it is important that we have compassion for the immense suffering that sparks the use of these strategies. In later chapters, we will present several emotion regulation strategies that provide alternative ways for survivors to manage their distress. The church can support trauma survivors and prevent revictimization in the way they respond to those who are struggling with self-harm and addiction. Conceptualizing these behaviors as attempts at managing pain allows us to create communities that provide safe companionship as trauma survivors work toward wholeness and healing. Self-harm and addiction can be extraordinarily isolating, especially in faith communities. A church's ability to walk alongside those recovering from addiction provides a safety net of support that protects the survivors from the charming and inviting grooming strategies of perpetrators.

CONCLUSION

The potential cascading aftermath of abuse in the life of a survivor is tragic and heartbreaking. Attachment deficits from dysfunctional family systems create a vacuum of healthy relationship models. Normal responses to trauma catalyze an escalating feedback loop of anxiety and self-medicating that provides temporary relief with terrible consequences and often impacts relationships. The exploitation of a person's body may distort their perception of their inherent worth and dignity as someone made in the image of God. These consequences of abuse make survivors vulnerable to the grooming strategies of perpetrators and increase their risk of revictimization. Trauma often begets future trauma, but there is hope in Christ even for those for those who have suffered many horrific forms of abuse.

Research shows that even amid the terrible distress of trauma, survivors experience resilience and growth (Sheridan & Carr, 2020). A supportive, patient community allows survivors to honestly wrestle with God and make sense of their experiences. This unraveling and reconstructing creates meaning from what once felt hopeless, paving the way for a purposeful life of both grief and joy. With thoughtful processing and safe relationships, survivors can say with the psalmist, "I believe that I shall look upon the goodness of the LORD in the land of the living" (Psalm 27:13). We can be confident that God sees the vulnerable, acts on their behalf, and executes judgment on their perpetrators. He has established the church to be the body of Christ and charged us to sacrificially serve and protect to help establish redeemed relational templates that communicate the kind, steadfast, just character of God.

PERSONAL REFLECTION

1. What character traits/behaviors displayed by a survivor would make it hard for you to believe their story? How can those be seen through a trauma-informed lens?

2. It can be challenging to read stories of abuse and revictimization. What thoughts, feelings, and physical sensations did you experience as you read Sarah's story?

3. How can you apply this information to better support trauma survivors in your community?

GROUP DISCUSSION

1. Considering the risk of revictimization, how can church communities create environments that are supportive, understanding, and protective for abuse survivors?

2. How does an understanding of emotional dysregulation help conceptualize survivors' use of coping mechanisms such as substance abuse or self-harm?

3. Reflect on the impact of trauma on a survivor's ability to discern healthy relationships from potentially harmful ones. How might past experiences of abuse shape a survivor's perception of what is acceptable or normal in relationships?

REFERENCES

Attrash-Najjar, A., Cohen, N., Glucklich, T., & Katz, C. (2023). "I was the only one talking about the abuse": Experiences and perceptions of survivors who underwent child sexual abuse as boys. *Child Abuse & Neglect*, 140, 106144. https://doi.org/10.1016/j.chiabu.2023.106144

Bowlby, J. (1988) *A secure base: Clinical applications of attachment theory.* London: Routledge.

Brewin, C. R., Gregory, J. D., Lipton, M., & Burgess, N. (2010). Intrusive images in psychological disorders: Characteristics, neural mechanisms, and treatment implications. *Psychological Review*, 117(1), 210-32. https://doi.org/10.1037/a0018113

Bunderson, K. (2020). Female sexual arousal during rape: Implications on seeking treatment, blame, and the emotional experience. [Doctoral dissertation, Alliant International University: California School of Professional Psychology].

Caprioli, S., & Crenshaw, D. A. (2017). The culture of silencing child victims of sexual abuse: Implications for child witnesses in court. *Journal of Humanistic Psychology*, *57*(2), 190-209. https://doi.org/10.1177/0022167815604442

Crittenden, P. M., & Heller, M. B. (2017). The roots of chronic posttraumatic stress disorder: Childhood trauma, information processing, and self-protective strategies. *Chronic Stress*, *1*, 2470547016682965. https://doi.org/10.1177/2470547016682965

Estévez, A., Jáuregui, P., Sánchez-Marcos, I., López-González, H., & Griffiths, M. D. (2017). Attachment and emotion regulation in substance addictions and behavioral addictions. *Journal of Behavioral Addictions*, *6*(4), 534-44. https://doi.org/10.1556/2006.6.2017.086

Goodman, G. S., Quas, J. A., Goldfarb, D., Gonzalves, L., & Gonzalez, A. (2019). Trauma and long-term memory for childhood events: Impact matters. *Child Development Perspectives*, *13*(1), 3-9. https://doi.org/10.1111/cdep.12307

Gurung, K. (2018). Bodywork: Self-harm, trauma, and embodied expressions of pain. *Arts and Humanities in Higher Education*, *17*(1), 32-47. https://doi.org/10.1177/1474022216684634

Hakamata, Y., Mizukami, S., Izawa, S., Okamura, H., Mihara, K., Marusak, H., Moriguchi, Y., Hori, H., Hanakawa, T., Inoue, Y., & Tagaya, H. (2022). Implicit and explicit emotional memory recall in anxiety and depression: Role of basolateral amygdala and cortisol-norepinephrine interaction. *Psychoneuroendocrinology*, *136*, 105598. https://doi.org/10.1016/j.psyneuen.2021.105598

Jaffe, A. E., DiLillo, D., Gratz, K. L., & Messman-Moore, T. L. (2019). Risk for revictimization following interpersonal and noninterpersonal trauma: Clarifying the role of posttraumatic stress symptoms and trauma-related cognitions. *Journal of Traumatic Stress*, *32*(1), 42-55.

Kalaf, J., Coutinho, E. S. F., Vilete, L. M. P., Luz, M. P., Berger, W., Mendlowicz, M., Volchan, E., Andreoli, S. B., Quintana, M. I., de Jesus Mari, J., & Figueira, I. (2017). Sexual trauma is more strongly associated with tonic immobility than other types of trauma—a population based study. *Journal of Affective Disorders*, *215*, 71-76. https://doi.org/10.1016/j.jad.2017.03.009

Katz, C., & Nicolet, R. (2022). "If only I could have stopped it": Reflections of adult child sexual abuse survivors on their responses during the abuse. *Journal of Interpersonal Violence*, *37*(3–4), NP2076-NP2100. https://doi.org/10.1177/0886260520935485

Katz, C., Tsur, N., Talmon, A., & Nicolet, R. (2021). Beyond fight, flight, and freeze: Towards a new conceptualization of peritraumatic responses to child sexual abuse based on retrospective accounts of adult survivors. *Child Abuse & Neglect*, *112*, 104905. https://doi.org/10.1016/j.chiabu.2020.104905

Lathan, E. C., Koon-Magnin, S., Selwyn, C. N., Isaak, H., & Langhinrichsen-Rohling, J. (2023). Rape myth acceptance and other barriers to formally reporting sexual assault among college students with and without sexual assault histories. *Journal of Interpersonal Violence*, *38*(9–10), 6773-797. https://doi.org/10.1177/08862605221137703

Lemaigre, C., Taylor, E. P., & Gittoes, C. (2017). Barriers and facilitators to disclosing sexual abuse in childhood and adolescence: A systematic review. *Child Abuse & Neglect*, *70*, 39-52. https://doi.org/10.1016/j.chiabu.2017.05.009

Li, S., Ran, G., & Chen, X. (2021). Linking attachment to empathy in childhood and adolescence: A multilevel meta-analysis. *Journal of Social and Personal Relationships*, *38*(11), 3350-77. https://doi.org/10.1177/02654075211031006

McElvaney, R., Lateef, R., Collin-Vézina, D., Alaggia, R., & Simpson, M. (2022). Bringing shame out of the shadows: Identifying shame in child sexual abuse disclosure processes and implications for psychotherapy. *Journal of Interpersonal Violence, 37*(19–20), NP18738-NP18760. https://doi.org/10.1177/08862605211037435

RAINN. (2020). *The Criminal Justice System: Statistics.* www.rainn.org/statistics/criminal -justice-system

Sheridan, G., & Carr, A. (2020). Survivors' lived experiences of posttraumatic growth after institutional childhood abuse: An interpretative phenomenological analysis. *Child Abuse & Neglect, 103*, 104430. https://doi.org/10.1016/j.chiabu.2020.104430

Siegel, D. J., Schore, A. N., & Cozolino, L. (2021). Interpersonal neurobiology and clinical practice (1st Ed.). W. W. Norton & Company.

Siegel, J. P. (2015). Emotional regulation in adolescent substance use disorders: Rethinking risk. *Journal of Child & Adolescent Substance Abuse, 24*(2), 67-79. https://doi.org/10.1080 /1067828X.2012.761169

Solberg, E. T., Halvorsen, J. E., & Stige, S. H. (2021). What do survivors of child sexual abuse believe will facilitate early disclosure of sexual abuse? *Frontiers in psychiatry, 12*, 639341. https://doi.org/10.3389/fpsyt.2021.639341

Stiller, A., & Hellmann, D. F. (2017). In the aftermath of disclosing child sexual abuse: Consequences, needs, and wishes. *Journal of Sexual Aggression, 23*(3), 251-65. https:// doi.org/10.1080/13552600.2017.1318964

Tashjian, S. M., Goldfarb, D., Goodman, G. S., Quas, J. A., & Edelstein, R. (2016). Delay in disclosure of non-parental child sexual abuse in the context of emotional and physical maltreatment: A pilot study. *Child Abuse & Neglect, 58*, 149-59. https://doi .org/10.1016/j.chiabu.2016.06.020

Wegner, R., Pierce, J., & Abbey, A. (2014). Relationship type and sexual precedence: Their associations with characteristics of sexual assault perpetrators and incidents. *Violence Against Women, 20*(11), 1360-82. https://doi.org/10.1177/1077801214552856

9

IMPACT ON CHILDREN AND ADOLESCENTS

DR. KRISTY M. FORD

If you give one of these simple, childlike believers a hard time,
bullying or taking advantage of their simple trust,
you'll soon wish you hadn't. You'd be better off dropped in
the middle of the lake with a millstone around your neck.

MARK 9:42 MSG

CHILDREN AND ADOLESCENTS present unique challenges for helpers, requiring an understanding of their specialized needs. Concerns about childhood trauma highlight the importance of establishing safety in the immediate sense, while developing systems for maintaining ongoing safety for this vulnerable population. Globally, trauma impacts an estimated one billion children and adolescents annually (Hillis et al., 2016) in the form of physical, sexual, or emotional violence or neglect (World Health Organization [WHO], 2022). Lifetime estimates range from two out of three children in the United States (SAMHSA, 2023) to 75 percent of children worldwide (WHO, 2022) who will experience some form of trauma before the age of sixteen. While safety needs must be prioritized in the present, in the long run, it is also important for helpers to consider how childhood trauma impacts physical, mental, emotional, and spiritual development and disrupts long-term health and well-being. By establishing safeguarding services that include trauma-informed care for children and adolescents, helpers can mitigate generational cycles of abuse by recognizing the early signs and symptoms of trauma and responding with appropriate programs and interventions to enhance resilience and build communities that support healthier relationships (Lyons-Ruth & Jacobvitz, 2008).

DEFINING TRAUMA AND ADVERSE CHILDHOOD EXPERIENCES

The LORD is close to the brokenhearted and
saves those who are crushed in spirit.

PSALM 34:18

Traumatic experiences for children and adolescents are most often conceptu-alized as interpersonal experiences of physical violence, sexual abuse, emo-tional abuse, boundary violations, and/or neglect within their own family system. However, trauma can also include witnessing these types of abuses perpetrated toward others, experiencing violence at the community level such as at school or in their neighborhood, or experiencing the sudden death of a loved one. To further expand considerations of what constitutes childhood trauma, children and adolescents worldwide may be exposed to natural di-sasters, terrorism, refugee or war experiences, military-related stressors, hunger, and/or life-threatening disease (SAMHSA, 2023). The exploitation of children through the commercialized sex trafficking industry and forced labor market is well documented, with estimates in the millions worldwide (World's Children, 2023).

As mentioned in an earlier chapter, adverse childhood experiences (ACEs) include experiences that have the potential to impact early brain growth as well as overall well-being and resiliency (Murphy et al., 2014). ACEs can include any of the above detailed traumatic experiences but are further expanded to include attachment relationship disruptions such as parental divorce, an incar-cerated loved one, or other stressor events that initiate family displacement, such as military deployment. Research indicates that ACEs are associated with disruptions in brain development; social, emotional, and cognitive impairment; high-risk behaviors; disability and disease; and even early death (Dube, 2018; Felitti et al., 1998). Childhood adversity also increases risk of future trauma and victimization (Quinn et al., 2017).

THE IMPACT OF TRAUMA ON THE BRAIN

I praise you because I am fearfully and wonderfully made;
your works are wonderful, I know that full well.

PSALM 139:14

While the human brain is resilient, often demonstrating a capacity to overcome negative life experiences and adapt as needed, children do not have the cognitive and emotional resources to process trauma or understand its implications fully (Zilberstein, 2014). Children from unhealthy, dysfunctional family systems or children who have had traumatic experiences may manifest their response to the trauma in numerous ways, such as behavioral problems, emotional dysregulation, or even physical symptoms. Additionally, these experiences shape the child's core beliefs and perceptions about themselves, others, and the world that can endure throughout the lifespan. This underscores the importance of creating safe and nurturing environments for children and providing them with the necessary support and resources to build resilience and heal from trauma.

The vulnerability of children. Children are particularly vulnerable to long-term impairments from trauma because their brains are still developing. When a caregiver or trusted person is inconsistent in meeting needs or is emotionally unavailable, these experiences can disrupt the sense of safety and trust. Both severe attachment deficits and traumatic events such as abuse can leave a severe and lasting impression on a child's developing brain. The brain undergoes significant growth and development during childhood (this period is marked by increased neuroplasticity), when the brain is highly influenced by environmental experiences. Traumatic experiences during this critical phase can have a profound consequence, impacting mental health, relationships, and overall quality of life (Zilberstein, 2014).

While trauma impacts children holistically, including disruptions of cognition, emotion, and sense of self, it is important to consider that these more obvious symptoms are evidence of trauma's impact at the most basic and physical level, the neurobiological level (Siegel et al., 2021). "After trauma, the world is experienced with a different nervous system" (van der Kolk, 2014, p. 53). Trauma induces a type of brain damage that disrupts normal communication between neurological systems, impacting overall brain function. Neural dis-integration refers to specialized areas of the brain that are not integrated, meaning they are not cooperating in the complex communication system with other specialized areas of the brain (Siegel et al., 2021). The brain reacts to trauma by dis-integrating neural networks, severely impacting overall brain development, often by overproducing or disrupting the availability of important neurochemicals. In addition, trauma can cause changes to structure and functioning of brain parts, including the amygdala, hippocampus, and prefrontal cortex (Noll, 2021). These changes can cause deficits throughout the lifespan without therapeutic intervention.

The fight, flight, freeze, and fawn response. We are wired for survival, and our brains almost instantaneously employ specific survival responses, including fight, flight, freeze, or fawn (Porges, 2021), which we learned about in an earlier chapter. In the following section, we will explore how these survival responses impact children's physical health, cognitive abilities, and behaviors.

During the state of fight/flight activation, stress hormones, including cortisol, are released to prepare the body for threat response. However, when trauma exposure is extreme or ongoing, they can reduce cognitive functioning and increase the risk of health issues. These hormones initiate fast-paced breathing for increased oxygen intake, increased blood flow to enhance strength and focus, and dilated pupils to allow in more light for the eyes to scan the environment. Stress hormones also reduce other functions deemed unnecessary for response to imminent danger, such as digestion, and block access to the more advanced areas of the brain responsible for information processing, problem solving, and future planning, inhibiting the ability to think clearly in that moment (Cozolino, 2014). This is useful for brief periods of engagement with any threat, assuming the body can then return to a regulated state after the danger is over, but these responses can get stuck in the "on" position, resulting in chronic activation of the brain's nervous system that presents as hyperarousal (jumpiness/irritability), nightmares, flashbacks, anxiety, panic, and dread (Lyons-Ruth et al., 2016). Chronic exposure to stress hormones is toxic to organ systems and can lead to significant inflammation and other health issues. Chronic blocked access to clear thinking makes it difficult for persistently traumatized children and adolescents to settle into basic self-care routines, generate strategies for problem solving, concentrate on schoolwork, and establish long-range life goals.

In addition to potential health and cognitive issues from intense or persistent trauma, children may also display problematic behaviors as reactions to ongoing threat activation. First, in a display of the behavioral response of *fight*, children might exhibit aggressive, defiant, or confrontational behavior as a way to protect themselves or regain control. This response activates the sympathetic nervous system, leading to an increased heart rate and heightened alertness. Next, the *flight* response involves avoidance or escapism, where children attempt to distance themselves from fearful or potentially threatening situations. This behavior stems from the need to seek safety and is associated with hyperarousal, causing restlessness and anxiety. Further, children may experience a state of *freeze*, characterized by a lack of emotional responsiveness or motor activity. This response often occurs when a child's brain subconsciously perceives that fighting or fleeing is impossible due to inescapable trauma. The child may respond to future perceived threats with a similar state of zoning out, helplessness, isolation, or dissociation. Lastly, the *fawn* response involves seeking to appease or please the perpetrator, often observed when the source of the trauma is someone the child is dependent on. Related behaviors include people pleasing, dependency, and trauma bonding with abusers.

The compounded impact of prolonged trauma. The more persistent and intense the trauma, the more these brain responses become rooted, manifesting in major alterations in the way the child views the world, self, and others, particularly when combined with low social support. Important brain processes such as reasoning, learning, and impulse control become impaired, potentially leading to distorted thinking, feeling, and behaving; disrupted memory systems; poor judgment; and disruptions of relational attachment capacity (Cozolino, 2014). Additionally, the brain is divinely designed as a self-protective machine and calculates the threat response of environmental cues. Intense or chronic trauma can cause an overgeneralization of potential dangers as the brain constructs ideas about the beliefs, intentions, and perspectives of others, which can become severely distorted when relational trust has been breached. Emotional memories, which are created and stored in the brain during strong emotional experiences, are easily triggered by new or ongoing events that activate the established beliefs about the world, self, and others associated with early trauma memories (van der Kolk, 2014). Clearly, the damage caused by childhood trauma can cause lifelong struggles in all areas of functioning.

HEALTHY BRAIN DEVELOPMENT AND SECURE ATTACHMENT

> *Children are a gift from the Lord; they are a reward from him.*
> *Children born to a young man are like arrows in a warrior's*
> *hands. How joyful is the man whose quiver is full of them!*

Psalm 127:3-5 NLT

Before continuing the exploration of the impact of trauma on children and adolescents, it is important to first understand what is required for a healthy brain to mature. Colonnesi et al. (2011) explain that as children experience parental attunement and have their needs met by their caregivers, they internalize important skills such as an ability to emotionally regulate and the general expectation that other people can be trusted. At birth, the developing brain of the infant seeks validations of love and safety, and, over time, children learn that others can be trusted to meet their needs as these expectations are met by caretakers. As the brain continues to develop, predictable physical and emotional safety results in neural systems that are well integrated, meaning that the brain is communicating effectively between systems and is functioning in a healthy way (van der Kolk, 2014). This ultimately results in what is experienced as growth and maturity over time, demonstrated in the ability to maintain self-regulation and impulse control, as well as the capacity to reason, problem solve, plan, and create.

In healthy functioning families, secure attachment schemas can be defined as positive mental representations developed by individuals who have experienced secure attachment relationships during their formative years, typically in early childhood (Lahousen et al., 2019). These schemas reflect their expectations and beliefs about themselves, others, and relationships. The pattern is established by a feedback loop that begins with a felt need, in the form of any dysregulated state such as hunger, fear, or loneliness, and ends with the meeting of that need, resulting in a re-regulated state as the desire is satiated (Lahousen et al., 2019). Secure attachment schemas support ongoing healthy relationships, as the growing child interprets the world as a safe place where others can be trusted and their needs will be met, enabling them to interact socially and reach out to the community for connection rather than seeking isolation. Parents do not need to be perfectly attuned to their child's needs to facilitate secure attachment, but they must effectively repent and repair ruptures or misattunement. When a parent properly attunes and quickly and effectively repairs when there are moments of disconnection, children learn that conflict can be safely managed. Brain development seeks security in relationships, and security in relationships supports ongoing brain development, enhancing overall mental health and the experience of positive emotions through healthy connections with others (Zilberstein, 2014). Children rely on caregivers and trusted loved ones for safety, nurturance, and emotional support. These relationships serve as the foundation for the child's sense of security and self-worth.

THE IMPACT OF TRAUMA ON ATTACHMENT SCHEMAS

Why, my soul, are you downcast? Why so disturbed within me?

PSALM 43:5

As discussed in the previous section, attachment schemas are cognitive frameworks that shape an individual's beliefs and expectations about relationships, formed through early interactions with primary caregivers (Siegel et al., 2021). These schemas are established based on secure or insecure relational interactions in early childhood development and ultimately influence how children will interact in relationships across their lifespan. Secure attachment schemas indicate that children learned the world was basically a safe place where others could be trusted to meet their needs. However, insecure attachment schemas are formed as basic needs in childhood are not met or, worse, the caretakers who should have met those needs were instead the initiators of the trauma as perpetrators of the abuse (Briere et al., 2017). Research in the area of interpersonal neurobiology (Siegel et al., 2021; Porges, 2021) suggests that beyond the physiological realm, the fight-or-flight response is related to how the brain processes and integrates social and emotional experiences. So, as the brain becomes dysregulated, it affects not only the child's ability to self-regulate but also their ability to interact with others effectively. Insecure attachment schemas combined with low social support are associated with higher likelihood of ACEs and traumatic experiences, as well as lower resiliency and the increased potential for ongoing trauma throughout the lifespan (Dube, 2018; Dube et al., 2001). As we briefly discussed in the systems chapter, insecure childhood attachment schemas fall into three main patterns: anxious, avoidant, and disorganized.

The anxious attachment schema. First, anxious attachment, sometimes called the preoccupied attachment style, typically originates from a lack of consistent support and reassurance from caregivers during the child's explorations and interactions with their environment. Children with this relational pattern anxiously seek to get their needs met by others. Children with anxious attachment tend to feel uncomfortable when confronted with new or unfamiliar situations or people. This fear is rooted in the uncertainty of how their caregivers will respond or if they will be there for support (Colonnesi et al., 2011). Because they haven't experienced consistent support for their explorations and emotions, these individuals often lack self-confidence. They may doubt their abilities, fear making decisions, and struggle with independence. Anxious attachment is associated with an overly activated attachment system. This means that they have a heightened sensitivity to potential threats to their emotional security, which can lead to exaggerated emotional responses that children have difficulty soothing on their own, especially in stressful situations.

The avoidant attachment schema. The next pattern, avoidant attachment, which is sometimes called the dismissive attachment style, is characterized by a fear of intimacy and vulnerability. Children with avoidant attachment actively try to ignore their own needs, as this pattern leads them to be highly self-reliant and hesitant to accept help from others or depend on them for support or comfort. Children who have developed this style have often experienced caregivers who were inconsistent in providing emotional safety and support when they were emotionally dysregulated. As a result, they develop a fear of intimacy and emotional closeness (Briere et al., 2017). Due to their past experiences with caregivers, children with avoidant attachment styles may find it challenging to trust others with their emotions, resulting in significant emotional independence. They are often skeptical of others' intentions and may fear becoming vulnerable in relationships as they have learned to rely on themselves to cope with distress. While maintaining boundaries is essential in any relationship, individuals with avoidant attachment may set emotional boundaries that are overly rigid, making it challenging for others to connect with them on a deep emotional level.

The disorganized attachment schema. Lastly, disorganized attachment is a complex and often challenging attachment style that can result from inconsistent, unpredictable, or even abusive caregiving experiences in childhood. Unlike secure, anxious, or avoidant attachment styles, disorganized attachment lacks a clear strategy for dealing with attachment figures. Children with disorganized attachment have experienced caregivers who provide unpredictable responses to their emotional needs. The caregivers may alternate between being a source of comfort and safety and a source of fear or even abuse. Further, in some cases of disorganized attachment, children may have been placed in the role of a caregiver, particularly when the caregiver is emotionally unstable or abusive. This role reversal can create confusion and anxiety for the child.

Children with disorganized attachment often display a chaotic mixture of behaviors in response to distress, including seeking proximity to the caregiver for comfort and then suddenly withdrawing when they become fearful (Fearon et al., 2010). This contradictory behavior reflects their internal conflict and confusion. Disorganized attachment is often associated with severe emotional dysregulation, as children struggle to manage their feelings and reactions due to the inconsistent caregiving they receive. Research has shown that disorganized attachment is associated with a higher risk of developing mental health issues, including anxiety, depression, and posttraumatic stress disorder (PTSD), and even attention-deficit hyperactivity disorder (ADHD; Ivarsson et al., 2016; Macdonald et al., 2008; Schore, 2002; Storebe et al., 2016). The challenging relational patterns of disorganized attachment underscore the critical importance of consistent, loving, and safe caregiving in childhood.

Without these elements, children may develop complex attachment patterns that can significantly impact their emotional well-being and relationships throughout their lives.

REESTABLISHING RELATIONAL SECURITY AND REGULATION

See that you do not despise one of these little ones.
For I tell you that their angels in heaven always
see the face of my Father in heaven.

MATTHEW 18:10

Thankfully, while traumatic events and insecure relational attachment serve to disrupt brain development and decrease overall resilience for children and adolescents, it is possible for safeguarders to support the initiation of increased secure attachment at any stage of development, contributing physical and emotional resources to overcome the barriers associated with ACEs and childhood trauma. By serving as models of safe and predictable caregivers, helpers can jumpstart the attachment feedback loop, generating circumstances in which children have the opportunity to learn at a deep neurobiological level that some people are, in fact, trustworthy. Research on *earned-secure attachment* by Saunders et al. (2011) indicates that someone other than the primary caregiver may offer the emotional support needed to jumpstart the attachment system and allow for new learning, accomplished by providing a listening ear during times of distress as well as offering genuine aid when more tangible needs are presented. However, relational attachment is more flexible and open to change during childhood comparable to adulthood, meaning that having a safeguarder as a child may increase the likelihood of overcoming the trauma of ACEs and demonstrating security in future relationships (Saunders et al., 2011).

Reinitiating the attachment cycle. Children and young people who come with felt needs provide helpers with an opportunity to meet those needs, encouraging them in the present moment to move from dysregulated to regulated physical and emotional states. For instance, addressing a physical need like feeding a hungry child alleviates the discomfort of hunger, allowing the body to relax and regain its balance. Likewise, when a child is frightened or lonely, offering emotional support through comforting words or a smile partially eases the emotional distress, providing the emotional self with room for regulation.

Co-regulation and self-regulation. When a calm and safe caregiver moves toward a dysregulated child or adolescent for the purpose of helping them in some way to become regulated, this is known as *co-regulation*. In a sense, the child's brain "borrows" safety and peace from the brain of the regulated adult, which is the foundation of the experience of trust (Porges, 2021). In other words, the child can sense that if the adult is regulated in this circumstance, that it is safe to relax and trust the caregiver to meet their needs. Over time, experiences that encourage the establishment of trust can retrain the attachment system, as the child or adolescent first relearns how to reach out to have their needs met through co-regulation, then learns to meet their own needs as their capacity grows for self-regulation. In co-regulation, cycles of emotional dysregulation and regulation become more predictable and less frightening, as the world is viewed as more trustworthy, and the self is viewed as more capable of self-regulation. As self-regulation is strengthened over time, children learn they can cope with a range of emotions without becoming overwhelmed or dysregulated, and they can make behavior choices that align with their goals and values.

WHAT CHILDREN NEED FOR SAFETY

> *He will cover you with his feathers, and under his wings you will*
> *find refuge; his faithfulness will be your shield and rampart.*
>
> PSALM 91:4

Children's safety is paramount to their overall development and well-being. Safety encompasses various aspects, including physical, emotional, and attachment safety, and it plays a fundamental role in shaping children's experiences (Porges, 2022). By providing foundational safety, caregivers and adults enable children to grow, learn, and thrive in an environment that nurtures their potential (Beachboard, 2022).

Safety in physical spaces. A safe and secure environment is essential for children. This includes childproofed spaces for young children and safe neighborhoods for older kids, as this allows for exploration, play, and learning without fear. First, a safe space prioritizes physical safety. For young children, this means taking steps to clear the environment of any potential danger such as having safe games and toys for play, establishing a room that is inviting and comfortable, and ensuring children are out of sight of potential perpetrators. In this secure setting, parents or caregivers can have peace of mind that children are less likely to encounter accidents or injuries or be exposed to perpetrators. Beyond physical safety, safe spaces contribute to emotional well-being. When children are in a secure environment, they can play, express themselves, and learn without the fear of getting hurt. This emotional safety promotes healthy psychological development.

Overall, a secure physical environment, whether at home, at school, or in the community, fosters trust and attachment. When children feel safe in their surroundings, they can form healthy attachments to their caregivers, teachers, and peers. Safe spaces are essential for children's physical and emotional well-being, autonomy, learning, and development. They provide a foundation for exploration, creativity, and social interaction, while also helping children develop a sense of boundaries, responsibility, and trust. Safe spaces serve as the nurturing environments in which children can thrive, building a strong foundation for their future.

Safety in emotionally connected and nurturing environments. Emotional well-being and development in children encompass a range of interconnected elements, emphasizing the importance of a nurturing and supportive environment. Providing a secure emotional environment is paramount, as children need to feel that their emotions are not only accepted but also valued. In such an environment, caregivers listen attentively, are emotionally available, validate the child's feelings, and respond with empathy.

Emotional nurturing helps children by encouraging them to express their emotions openly and without fear. When children are confident that their feelings are acknowledged and respected, they become more adept at articulating their emotional experiences. This supports the development of emotional intelligence as children learn to recognize and understand their own feelings, as well as the emotions of others. This is a fundamental skill that sets the stage for healthy relationships and effective communication, as being present and accessible helps children feel secure and loved. Attachments serve as emotional anchors, fostering a sense of trust and safety. These attachment bonds further provide emotional resilience, helping children bounce back from adversity and setbacks.

Safety in guidance and discipline. Children need guidance in managing and expressing their emotions. Teaching them strategies for recognizing and dealing with their feelings is a vital aspect of emotional nurturing. Learning to manage emotions equips children with effective coping mechanisms. Managing emotions does not mean stifling their emotional expression—actually, just the opposite. Children should never be scolded for crying or even for being upset. They interpret the world differently than adults who have the benefit of experience and perspective. The more they are free to feel their emotions and release them through crying, communication, and other ways, the more control they will have over them. For example, using play to work through emotions allows them to express and process what they may find difficult to articulate verbally. Caregivers should be emotionally available to children, offering support and guidance, while modeling emotion regulation skills.

Children, especially those who have experienced trauma, may exhibit behavioral outbursts. In these moments, caregivers and adults must respond with patience, understanding, and compassion. While we are prone as parents, teachers, and ministry leaders to focus on training children to display appropriate external behaviors, it is crucial to understand that tantrums and oppositional acts are often just symptoms of internal distress. Providing empathy and helping the child to work through their intense emotions is much more effective than harsh discipline. Empathetic responses to outbursts aid children in becoming more regulated, which allows them to communicate the root causes of their distress.

Empathetic responses can also include boundaries and consequences for inappropriate behaviors. Boundaries help children understand what is expected of them, creating a structured and secure environment. Knowing the limits of acceptable behavior offers a sense of predictability and safety. Communicating these boundaries with love and consistency is crucial. When caregivers and adults enforce rules and boundaries with empathy and understanding, children feel safe and supported. They learn that boundaries are in place not to restrict them but to protect and guide them.

Safety in predictable routines. Predictable routines play a fundamental role in promoting a child's well-being and development. These routines are a set of regular, structured activities and events that follow a consistent schedule or pattern. Consistency offers children a sense of security and predictability. Knowing what to expect provides comfort, reducing anxiety and stress, as children thrive in environments where they can anticipate what happens next. For example, a bedtime routine with the same steps every night can signal to a child that it is time to wind down and prepare for sleep. Predictable routines also assist children in regulating their emotions. When they know what to expect, they can prepare mentally and emotionally for changes or transitions. Allowing children to return to a familiar routine such as going back to school after natural disaster fosters resiliency from a familiar and stable environment (Osofsky & Osofsky, 2018).

Safety in play and social connection. Safety in play and social connections is essential for children's healthy development. Interactions with peers and positive social relationships contribute to emotional safety. These interactions help them learn social skills, cooperation, empathy, and conflict resolution. Positive interactions with friends contribute to their overall well-being, boosting self-esteem and fostering a sense of belonging. Further, healthy social connections are a cornerstone of building self-esteem in children. When they engage in positive relationships with their peers, children gain a sense of self-worth. They learn to appreciate themselves through the eyes of others and develop a positive self-concept.

Adequate guidance and supervision during play is essential, especially for younger children. It ensures their physical safety during activities and interactions. Supervision also helps prevent accidents and harmful situations, creating a secure environment where children can explore, learn, and grow without fear. Caregivers should pay attention to instances when children are showing strong resistance or anxiety about going to certain places or being around certain older children or adults. While this does not necessarily indicate abuse, it is important to attune to these strong messages from children. Establishing safety in play and social connections is a fundamental part of supporting a child's development.

Overall, in consideration of children's safety needs, taking responsibility as a safeguarder to establish environments that ensure this safety is no simple task.

From creating physically safe and emotionally nurturing spaces to guiding their emotional development and establishing predictable routines, safety is essential for fostering a child's growth and critical in supporting recovery from trauma. These foundational elements empower children to explore, develop, and form secure attachments, perhaps for the first time. By prioritizing safety, safeguarders offer children a strong foundation on which they can build healthy, fulfilling lives, equipped with the resilience and skills needed to navigate future challenges.

PERSONAL REFLECTION

1. Reflect on your own childhood experiences. How do you believe they have shaped your personality, values, and relationships as an adult?

2. Reflect on your relationships with your parents/caregivers growing up. How have these relationships shaped your sense of security, attachment styles, and ability to regulate your emotions?

3. If you are a parent, aunt/uncle, friend, or minister who interacts with children, how can you grow in fostering secure attachment with the children in your life?

GROUP DISCUSSION

1. With attachment theory in mind, in what ways can your local church, school, or community grow in the way it supports healthy child development?

2. How does trauma impact a child's ability to regulate their emotions? How does this impact the way you conceptualize a child's behavior?

3. How can you better equip the parents in your communities to promote secure attachment and healthy child development?

REFERENCES

Beachboard, C. (2022). Creating safe environments for students recovering from trauma. In C. Beachboard, *The school of hope: The journey from trauma and anxiety to achievement, happiness, and resilience.* Corwin Press.

Briere, J., Runtz, M., Eadie, E., Bigras, N., & Godbout, N. (2017). Disengaged parenting: Structural equation modeling with child abuse, insecure attachment, and adult symptomatology. *Child Abuse & Neglect, 67,* 260-70. https://doi.org/10.1016/j.chiabu .2017.02.036

Colonnesi, C., Draijer, E. M., Stams, G. J. J. M., Van derBruggen, C. O., Bogels, S. M., & Noom, M. J. (2011). The relation between insecure attachment and child anxiety: A meta-analytic review. *Journal of Clinical Child and Adolescent Psychology, 40*(4), 630-45.

Cozolino, L. (2014). *The neuroscience of human relationships. Attachment and the developing social brain* (2nd Ed.). Norton & Company.

Dube, S. R. (2018). Continuing conversations about adverse childhood experiences (ACEs) screening: A public health perspective. *Child Abuse & Neglect, 85,* 180-84.

Dube, S. R., Anda, R. F., Felitti, V. J., Chapman, D., Williamson, D. F., & Giles, W. H. (2001). Childhood abuse, household dysfunction and the risk of attempted suicide throughout the life span: Findings from adverse childhood experiences study. *Journal of the American Medical Association, 286,* 3089-96.

Fearon, R. P., Bakermans-Kranenburg, M. J., van Ijzendoorn, M. H., Lapsley, A. M., & Roisman, G. I. (2010). The significance of insecure attachment and disorganization in the development of children's externalizing behavior: A meta-analytic study. *Child Development, 81,* 435-56.

Felitti, V. J., Anda, R. F., Nordenberg, D., Williamson, D. F., Spitz, A. M., Edwards, V., . . . Marks, J. S. (1998). Relationship of childhood abuse and household dysfunction to many of the leading causes of death in adults: The adverse childhood experiences (ACE) study. *American Journal of Preventive Medicine, 14*(4), 245-58.

Hillis, S., Mercy, J., Amobi, A., & Kress, H. (2016). Global prevalence of past-year violence against children: A systematic review and minimum estimates. *Pediatrics, 137*(3), e20154079. https://doi.org/10.1542/peds.2015-4079

Ivarsson, T., Saavedra, F., Granqvist, P., & Broberg, A. G. (2016). Traumatic and adverse attachment childhood experiences are not characteristic of OCD but of depression in adolescents. *Child Psychiatry and Human Development, 47*(2), 270-80.

Lahousen, T., Unterrainer, H. F., & Kapfhammer, H. P. (2019). Psychobiology of attachment and trauma: Some general remarks from a clinical perspective. *Frontiers in Psychiatry, 10,* 914. https://doi.org/10.3389/fpsyt.2019.00914

Lyons-Ruth, K., & Jacobvitz, D. (2008). Attachment disorganization: Genetic factors, parenting contexts, and developmental transformations. In J. Cassidy & P. R. Shaver (Eds.), *Handbook of attachment: Theory, research, and clinical applications* (2nd ed; pp. 667-97). Guilford Press.

Lyons-Ruth, K., Pechtel, P., Yoon, S. A., Anderson, C. M., & Teicher, M. H. (2016). Disorganized attachment in infancy predicts greater amygdala volume in adulthood. *Behavior Brain Research, 308,* 83-93.

Macdonald, H. Z., Beeghly, M., Grant-Knight, W., Augustyn, M., Woods, R. W., Cabral, H., & Frank, D. A. (2008). Longitudinal association between infant disorganized attachment and childhood posttraumatic stress symptoms. *Development and Psychopathology, 20,* 493-508.

Murphy, A., Steele, M., Rishi, S., Dube, J. B., Bonuck, K., Meissner, P., Goldman, H., & Steele, H. (2014). Adverse childhood experiences (ACEs) questionnaire and adult attachment interview (AAI): Implications for parent child relationships. *Child Abuse & Neglect, 38*(2), 224-33.

Noll, J. G. (2021). Child sexual abuse as a unique risk factor for the development of psychopathology: The compounded convergence of mechanisms. *Annual Review of Clinical Psychology, 17*(1), 439-64. https://doi.org/10.1146/annurev-clinpsy-081219 -112621

Osofsky, J. D., & Osofsky, H. J. (2018). Challenges in building child and family resilience after disasters. *Journal of Family Social Work, 21*(2), 115-28. https://doi.org/10.1080/105 22158.2018.1427644

Porges, S. W. (2021). *Polyvagal safety: Attachment, communication, self-regulation.* W. W. Norton.

Porges, S. W. (2022). Polyvagal theory: A science of safety. *Frontiers in Integrative Neuroscience, 10,*1-15. https://doi.org/10.3389/fnint.2022.871227

Quinn, K., Pacella, M. L., Dickson-Gomez, J., & Nydegger, L. A. (2017). Childhood adversity and the continued exposure to trauma and violence among adolescent gang members. *American Journal of Community Psychology, 59*(1-2), 36-49. https://doi .org/10.1002/ajcp.12123

SAMHSA. (2023, March 17). *Understanding child trauma.* SAMHSA. www.samhsa.gov /child-trauma/understanding-child-trauma

Saunders, R., Jacobvitz, D., Zaccagnino, M., Beverung, L. M., & Hazen, N. (2011). Pathways to earned-security: The role of alternative support figures. *Attachment & Human Development, 13*(4), 403-20.

Schore, A. N. (2002). Dysregulation of the right brain: A fundamental mechanism of traumatic attachment and the psychopathogenesis of posttraumatic stress disorder. *Australian and New Zealand Journal of Psychiatry, 36*(1), 9-30.

Siegel, D. J., Schore, A. N., & Cozolino, L. (2021). *Interpersonal neurobiology and clinical practice.* W. W. Norton.

Storebe, J. O., Rasmussen, P. D., & Simonsen, E. (2016). Association between insecure attachment and ADHD: Environmental mediating factors. *Journal of Attention Disorders, 20*(2), 187-96.

van der Kolk, B. A. (2014). *The body keeps the score: Brain, mind, and body in the healing of trauma.* Penguin.

World's Children. (2023). Child trafficking statistics. https://www.worldschildren.org /child-trafficking-statistics/

World Health Organization. (2022, September). *Child maltreatment.* World Health Organization. https://www.who.int/news-room/fact-sheets/detail/child-maltreatment#:~:text =Nonetheless%2C%20international%20studies%20reveal%20that,sexually%20 abused%20as%20a%20child

Zilberstein, K. (2014). Neurocognitive considerations in the treatment of attachment and complex trauma in children. *Clinical Child Psychology and Psychiatry 19*(3) 336-54.

SECTION IV

VULNERABLE POPULATIONS

10

VULNERABILITY OF CHILDREN TO GROOMING STRATEGIES

DR. KATHRYN STAMOULIS

SEXUAL GROOMING IS considered to be a core part of childhood sexual abuse. Grooming refers to deliberate actions taken by a perpetrator to build trust with a child with the intent to be sexually abusive. Through grooming, a perpetrator forms an emotional connection with a minor in order to reduce the minor's inhibitions to make them compliant for sexual activity. This manipulation molds the victim into a cooperating participant and often, when successful, leads the victim to believe they are in a romantic relationship, not a victim of abuse, thus reducing the likelihood of a disclosure. Concurrently, perpetrators often present a helpful and nonthreatening persona to victims' family members to establish a sense of trust and safety in those adults, create opportunities to access the child, and decrease the chances of being caught.

Grooming is a methodical process in which "groomers" (i.e., perpetrators) work to create emotional intimacy, with the intent of being sexually abusive. In 2020, the *Journal of Child Sexual Abuse* published a comprehensive, validated model of in-person sexual grooming called the Sexual Grooming Model (Winters, Jeglic, & Kaylor, 2020). The Sexual Grooming Model contains five stages: victim selection, gaining access and isolating, trust development, desensitization to sexual content and physical contact, and post-abuse maintenance.

VICTIM SELECTION

Perpetrators often identify a potential victim by selecting a child who is vulnerable, either because of psychological reasons or because of unfortunate family circumstances. The aim of a perpetrator is to find a child who will not advocate for themselves when uncomfortable and will not reach out to parents or trusted adults with their concerns.

Children are vulnerable by nature. They rely on adults for survival, but there are risk factors that make them more likely to be targeted by perpetrators. So, what makes a child especially vulnerable?

Lack of parental supervision. Children who are not closely supervised at home are more likely to be exploited than children with attentive parents (Olson et al., 2007). Lack of supervision could be due to a parent who is neglectful or abusing drugs or alcohol. Other times, through no fault of their own, a parent is unable to closely monitor their child. This could be, for example, because they have to work multiple jobs to make ends meet, or they are busy tending to a sick child or parent and are overwhelmed with caretaking. Spending time alone puts the child at risk because a perpetrator has more opportunities to get close. Additionally, when a child is not getting the care they need at home, they often seek attention or even distraction from home troubles elsewhere.

Lack of financial resources. Economic hardship creates stress and threatens adequate family functioning. Children who come from financially strained homes are more likely to be victimized (Conrad-Hiebner & Byram, 2020). Parents are often working many hours or are spending time trying to satisfy basic needs. There can be food insecurity, uncomfortable or dangerous living quarters, and lack of access to things like books, electronics, and entertainment. Perpetrators often zero in on these children because they and/or their parents are easier to manipulate with money, gifts, resources, and acts of service. Often, a child does not want to be a financial burden to their family by asking for toys, ice cream, money, or items that may help them fit in with peers. Perpetrators exploit this.

Low self-esteem. Children with low self-esteem feel they are unworthy of respect and boundaries. There is a psychological need to feel worthy or special, and perpetrators exploit that need. Therefore, children with low self-esteem are more susceptible to those who offer flattery, gifts, and attention. They are more willing to put aside their discomfort and unease in order to have the company of someone who is giving them attention, praise, or validation. Low self-esteem is also related to insecure attachment, amplifying the importance of safe, attuned parenting to reduce a child's risk of being targeted by a perpetrator (Passanisi et al., 2015).

Children with identity issues. Children in the process of understanding their gender identity or questioning their sexual orientation are at greater risk. These children often feel alienated from their community. The fear, uncertainty, or shame they may feel often leads to little emotional support. A perpetrator may pick up on this vulnerability and need for guidance and present themselves as the only person who understands and accepts them. As noted by Super and Jacobson (2011), if children are violated by a perpetrator of the same gender, they may not open up to their parents or others for fear of rejection. Additionally, a perpetrator may threaten to disclose the child's secret if they don't comply.

Children with disabilities. Children with disabilities are significantly more likely to be sexually abused than their typically developing peers (Amborski et al., 2021). There are many reasons for this, including the need of bodily personal care, a desire to fit in with others, communication difficulties, physical limitations that prevent escape, and lack of education or understanding of healthy sexuality and sexual abuse. Many adults hold the myth that a disability shields a child from sexual abuse, and therefore, they do not provide education or look for warning signs of abuse.

These vulnerabilities are not exhaustive and often overlap. Each vulnerability that a young person has puts them at greater risk of abuse (Whittle et al., 2013).

GAINING ACCESS AND ISOLATING

The next step in the grooming process is gaining access and isolating the victim. There are two major ways that adults gain access to children in person. The first is through youth-serving organizations, such as schools, sport teams, extracurriculars, and religious groups. In such organizations, there is an expectation that adults and children associate. The second way perpetrators access children is by gaining the trust of the child's guardians. When a friend, neighbor, or babysitter, for example, has become a part of a family's support system, they often have unfettered access to the children in that home. A perpetrator who has gained the trust of a child's family may assume a father-figure role for the child, offer to help out around the house, or suggest overnight stays (Lanning, 2010).

Once a perpetrator has access to the child, they aim to spend a lot of time together so a relationship forms (Mooney & Ost, 2013). Abuse happens behind closed doors, not out in the open, so perpetrators concoct reasons to spend time alone with a victim. In addition to physical time spent together, a perpetrator will often use technology to further access the child in a covert way. This could mean texting, emailing, private messaging via social media, or communication over video game networks.

At the same time the relationship is forming, perpetrators work to emotionally separate a child from those who could protect them. They will often try to create fissures between parent and child. They will present themselves as the only one who understands the child. They will paint the child's parent in a negative light or exploit the natural distance from parents that occurs in adolescence. They may try to get the child to retreat from their peer group. The more isolated a child is from friends and family, the more power the perpetrator has.

TRUST DEVELOPMENT

Trust development is crucial in the grooming process. A perpetrator does not want a child to view them as dangerous and deviant, so they often present themselves as charming, kind, and likeable (Craven et al., 2006). With compliments, secret sharing, gift giving, and favoritism, the victim often becomes besotted with the perpetrator. All of this attention makes a victim feel as though they are in a caring and special relationship. Quite often, a perpetrator has already ingratiated themselves into the victim's community or family and automatically has an air of trust around them.

Further, there is inherent trust of people in positions of power. This is called the authority bias. The authority bias is the tendency to be highly influenced by the opinion and actions of people in positions of power (teachers, clergy, coaches, celebrities, etc.), even when it is in direct opposition to one's own interests. Psychologist Stanley Milgram famously studied this bias in the 1960s when he sought to investigate the rate at which adult men would obey an authority figure (a man in a white lab coat) who directed them to shock an innocent person at an increasing rate. He predicted only a scant few with "psychopathic" tendencies would continue to shock the person given that the results could ultimately be deadly (if the shock had been real). He was stunned when 65 percent of the men did not cease giving shocks, even though the men noted that they were distressed by the victims' suffering and screams. Milgram concluded that people often obey out of a desire to appear cooperative, even if it conflicts with their better judgment (Milgram, 1963).

For children, a perpetrator does not necessarily have to hold a powerful place in the community because adults already hold more power than a child. Children are taught to listen to adults because adults "know what's best." Some families employ a hierarchal system in which the father (or other parent) is the unquestioned authority whom children must obey, sometimes even cheerfully obey. Children are socialized at a young age to follow the direction of adults, show respect, and not question authority. Children often comply with a perpetrator's request because they have been conditioned to obey their elders. They don't recognize that it is in the realm of possibility to say no. Instead, victims often go along with the abuse because they trust the abusers more than they trust themselves.

DESENSITIZATION TO SEXUAL CONTENT AND PHYSICAL CONTACT

After trust is formed, the perpetrator prepares the child for abuse by desensitizing them to sexual content. It is a strategy of escalation. In an effort to push boundaries, a perpetrator may start small, by sharing a sexual joke or incorporating sex into discussions. This can progress to sharing sexual interests, sending intimate photographs, or exposing the minor to pornography.

In terms of physical contact, perpetrators often start with nonsexual touching, a hand on the shoulder or a pat on the back. If the child doesn't retreat, the touching then escalates into more sexualized touching. The goal is to normalize touching so the victim doesn't run or resist. With the child desensitized to touch, physical sexual abuse occurs (Winters et al., 2020).

While abuse often moves into molestation or rape, it doesn't always. Sometimes a perpetrator will toe the line so they can avoid legal prosecution. Other times, the perpetrator deems progressing too risky. Abuse exists on a continuum, and anything that sexualizes a child is psychologically damaging. Even if nothing physical occurs, the grooming in and of itself is abusive and causes harm to the child emotionally and in their understanding of what to expect from adults or other relationships. In fact, some victims report the prolonged psychological manipulation and breach of trust as harder to recover from than the physical assaults.

POST-ABUSE MAINTENANCE

After abuse occurs, victims are told not to tell anyone what happened. Silence ensures that the abuser will not be caught and therefore has the opportunity to continue the abuse. The manipulation tactics used in this phase vary. A perpetrator may blame the victim, making them feel responsible and ashamed and therefore less likely to disclose to their parents for risk of being viewed as bad or sinful (Raine & Kent, 2019). They may threaten to disclose secrets shared. They may promise love and marriage in the future. They may guilt them by saying their family will break up, they will be fired, arrested, and so on. They reinforce that the victim will face rejection, abandonment, humiliation, or family destruction if the abuse is revealed.

When grooming is "successful," children may appear cooperative, and this can lead them or others to believe they were complicit in their own abuse. Some victims of childhood sexual abuse don't even realize they were groomed until later in adulthood. Even if a child or adolescent seemingly gives permission or acts willingly, this never implies consent. A child is never accountable nor capable of giving consent for any sexual interactions with adults.

RELATIONSHIP OF NEURODEVELOPMENT TO ABUSE

Grooming is a subtle art, a calculated manipulation that occurs over time. We cannot expect children to protect themselves against grooming. The child and adolescent brain is not equipped to understand sexual grooming. Children don't have the cognitive ability to interpret manipulation, or the experience to realize seemingly kind and loving people can have malicious intent. Not only do children usually have limited physical strength compared to adults, but their lack of life experience and their still-developing brain limits their ability to protect themselves. Although even the brain of a young child can identify threats of danger in the environment, "the long period of childhood is needed for children to recognize the signs of danger and to organize self-protective strategies" (Crittenden & Heller, 2017, p. 2). Therefore, children need adults to provide this protective safeguarding role.

CONCLUSION

A study by Winters and Jeglic (2017) found that most adults are unable to identify potentially predatory grooming behaviors of sexual perpetrators prospectively. The authors of the study suggest it may be because adults are unaware of what classifies grooming behavior. Thus, we need to educate parents and community members, and encourage them to remain cognizant that potential perpetrators may be targeting vulnerable children. Additionally, parents should inform their children about potential perpetrators in an age-appropriate manner. With education and awareness, people may be able to spot grooming behaviors and intervene before abuse occurs.

PERSONAL REFLECTION

1. What thoughts, feelings, and physical sensations did you experience as you read the strategies used by perpetrators to target victims?

2. How does the fact that children's brains are not fully developed until adulthood contribute to their vulnerability to grooming?

3. Grooming can also happen with adult victims. What are some ways grooming would look the same and ways it would look different with adults?

GROUP DISCUSSION

1. What are some ways to educate parents and children on the risk of grooming?

2. What aspects of church life or doctrine/theology could make children vulnerable to grooming strategies?

3. How can churches address risk factors such as low socioeconomic status and other child vulnerabilities?

REFERENCES

Amborski, A. M., Bussières, E., Vaillancourt-Morel, M., & Joyal, C. C. (2021). Sexual violence against persons with disabilities: A meta analysis. *Trauma, Violence, & Abuse, 23*(4), 1330-43.

Conrad-Hiebner, A., & Byram, E. (2020). The temporal impact of economic insecurity on child maltreatment: A systematic review. *Trauma, Violence, & Abuse, 21*(1), 157-78.

Craven, S., Brown, S., & Gilchrist, E. (2006). Sexual grooming of children: Review of literature and theoretical considerations. *Journal of Sexual Aggression, 12*(3), 287-99.

Crittenden, P. M., & Heller, M. B. (2017). The roots of chronic posttraumatic stress disorder: Childhood trauma, information processing, and self-protective strategies. *Chronic Stress, 1*, 2470547016682965–2470547016682965. https://doi.org/10.1177/2470547016682965

Lanning, K.V. (2010). *Child molesters: A behavioral analysis for professional investigating the sexual exploitation of children* (5th Ed.). National Center for Missing and Exploited Children.

Milgram, S. (1963). Behavioral study of obedience. *Journal of Abnormal and Social Psychology, 67,* 371-78.

Mooney, J., & Ost, S. (2013). Group localised grooming: What is it and what challenges does it pose for society and law? *Child and Family Law Quarterly, 25*(4), 1-20.

Olson, L. N., Daggs, J. L., Ellevold, B. L., & Rogers, T. K. K. (2007). Entrapping the innocent: Toward a theory of child sexual predators' luring communication. *Communication Theory, 17*(3), 231-51.

Passanisi, A., Gervasi A. M., Madonia, C., Guzzo, G. & Greco, D. (2015). Attachment, self-esteem and shame in emerging adulthood. *Procedia - Social and Behavioral Sciences,* (191), 342-346.

Raine, A., & Kent, S. A. (2019). The grooming of children for sexual abuse in religious settings: Unique characteristics and select case studies. *Aggression and Violent Behavior, 48,* 180-89.

Super, J. T., & Jacobson, L. (2011). Religious abuse: Implications for counseling lesbian, gay, bisexual, and transgender individuals. *Journal of LGBT Issues in Counseling, 5*(3-4), 180-96.

Whittle, H., Hamilton-Giachritsis, C., Beech, A., & Collings, G. (2013). A review of young people's vulnerabilities to online grooming. *Aggression and Violent Behavior, 18*(1), 135-46.

Winters, G. M., & Jeglic, E. L. (2017). Stages of sexual grooming: Recognizing potentially predatory behaviors of child molesters. *Deviant Behavior, 38*(6), 724-33.

Winters, G. M.,. Jeglic, E. L., & Kaylor, L. E. (2020). Validation of the Sexual Grooming Model of child sexual abusers. *Journal of Child Sexual Abuse, 29*(7), 855-75.

11

OLDER ADULTS AND PERSONS WITH DISABILITIES

DR. KATHIE T. ERWIN

I have shown you in every way, by laboring like
this, that you must support the weak.

ACTS 20:35 NKJV

WHEN WE THINK OF who is most vulnerable in our society, we naturally consider children as the population needing protecting; however, older adults and adults with both intellectual and/or physical disabilities are also more susceptible to abuse. Children with disabilities are at an even higher risk for abuse than children without disabilities. In the United States, there are an estimated 5.7 million adults over eighty-five years old (Caplan, 2023) and approximately 7.39 million people who have intellectual or developmental disabilities (Residential Information Systems Project, 2019). These groups are rightly included in many mandatory reporting policies and should be a part of safeguarding training. In this chapter, we will explore the factors which make older adults and persons with disabilities more vulnerable, how to recognize trauma in each of these populations, and how safeguarders can provide protective measures and compassionate care to victims of abuse.

OLDER ADULTS

Vulnerability factors. There is no set age when an aging adult becomes a vulnerable person, since people age differently in their physical and cognitive abilities. Similar to early childhood, aging brings a period of dependency that may be complicated by physical limitations, long-term illness, or dementia. There are also many losses inherent in aging, including the death of a loved one, the ending of a career, and the loss of income-producing financial stability. These losses can lead to loneliness, isolation, depression, and feeling a lack of purpose and connection.

Older adult believers naturally seek refuge in the church for spiritual comfort as well as safety. Typically, they are relegated to a class or social group specifically designated for older adults. They are less likely to be asked to serve in ministry, participate in a church program, or be active with outreach committees. They are often deemed "unsuitable" for what may be interim confusion exacerbated by lack of sleep, chronic physical pain, medication reactions, or polypharmacy (medication excesses or mixing prescription with over-the-counter medications leading to a negative effect). Mobility limitations, medical problems, and financial losses are barriers for older adults who desire to be more active in their church. Memory impairment can also lead to others becoming frustrated with older adults' limited concentration, so they choose not to connect with the person who desperately needs that acceptance. Once an older adult has been characterized as "not with it" due to slower responses or "unable to keep pace" on a project because of mobility limitations, that label sticks like a badge of dishonor, and no further efforts are made to include that person in meaningful service or social opportunities. This marginalization makes them further susceptible to perpetrators and others who wish to take advantage of them.

Recognizing trauma in older adults. Older adults are at high risk of negative consequences from traumatic experiences including mental and physical health issues (Hansen, Ghafoori, & Diaz, 2020). Decades ago, when less was known about psychological trauma, older adults who expressed trauma symptoms such as flashbacks or losing awareness of time were dismissed as "senile." Equally dismissive was the belief that because older adults already lived through so many life challenges, they were somehow less impacted by current traumatic situations. While personal resilience and strong faith are protective factors, facing a new trauma is a shock to the mind, body, and spirit at any age. When that trauma involves a trusted person, the impact is even more devastating.

Recognizing the difference between trauma and other aging issues is critically important yet can be difficult. Most older adults have been indoctrinated from childhood to "never air our dirty laundry in public." That is a familial imperative that has prevented many trauma victims from seeking help, because they must protect the "family secret." Too often, that secret involves sexual, physical, or emotional abuse within the family of origin or committed by persons in the church who were close to and trusted by the family. This "secret" may also extend to other members of the faith community, including clergy (priests, pastors, or other church leaders), teachers, or lay leaders.

For other older and disabled adults, the emotional and physical abuse from caregivers, family, and church leaders may have started at younger ages and continued throughout their lives. From childhood forward to older adult years, persons with cognitive disabilities or physical disabilities can be at higher risk as they are often not believed when expressing discomfort or fear around family members or caregivers. Particularly for those with limited verbal abilities, their efforts to show distress can be misinterpreted as temperamental or refusal to cooperate.

Another type of abuse that is only recognized in some jurisdictions as part of the elder abuse statute is emotional abuse, which includes financial coercion. In a recent study by Hansen and colleagues (2020), results indicated that older adults' resiliency to trauma and openness to treatment were correlated with their quality of life in areas such as perceived access to health care, financial security, and environmental safety. Older adults who are dependent on family or institutional caregivers are easy prey for those who want to cheat or steal for financial gain. Older adults with physical disabilities can also become even more isolated from their church community due to transportation challenges and lack of a support person to assist them.

Protecting and caring for older adults: Mandatory reporting. Mandatory reporter laws that protect children often extend to other vulnerable populations like disabled and older adults. Any older person with physical limitations, mental health issues, cognitive impairment, or disconnection from family and community needs protection within the church. This is a key issue for every church, church-affiliated school, and ministry to address and annually review.

In the United States, each state has reporting requirements for elder abuse, although some state statutes do not clearly define neglect or include financial exploitation. In other countries, the protections against elder abuse may also differ in defining elder abuse and specifying which actions are prohibited and which may potentially be prosecuted under that law.

Another issue that can vary by locality is in defining who is the person "in a position of trust." *Position of trust* is used as a legal term in areas of employment, healthcare, and other roles in which there is an expectation of functioning with integrity and high ethical standards to ensure the safety and well-being of the individuals being served. This commonly used phrase addresses settings where adults routinely work with children and also may refer to caregivers, trustees, or other managers who may or may not be relatives of the older adult. Ministries need to carefully define and screen those persons who are given "positions of trust" within their ministry and thoroughly educate them on mandatory reporting regulations in their area.

The role of mandatory reporter must be clearly explained to all pastors, leaders, and ministry volunteers and reviewed annually and applied consistently. At a minimum, there needs to be an annual training of staff and volunteers on the mandatory reporting policy from a legal and church-based perspective. Many ministries do this training well as applied to children and minors in their church programs or faith-based schools, but they forget the other vulnerable populations of older adults and children and adults with cognitive and/or physical challenges and potential areas of harm, including financial, physical, sexual, and psychological. Ministry training also needs to address ageism as a prejudice toward older adults and potential risk factor for abuse. Dr. Robert Butler (1975), who was the first to coin the term *ageism*, defined ageism as an attitude that "allows younger adults to cease to identify with their elders as human beings" (p. 12). When older adults are hesitant to discuss their living environment or care needs, it may be an unspoken cry for safeguarding support.

CASE STUDY

Emma is a seventy-nine-year-old woman who started attending church ten years ago. Since retiring five years ago, she has been a regular volunteer with the cafeteria staff at the church K-8 school.

In the past year, she has been withdrawn and talks less with the other volunteers. She wants to taste all the food and pick up cookies without gloves. She was moved away from the food lines and into the kitchen clean-up area. Susan, the volunteer coordinator, was asked to talk with her about behavioral changes. Emma seemed confused by the questions as she is having more difficulty tracking conversations. Susan decided to visit Emma's home on Saturday. She found Emma crying over a large jigsaw puzzle as her husband, Arthur, shouted for her to "finish faster." Susan asked why Arthur was angry. He explained that he is helping Emma restore her memory by making her finish a puzzle every day before she is allowed to have lunch. Susan tried to explain to Arthur that Emma is showing signs of memory impairment and needs both medical and mental status evaluation. She went on to say withholding food is an abusive behavior. Arthur screamed in a threatening way and told Susan to leave.

Susan knew this was an urgent safeguarding situation. She returned to the pastoral office to tell what she saw. They agreed that Susan should make a report to local law enforcement of possible elder abuse and neglect. The pastor also added Emma's name to the visitation ministry list to check in with her weekly and arrange transportation for her to continue volunteering at the church.

PERSONS WITH DISABILITIES

Vulnerability factors. According to the Americans with Disabilities Act (ADA, 1990), a disability involves a physical or mental impairment that leads to significant impairment in major life activities. Physical disabilities include challenges to the structure and/or operation of the body. Mental disabilities include neurodevelopmental impairments, such as intellectual disabilities (ID), autism, and motor and communication disabilities. Persons with physical and mental disabilities are at higher risk of being victimized due to their dependency on others for care (Brendli et al., 2022; Carrellas et al., 2021; Daigneault et al., 2023). For example, persons with multiple sclerosis (MS) are at higher risk than the general population for physical and sexual abuse (Shapiro et al., 2013). Utilizing data from the US Census Bureau 2018 National Survey of Children's Health, Brendli et al. (2022) found that children with intellectual disabilities were 2.84 times as likely to experience victimization as children without disabilities. Another study examining the experiences of children with ID in the child welfare system found that they were more likely to be victims of sex trafficking than children without disabilities in that welfare system (Carrellas et al., 2021).

Codina and Pereda (2022) conducted research examining the lifetime prevalence of sexual abuse in people with intellectual disabilities. They found that a person's risk for victimization increased as they had other high-risk intersecting identities, including being a woman, being named legally incapable, and having a mental health diagnosis. Participants were most often victimized in their homes by male perpetrators known to them. The study found that people with ID have an increased likelihood of experiencing the long-term negative effects of trauma and are less likely to receive mental health treatment, and only 7 percent of the reports of victimization in this study had been reported to law enforcement. According to these authors and other researchers (Meer & Combrinck, 2015; Milligan & Neufeldt, 2001; Nario-Redmond et al., 2019), the way persons with ID have been dehumanized, objectified, and falsely assumed to be asexual has increased the risk that "potential perpetrators may consider consent to be dispensable in sexual interactions" (Codina & Pereda, 2022, p. 2).

Factors increasing the risk of victimization in persons with disabilities and potentially impacting their recovery include impairments in verbal and social skills, interpretation of events, and limited capacity to recognize grooming and other early abuse signs. The societal marginalization and devaluation of persons with disabilities may decrease their self-esteem and recognition of abuse. One study of predominantly minority women with disabilities found that risk increases with lower mobility, higher social isolation, and higher depression levels (Nosek et al., 2006). According to other research studies, additional variables that increased risk of victimization include the perception of people with disabilities as asexual and as easily overpowered mentally and/or physically as well as the presence of emotional or economic dependency and learned helplessness (Shapiro et al., 2013).

Victims who have disabilities may be less likely to report the abuse and more likely to stay in abusive relationships. Their hesitations to report the abuse often involve fears of retaliation or abandonment from their caregivers and support systems (Shapiro et al., 2013). This can include fear of rejection from church communities as well. Lower self-esteem, fear of being alone, or difficulty finding a romantic partner may all contribute to victims hiding the abuse and staying in abusive relationships. According to the Abuse Pathways Model (Hassouneh-Phillips, 2005), persons with disabilities often experience a "trade-off" between staying or leaving an abusive relationship. Based on this model, people are more likely to remain in an abusive relationship based on (1) their cumulative trauma history and psychosocial vulnerabilities (attachment deficits, previous childhood abuse, substance abuse, etc.) and (2) their specific desirability-related factors (Hassouneh-Phillips, 2005). The author of this model stated, "vulnerability factors tended to shift the balance of power in relationships in favor of actual or potential abusers" (p. 77).

Perpetrators exploit potential weaknesses and may target people with disabilities due to perceived impairments in physical strength, cognitive ability, health issues, and dependency on others. Perpetrators may view persons with disabilities as less likely to resist the abuse, more likely to be coerced into compromising situations, and less likely to report the abuse (Martin et al., 2006). Abuse may also have a more detrimental impact on persons who already experience compromised immune systems and mental health issues.

Recognizing trauma in persons with disabilities. Persons with ID range on a spectrum of neurological functioning, and their symptom risk may vary based on the severity of their disability and subsequent need for care, age, and the strength of their support system, among other variables. They have a similar risk for posttraumatic stress symptoms of intrusive thoughts, hyperarousal, and avoidance as their counterparts without ID but may experience higher rates of conduct disorders, self-harm, inappropriate sexualized speech, and fears about personal safety (Smit et al., 2019). They may also suffer with depression, anxiety, and hopelessness as a result of the abuse.

Protecting and caring for persons with disabilities. People with intellectual disabilities have a higher prevalence of long-term health difficulties, are more likely to die of preventable causes, and have a life expectancy of twenty-five years lower than the general population (Ali et al., 2013). A qualitative study examining patients with intellectual disabilities and their caregivers' experiences of the health system found that though they had increased medical needs due to comorbid health conditions, they experienced significant barriers to accessing appropriate healthcare (Ali et al., 2013). Participants reported feeling ignored by the healthcare provider if their caregiver was present and expressed difficulty understanding medical information they received from their provider. This resulted in a lack of meaningful informed consent, as the patients often did not understand the side effects of their medication or risk factors for surgical procedures and reported feeling pressured into consenting by their provider. This has significant implications for providing effective care, as it highlights the need for safeguarders to attune to the client, exhibit warmth, and communicate effectively to ensure mutual understanding. While this is important in all safeguarding relationships, the need to intentionally create a collaborative relationship is magnified when there is such a significant power differential and risk for coercion. Dekker et al. (2022) studied public stigma and discriminatory attitudes toward people with intellectual disabilities following the COVID-19 pandemic and found that participants with less frequent face-to-face interaction with people with intellectual disabilities were more prone to discriminate. This suggests the benefit of increased exposure to people with intellectual disabilities to promote equitable and appropriate care.

Research shows that exposure to childhood trauma increases a person's risk of addiction, depression, anxiety, cancer, autoimmune disease, and a number of other health problems (Felitti et al., 1998), thus compounding the challenges that persons with ID already face. Considering people with intellectual disabilities' increased risk of traumatic experiences and reduced access to professional counseling services, it is important that safeguarders develop competencies to serve this population and advocate for policy that enhances their protection against abuse.

CONCLUSION

Older adults and persons with disabilities are vulnerable to emotional, financial, and sexual abuse from family members as well as caregivers, coaches, teachers, neighbors, or clergy. Some persons use their positions of power, authority, and even reverence to control and abuse those who are least able to defend themselves. Older adults and persons with disabilities are often not believed when they do report, a similar obstacle to child reporting. Safeguarders should attend to nonverbal expressions of fear, hypervigilance, clinging, shaking, or cowering as potential signs for concern and response.

PERSONAL REFLECTION

1. Reflect on your own thoughts and feelings toward aging. What is your experience with aging? What are your fears around aging? What are you looking forward to about aging?

2. What thoughts, feelings, and physical sensations do you experience when interacting with older adults? People with intellectual or physical disabilities? How might these impact how you engage with this population?

3. What would you do if you noticed potential signs of abuse in a person in the church with a cognitive disability?

GROUP DISCUSSION

1. What does it look like to honor older adults and people with disabilities as valuable members of the body of Christ?
2. In what ways can you help protect them from harm?
3. In what way can you provide avenues for them to steward their gifts and strengths?

REFERENCES

Ali, A., Scior, K., Ratti, V., Strydom, A., King, M., & Hassiotis, A. (2013). Discrimination and other barriers to accessing health care: Perspectives of patients with mild and moderate intellectual disability and their carers. *PLoS ONE, 8*(8), e70855. https://doi .org/10.1371/journal.pone.0070855

Americans with Disabilities Acts. (1990). https://www.ada.gov/

Brendli, K. R., Broda, M. D., & Brown, R. (2022). Children with intellectual disability and victimization: A logistic regression analysis. *Child Maltreatment, 27*(3), 320-24. https:// doi.org/10.1177/1077559521994177

Butler, R. N. (1975). *Why survive? Growing old in America.* Harper & Row.

Caplan, Z. (2023, May 25). *U.S. older population grew from 2010 to 2020 at fastest rate since 1880 to 1890.* United States Census Bureau. www.census.gov/library/stories /2023/05/2020-census-united-states-older-population-grew.html

Carrellas, A., Resko, S. M., & Day, A. G. (2021). Sexual victimization and intellectual disabilities among child welfare involved youth. *Child Abuse & Neglect, 115*, 104986. https://doi.org/10.1016/j.chiabu.2021.104986

Codina, M., & Pereda, N. (2022). Characteristics and prevalence of lifetime sexual victimization among a sample of men and women with intellectual disabilities. *Journal of Interpersonal Violence, 37*(15–16), NP14117-NP14139. https://doi.org/10.1177 /08862605211006373

Daigneault, I., Paquette, G., De La Sablonnière-Griffin, M., & Dion, J. (2023). Childhood sexual abuse, intellectual disability, and subsequent physical and mental health disorders: A matched cohort study. *American Journal on Intellectual and Developmental Disabilities, 128*(2), 134-44. https://doi.org/10.1352/1944-7558-128.2.134

Dekker, M. R., Hendriks, A. H. C., Frielink, N., & Embregts, P. J. C. M. (2022). Public stigmatization of people with intellectual disability during the COVID-19 pandemic. *American Journal on Intellectual and Developmental Disabilities, 127*(6), 485-94. https:// doi.org/10.1352/1944-7558-127.6.485

Faccini, L., & Saide, M. A. (2011). Psychologists' experience with interviewing and analyzing abuse allegations of adults with intellectual disabilities. *Sexuality and Disability, 29*(3), 291-96. https://doi.org/10.1007/s11195-011-9206-8

Felitti, V. J., Anda, R. F., Nordenberg, D., Williamson, D. F., Spitz, A. M., Edwards, V., Koss, M. P., & Marks, J. S. (1998). Relationship of childhood abuse and household dysfunction to many of the leading causes of death in adults. *American Journal of Preventive Medicine, 14*(4), 245-58. https://doi.org/10.1016/S0749-3797(98)00017-8

Hansen, M. C., Ghafoori, B., & Diaz, M. (2020). Examining attitudes towards mental health treatment and experiences with trauma: Understanding the needs of trauma-exposed middle-aged and older adults. *Journal of Community Psychology, 48*(5), 1452-68. https://doi.org/10.1002/jcop.22339

Hassouneh-Phillips, D. (2005). Understanding abuse of women with physical disabilities: An overview of the abuse pathways model. *Advances in Nursing Science, 28*(1), 70-80. https://doi.org/10.1097/00012272-200501000-00008

Martin, S. L., Ray, N., Sotres-Alvarez, D., Kupper, L. L., Moracco, K. E., Dickens, P. A., Scandlin, D., & Gizlice, Z. (2006). Physical and sexual assault of women with disabilities. *Violence Against Women, 12*(9), 823-37. https://doi.org/10.1177/1077801206292672

Meer T., & Combrinck H. (2015). Invisible intersections: Understanding the complex stigmatization of women with intellectual disabilities in their vulnerability to gender-based violence. *Gender & Disability, 29*(2), 14-23. https://doi.org/10.1080/10130950.2015.1039307

Milligan M. S., & Neufeldt A. H. (2001). The myth of asexuality: A survey of social and empirical evidence. *Sexuality and Disability, 19*(2), 91-109. https://doi.org/10.1023/A:1010621705591

Nario-Redmond, M. R., Kemerling, A. A., & Silverman, A. (2019). Hostile, benevolent, and ambivalent ableism: Contemporary manifestations. *Journal of Social Issues, 75*(3), 726-56. https://doi.org/10.1111/josi.2019.75.issue-3/issuetoc

Nosek, M. A., Hughes, R. B., Taylor, H. B., & Taylor, P. (2006). Disability, psychosocial, and demographic characteristics of abused women with physical disabilities. *Violence Against Women, 12*(9), 838-50. https://doi.org/10.1177/1077801206292671

Plummer, S.-B., & Findley, P. A. (2012). Women with disabilities' experience with physical and sexual abuse: A review of the literature and implications for the field. *Trauma, Violence & Abuse, 13*(1), 15-29. https://doi.org/10.1177/1524838011426014

Residential Information Systems Project. (2019). Research and Training Center on Community Living, Institute on Community Integration. University of Minnesota. http://risp.umn.edu

Shapiro, J., Wiglesworth, A., & Morrison, E. H. (2013). Views on disclosing mistreatment: A focus group study of differences between people with MS and their caregivers. *Multiple Sclerosis and Related Disorders, 2*(2), 96-102. https://doi.org/10.1016/j.msard.2012.09.006

Smit, M. J., Scheffers, M., Emck, C., van Busschbach, J. T., & Beek, P. J. (2019). Clinical characteristics of individuals with intellectual disability who have experienced sexual abuse. An overview of the literature. *Research in Developmental Disabilities, 95*, 103513-103513. https://doi.org/10.1016/j.ridd.2019.103513

SECTION V

SKILL DEVELOPMENT

12

EMPATHETIC ALLIANCE

CYNTHIA MALCOLM FISHER AND
TAYLOR PATTERSON

"THE MOST FUNDAMENTAL CHARACTERISTICS of the conditio humana are attachment and the ability to form stable bonds with significant others" (Lahousen et al., 2019, p. 13). We were divinely designed by God for connection to him and to other people. Our relationships shape the structure of our brains and inform the functioning of our minds throughout our lifetime (Schore, 2021). In fact, connection to others, especially safe attachments in early childhood, is just as essential as nourishment for our survival. Research in the early twentieth century demonstrated this importance. These experiments include Spitz's study (1946) of human, orphan infants and Harlow's rhesus monkeys (1958) who were all provided adequate nourishment but lacked emotional care and social contact. In both studies, the mortality rate significantly increased without significant human connection (Lahousen et al., 2019).

Healthy, supportive relationships are the number one factor for healing from abuse and increasing resilience. Abuse occurs through a destructive human interaction. On the other hand, healing comes through empathetic engagement. Allen (2018) describes the core of trauma as "feeling alone in the midst of unbearably painful emotion" (p. 163). This feeling of isolation provides evidence of the crucial role the church needs to play with trauma survivors. Jesus shares the story of the good Samaritan as an example of how we attend to those who are alone and traumatized. When a man was robbed, beaten, and left on the side of the road, Jesus affirmed the proactive and intentional actions of the Samaritan who helped rescue him as opposed to the others who passed him by without caring for him in his distress.

How we respond to victims, whether it is in a ministry setting or over coffee, not only impacts that individual but also has a ripple effect in the culture of the church. Therefore, building our own character traits that facilitate connection is a foundational aspect of spiritual formation. These traits that foster a safe and healing relationship include empathy, humility, patience, and trustworthiness. Before we explore these traits and their corresponding skills, it is essential to understand how shame can hinder our empathetic engagement.

TRAUMA AND SHAME

A threat to our suitability for connection is experienced as a threat to our existence. Sexual abuse victims are vulnerable to feelings of low self-worth due to stigmatization from perpetrator grooming, the taboo of sexual assault, and family members' and church members' attitudes toward sexual abuse (Finkelhor & Browne, 1985). This stigmatization results in shame, an emotional experience causing fears of social rejection (Aakvaag et al., 2019). Survivors experience additional wounding and increased shame when their fellow church members or trusted leaders disbelieve their reports of abuse, suggest there was something they could have done to prevent the abuse, or misapply Scripture to persuade them to stay in unsafe situations. Careless words, judgment, or poor counsel can set back a person's recovery and often increase their feelings of worthlessness and shame, leading to increased anxiety, depression, posttraumatic stress, risk of future victimization, and, for some, thoughts of suicide (Aakvaag et al., 2019; Alix et al., 2017). Due to the trauma already endured, shame is an accompanying burden that often can be a roadblock to sharing trauma stories with others.

There is a definitive distinction between shame and guilt. Guilt is the emotional response to regrettable actions or behaviors that were perceived as wrong or inconsistent with values and can lead to a necessary repair of the offense (Kealy et al., 2017). Shame is a self-devaluing emotional response integrated into one's identity and self-worth due to perceptions of the self as bad, sinful, unlovable, dirty, or other deplorable traits (Brown, 2015). Shame is intrinsically painful and emotionally dysregulating. It can result in an expectation of rejection or abandonment, difficulty perceiving safety, and an increased risk of isolation from others and possibly hiding from God. Shame is also weaponized by perpetrators, making their victims more susceptible to becoming secret keepers and less likely to report the abuse. Clearly, shame is an important target for safeguarding. Thankfully, shame can be mitigated through an empathetic connection and unconditional support for abuse victims (Alix et al., 2017).

CHARACTER TRAITS FOR HEALING RELATIONSHIPS

Empathy. Empathy, or the ability to lean in to the suffering of others in an effort to ease their pain, is necessary for effective engagement with trauma survivors and is a skill that can be developed (Sacdalan, 2021). Empathy includes an affective dimension (feeling the emotions of others) and a cognitive dimension (understanding the perspective of others), both of which are necessary for understanding how someone is suffering and responding in an appropriate manner (Thompson et al., 2022). Empathy requires our constant presence amidst suffering and understanding of the other's emotions and lived experiences of events. A wonderful example of this is Jesus weeping with Lazarus's sister before raising Lazarus from the dead (John 11:35). He was not apathetic to her suffering, but in his humanness, Jesus wept over the loss of Lazarus. Jesus modeled incredible compassion and empathy in his grief. Empathy means demonstrating care for someone's experience while also providing comfort and connection through skills of attunement and co-regulation.

Skill: Attunement. Attunement is a form of empathy that includes resonating with the emotions of others and being in sync with those emotions to the degree that the helper is able to match and reflect back that emotional state both verbally and nonverbally. For example, when a ten-year-old child comes home from school crying because he was bullied on the school bus, an attuned parent would not laugh in response to his distress. Instead, they would show sadness and concern on their face and sit next to the child to show their responsiveness. When safeguarders are attuned to survivors' emotional experiences, they communicate openness and warmth. Attunement is interactive. It requires an active presence to perceive cues of the survivor's socioemotional experience and participate in a nonjudgmental way in the person's internal world (Elias-Juarez & Knudson-Martin, 2017; Schomaker & Ricard, 2015). Attunement includes bearing witness to someone's trauma story and using social cues to communicate acceptance and care. The next chapter will include specific steps on how to stay attuned and track with a survivor's emotional state.

Skill: Co-regulation. Co-regulation refers to the ability to help someone else regulate their emotions through our own self-regulation. In any given interaction, both participants influence each other's emotions moment to moment (Hilpert et al., 2020). Co-regulation provides an opportunity to tolerate intense feelings together. It communicates to the trauma survivor that you can handle their strong affect without being overwhelmed by it (and, therefore, they can too), and that you will not abandon them in their state of suffering. Survivors with complex trauma often find it challenging to self-regulate their heightened emotions. A safeguarder who is skilled in co-regulation can identify when a survivor is feeling more anxious and help them get to a more relaxed state. When someone shows signs of emotional dysregulation, such as talking quickly, fidgeting, or taking shallow breaths, these practical steps can assist in helping them become calm and regulated.

- *Mirror.* Reflect back to them their emotional state through your own facial expressions and body language. This will demonstrate that you see their suffering and validate their current emotional experience.

- *Model.* Slow the pace of your speech and take long, deep breaths to demonstrate your own emotional regulation, which they can then use as their own to reduce their arousal.

- *Check in.* If a survivor is still in distress, ask them to share with you how they are feeling in that moment. Acknowledge their anxiety and ask them to pause and take deep breaths with you. You can also ask them if they need to move or take a walk. These essential regulation skills are developed further in a later chapter.

Skill: Adopt a strengths-based perspective. When considering the pain that abuse causes, it can be tempting to focus on the brokenness of trauma victims. Recognizing and acknowledging their incredible resilience provides survivors hope that they can overcome any challenges that may come during the healing process. Validate that they have *survived* terrible abuses and that whatever coping mechanisms they used served a purpose when danger was present. A strengths-based approach not only recognizes and acknowledges their resiliency but also uses it to help survivors see themselves through the lens of strength and courage to build their confidence, reduce shame, and empower them to pursue future goals.

Humility. Humility is the ability to perceive oneself accurately, considering both abilities and limitations as well as prioritizing the well-being of others (Van Tongeren et al., 2019). Humility aids safeguarders in providing more collaborative care, acknowledging that the survivor is the expert of their own experiences. There are many Scriptures on the benefits of walking in humility, including wisdom (Proverbs 11:2), God's favor (James 4:6), and victory (Psalm 149:4). Humility also helps us to exercise patience and build trust with survivors. A posture of curiosity and practice of cultural humility are essential skills to promote a safe environment through humility.

Skill: Posture of curiosity. A safeguarder who adopts a posture of curiosity is focused on understanding the survivors' perspectives and seeing the world through their eyes. Curiosity demonstrates a genuine interest in the survivor's story and reinforces that you are there to listen and not to judge. Being mindful of your own beliefs, thoughts, and feelings aids in taking a curious and nonjudgmental posture and avoiding rigidity in your approach. I realized the importance of this as a team of supervisors and I were working with counselors in Ukraine amidst the Russian attacks. Practicing curiosity helped us connect with the counselors as they recalled the horrific events taking place around them and to not assume what they needed. As they were dealing with ongoing sirens and bombing, I presumed that we should cancel supervision. When I asked them if this would work for them, they disagreed and told me how it helped them to connect with people outside of the war zone. They looked forward to our meetings, and the scheduled supervision felt like how "normal" life used to be for them. Through curiosity, we were better able to meet their needs.

Skill: Practicing cultural humility. Cultural competence is the ability to interact with and understand the racial, ethnic, religious, and social backgrounds of diverse people groups, including their beliefs, customs, traditions, and values (Zhu et al., 2021). Cultural humility incorporates cultural competency and adds elements of lifelong self-exploration, teachability, and evaluation of one's own beliefs and biases against others (Zhu et al., 2021). The self-critiquing posture of cultural humility necessitates not only learning about others' cultural identities but also reflecting on our own conscious and unconscious biases.

Continued awareness of one's own biases about religious expectations, culture, traditions, gender, and identity is part of practicing cultural humility and promoting emotional safety (Yeager & Bauer-Wu, 2013, Zhu et al., 2021). Scripture is clear on treating others without blame or prejudice. James 2:1 instructs the reader to "show no partiality," honoring all members of the church as worthy of dignity and respect.[1] Similarly, Galatians 3:28 states that we are all one in Christ, eliminating status distinctions between rich and poor, male and female, and ethnic groups. Those in positions of authority within the church are commanded to "care for the church of God, which he obtained with his own blood" (Acts 20:28). Cultural humility also increases our self-awareness of how our own family, culture, background, and experiences influence how we relate with the people we are helping. For example, you may have been raised by parents who treated wealthy people in positions of power with great respect and admiration. This may have impacted the way you view people from various socioeconomic levels of society.

Skill: Empowerment. Humility requires correct management of power in relationships. In an earlier chapter, we learned about the abuse of power and resulting harm. Power differentials exist between the safeguarder and those who are seeking help. The helper, who may be a counselor, clergy, or church leader, has more "authority" and leadership within the venue they serve. It is essential not to lose sight of the survivor's vulnerability as they seek help from safeguarders. Safeguarders must steward their role humbly and with faithfulness, taking extra measures to help survivors feel safe. The opposite of abuse of power is empowering others. Empowerment includes communicating that you believe in their ability to take brave steps and make decisions. It also means collaborating with the survivors in making choices in their relationship with you—how often to meet and where to start in conversations. Some survivors may even prefer a different safeguarder than you based on gender or other characteristics of their perpetrator. It is important not to take these requests personally and to take whatever actions are needed to help the survivor feel safe and comfortable.

Skill: Avoiding defensiveness. Another skill related to humility is the ability to hear feedback without getting defensive. As a survivor starts growing in regaining boundaries and dignity, they learn skills that allow them to have more of a voice when they feel emotionally safe. If a survivor provides you feedback on what they need differently during your sessions, it is vital to

---

[1]Scripture quotations in this chapter, unless otherwise noted, are from the ESV.

maintain a posture of nondefensiveness. Being able to hear them and acknowledge their perspective reinforces their ability to use their voice and self-
advocate in other situations.

Patience. Healing from trauma takes time. There is no "quick fix" to the
wounds caused by abuse, and pushing a survivor to quickly heal re-creates a
relationship where they are being controlled by someone else's agenda. Helpers
can sometimes feel discouraged and angry over the lack of progress in a person's healing or emotional resiliency and worry that it reflects on their inef-
fectiveness as a helper. Often, support can wane when a safeguarder feels the
survivor is not making changes and taking steps fast enough. For people who
have not experienced abuse, there may be frustration as to why a survivor
makes certain choices or refuses to take action against a perpetrator of abuse.
The safeguarder may carelessly or naively view the survivor as weak or frail.
However, safeguarders who are intentional about practicing patience can empower survivors to do trauma recovery work at their own pace.

Skill: Recognizing that trauma recovery is not a linear process. When a safeguarder is working with a survivor, their recovery trajectory can often be five
steps forward and three steps back. The trajectory is still moving forward, but
there can be many bumps and setbacks along the way. Some adult survivors of
domestic violence may return to their perpetrator, or others may relapse into
addiction, causing feelings of hopelessness for both the safeguarder and the
survivor. Safeguarders who are patient with this process will continue to provide
support through all the hills and valleys of the healing process. Knowing that
this is often a part of recovery can help us resist our natural inclination to give
up and walk away. A crucial aspect of providing a safe environment is our
steady, unwavering support and meeting the survivor where they are at each
day. As safeguarders, you are not responsible for a survivor's change and recovery; you are accountable to God to do your part along their journey.

Skill: Celebrate small evidences of change and healing. If we recognize that
change is nonlinear, we are able to see the significance of "small changes" in
their lives. Celebrating those with the survivor can keep them engaged in their
recovery and give them hope for their future growth. An example of a small
win may be a survivor who was only able to sleep a few hours at a time now
able to sleep six consecutive hours because they are feeling safer and less alone.
Other small steps include being able to get out of bed to arrive at an appointment on time or joining a support group. Acknowledging and celebrating

these victories builds resilience in the survivor and also in you as a safeguarder, which can protect against burnout and compassion fatigue (discussed later in this text).

Trustworthiness. Abuse is a breach of trust and a violation of connection. In order for safeguarding to be a reparative relationship, the safeguarder must be a trustworthy helper. Trust is earned gradually over time and with consistency. Trusting someone may elicit further feelings of vulnerability in the abuse survivor and require them to lower defenses of protection they put in place such as social isolation and suppression of the trauma memories. Some of the safeguarding skills necessary to build trust are nonjudgmental engagement, confidentiality, and sensitivity to physical touch. An essential part of exercising trustworthiness is being consistent with who you are and how you treat all people in every area of your life. With church leaders who have abused their power, they wear many different masks, and it is hard for survivors to know which is the true persona. Survivors need a safeguarder who is genuine in all situations. To walk in these virtues and implement these skills, it is imperative that you come from a place of sincerity and allow the Holy Spirit to refine you as a leader and a caregiver.

Skill: Nonjudgmental engagement. Engaging with survivors with a nonjudgmental posture promotes safety and protects against further shaming. Pointing out their mistakes or poor choices related to their recovery in the midst of their pain only furthers their suffering. It also engages their brain's threat response system, viewing you as a potential emotional threat, and reinforces their walls as opposed to helping lower them. Survivors do not need to hear platitudes or dismissals of their fear or anger at God but, instead, have a place where they can fully share their thoughts and feelings without condemnation. By maintaining empathy and withholding judgment, you will communicate you can tolerate even their most agonizing moments without threat of rejection or abandonment.

Skill: Maintaining confidentiality. Trust with survivors is built over time through our discretion and maintaining confidentiality. The way we hold their private stories matters. The book of Proverbs has many stern warnings on this topic: "Do not reveal another's secret, lest he who hears you bring shame upon you, and your ill repute have no end" (Proverbs 25:9-10). These are not our stories to tell unless it is in the context of mandatory reporting and stopping the abuse. The Bible takes a high view against slander and gossip. "Whoever derides their neighbor has no sense, but the one who has understanding holds their tongue. A gossip betrays a confidence, but a trustworthy person keeps a secret" (Proverbs 11:12-13 NIV). Cases of abuse that become public within the church or are broadcasted in the media can be especially difficult for survivors to navigate. As safeguarders, we do our part to preserve their privacy and support them as they come under the microscope of scrutiny. Kindness in your general speech about abuse and abuse victims is another way to build trust and identify yourself as a safe person in the community. We will cover the topic of confidentiality in more detail in a later chapter.

Skill: Sensitivity to physical touch. A final skill related to trustworthiness is awareness and sensitivity of our physical contact with others. Trauma survivors can sometimes experience an intense fight, flight, or freeze response upon physical touch, especially when in an enclosed space or by someone in a position of authority. Remembering how the survivor's body was violated by abuse can help safeguarders be mindful of giving space and asking permission before physical contact such as a pat on the shoulders or even sitting close to a survivor. Always ask permission before giving a hug or arm around the shoulder and opt for less physical contact in most cases. Reassuring words and facial expressions can substitute for touch and can empower the survivor to feel in control of their physical space, allowing them to stay emotionally regulated. Being sensitive and mindful of the use of touch builds trust as it increases their sense of security, autonomy, and belief that you are a safe person who will not take advantage of them.

CONCLUSION

Empathetic engagement is a powerful healing agent. The virtues and corresponding skill development in this chapter provide a strong foundation for character formation for every person called to a ministry or other helping position. In the following chapters we will learn additional skills such as effective listening, emotion regulation, and boundary setting, which all contribute to building safe and therapeutic relationships with trauma survivors and others who need our care.

PERSONAL REFLECTION

1. When you think of the virtues or qualities of a healthy safeguarder (calm and regulated, humble, compassionate, patient, and trustworthy), which

virtue takes more intentionality for you? Identify ways you can grow in this virtue.

2. What are some ways that you can co-regulate with trauma survivors?

3. How did your family view people religiously, racially, or ethnically different from you? How has this shaped your biases? How can you grow in cultural humility?

GROUP DISCUSSION

1. What are ways safeguarders can adjust the physical meeting spaces with trauma survivors to promote safety and engagement?

2. How can the church better differentiate between the use of guilt and shame?

3. Empathy involves empowerment. What are some ways the church can empower more vulnerable members

REFERENCES

Aakvaag, H. F., Thoresen, S., Strøm, I. F., Myhre, M., & Hjemdal, O. K. (2019). Shame predicts revictimization in victims of childhood violence: A prospective study of a general Norwegian population sample. *Psychological Trauma*, *11*(1), 43-50. https://doi.org/10.1037/tra0000373

Alix, S., Cossette, L., Hébert, M., Cyr, M., & Frappier, J.-Y. (2017). Posttraumatic stress disorder and suicidal ideation among sexually abused adolescent girls: The mediating role of shame. *Journal of Child Sexual Abuse*, *26*(2), 158-74. https://doi.org/10.1080/10538712.2017.1280577

Allen, J. G. (2018). *Mentalizing in the development and treatment of attachment trauma* (1st Ed.). Routledge.

Brown, B. (2015). *Daring greatly*. Penguin Random House.

Elias-Juarez, M. A., & Knudson-Martin, C. (2017). Cultural attunement in therapy with Mexican-heritage couples: A grounded theory analysis of client and therapist experience. *Journal of Marital and Family Therapy*, *43*(1), 100-114. https://doi.org/10.1111/jmft.12183

Finkelhor, D., & Browne, A. (1985). The traumatic impact of sexual abuse: A conceptualization. *American Journal of Orthopsychiatry*, *55*(4), 530-41. https://doi.org/10.1111/j.1939-0025.1985.tb02703.x

Harlow, H. F. & Zimmermann, R. R. (1958). The development of affective responsiveness in infant monkeys. *Proceedings of the American Philosophical Society*, *102*, 501-9.

Hilpert, P., Brick, T. R., Flückiger, C., Vowels, M. J., Ceulemans, E., Kuppens, P., & Sels, L. (2020). What can be learned from couple research: Examining emotional co-regulation processes in face-to-face interactions. *Journal of Counseling Psychology*, *67*(4), 475-87. https://doi.org/10.1037/cou0000416

Kealy, D., Spidel, A., & Ogrodniczuk, J. S. (2017). Self-conscious emotions and suicidal ideation among women with and without history of childhood sexual abuse. *Counselling and Psychotherapy Research*, *17*(4), 269-75. https://doi.org/10.1002/capr.12140

Lahousen, T., Unterrainer, H. F., & Kapfhammer, H. P. (2019). Psychobiology of attachment and trauma—some general remarks from a clinical perspective. *Frontiers in Psychiatry*, *10*, 914. https://doi.org/10.3389/fpsyt.2019.00914

McAuliffe, G. (2020). *Culturally alert counseling: A comprehensive introduction*. Sage.

Sacdalan, D. B. (2021). Empathy. *Journal of Patient Experience*, *8*, 237437352199696-2374373521996767. https://doi.org/10.1177/2374373521996967

Schomaker, S. A., & Ricard, R. J. (2015). Effect of a mindfulness-based intervention on counselor-client attunement. *Journal of Counseling and Development*, *93*(4), 491-98. https://doi.org/10.1002/jcad.12047

Schore, A. N. (2021). The interpersonal neurobiology of intersubjectivity. *Frontiers in Psychology*, *12*, 648616-648616. https://doi.org/10.3389/fpsyg.2021.648616

Spitz, R. A. (1946). Hospitalism: A follow-up report. *The Psychoanalytic Study of the Child*, *2*, 113-17. https://doi.org/10.1080/00797308.1946.11823540

Thompson, N. M., van Reekum, C. M., & Chakrabarti, B. (2022). Cognitive and affective empathy relate differentially to emotion regulation. *Affective Science*, *3*(1), 118-34. https://doi.org/10.1007/s42761-021-00062-w

Van Tongeren, D. R., Davis, D. E., Hook, J. N., & Witvliet, C. vanOyen. (2019). Humility. *Current Directions in Psychological Science: A Journal of the American Psychological Society*, *28*(5), 463-68. https://doi.org/10.1177/0963721419850153

Yeager, Katherine A., & Bauer-Wu, S. (2013). Cultural humility: Essential foundation for clinical researchers. *Applied Nursing Research*, *26*(4), 251-56.

Zhu, P., Luke, M., & Bellini, J. (2021). A grounded theory analysis of cultural humility in counseling and counselor education. *Counselor Education and Supervision*, *60*(1), 73-89. https://doi.org/10.1002/ceas.12197

13

LISTENING AND RESPONDING

DR. PENSIRI NUK KONGKAW-ODEN
AND DR. LISA COMPTON

ONE OF THE GREATEST GIFTS we can give someone is to listen well to their stories and respond in a way that promotes healing. Listening encourages expression of distressing thoughts and strong emotions, offers validation to the survivor's experiences, reduces feelings of isolation, creates opportunity for empathetic engagement and bearing witness to their pain, reduces shame through normalizing trauma responses, and aids in organizing memories into a cohesive narrative. God created us as relational beings, and even our physiology is dependent on communication and interactions with others. According to Schore (2021), our brains are literally molded throughout our lifespan by our experiences and our engagements with others, particularly when those engagements involve emotional connection. We were designed by God for meaningful relationships, and these relationships facilitate healing when the trauma survivor feels heard by an attuned, empathetic listener.

SELF-REGULATION

In order to listen well, we must first be able to attend to our own internal experiences while witnessing client stories. Recollections of trauma affect all of us; even the most seasoned counselors who have treated trauma for years can be triggered by the horrors that their clients have had to endure. For example, when listening to the story of a firefighter in my counseling office describe the young child he was unable to save from the burning apartment, I felt my stomach twist into knots and gripped the armrest of my chair just to hold on to something so I would not collapse to the floor. I took several deep breaths, rolled my tense shoulders back, and focused on the cool plastic of the armrest for a moment to reset my nervous system activation. I was then able to listen attentively to his story. I met with my supervisor the following day to process my vicarious trauma from that session. In order to stay present cognitively and emotionally with others, we need to recognize our own distress reactions and then practice the grounding and regulation exercises that will be covered in the next chapter.

Sometimes, it is not the trauma details of the story that trigger us but the strong emotional reactions of the survivors that cause us disturbance. Trauma survivors rightly experience rage and intense grief from the violence, betrayal, and powerlessness of abuse. They may express these feelings with shouting, cussing, sobbing, or even anger misdirected at you. These reactions may not only be uncomfortable for us but also trigger our own past experiences, such as living with an alcoholic mother. Again, it is important to be aware of our internal reactions and attend to our own regulation in order to stay present, listen well, and allow the survivor to know this is a safe place to express and process their strong emotions. This is also true in safeguarding. By resetting our central nervous system to return to a calmer state, we can provide co-regulation for the people we are trying to support.

COMMUNICATING EMPATHY

Listening is not only information gathering but also an opportunity to demonstrate empathy. Empathy allows us to step into the survivor's world and understand their perspective and their experiences. If we just focus on gathering the facts about what happened to the person as opposed to understanding how the person experienced the event, we fail to show our care and concern. The Bible tells us to actively participate in the joys and sorrows of others: "Rejoice with those who rejoice, and weep with those who weep" (Romans 12:15).[1] We can match the emotional state of those we are helping and then connect with them in their pain. Instead of using statements that come across as emotionally disconnected, such as "I'm so sorry that happened to you," offer an empathetic response that shows you witnessed their emotion, such as "That sounds like it must have been a very painful and lonely experience. Can you tell me more about what that was like for you?" By conveying empathy, we communicate that they are not alone on their healing journey.

---

[1]Scripture quotations in this chapter, unless otherwise noted, are from the NKJV.

Christians often prioritize speaking with the intent to change someone's beliefs and behaviors over empathetic listening. For example, you might feel that someone struggling just needs to hear the "truth" or be given advice in order to make changes in his or her life. However, sage advice is often ill received when the individual needs support instead of correction. The Bible warns of the damage that can come from not attending to the emotional condition of a hurting person. "Like one who takes away a garment in cold weather, and like vinegar on soda, is one who sings songs to a heavy heart" (Proverbs 25:20). Maybe you can remember a time when someone tried to offer advice or to cheer you up when you were hurting, and it actually stung more than comforted. This often occurs at funerals when well-meaning Christians try to console the bereaved with statements such as "I guess God needed another angel in the choir" or "Well, at least you still have [fill in the blank]." Not only is the first example incorrect theologically but both statements convey an intolerance of their emotional pain. As Brené Brown, researcher and author, states, "Empathy never begins with the words 'At least'" (RSA, 2013).

We do not need to have experienced the same things as the person we are helping in order to express empathy. How do we offer support to someone who has been sexually assaulted when we have not experienced that ourselves? We may not have experienced the exact same trauma, but we have experienced pain from other events in our lives and connect with their hurt and understand the pain from their perspective. Empathy comes from listening well and allowing ourselves to engage with what the survivor is both saying and feeling. Our empathy naturally leads to compassion—taking action out of our care and concern through advocacy and means to help meet the survivor's needs (Lahousen et al., 2019). Jesus modeled compassion for people's pain as he healed their ailments: "[Jesus] was moved with compassion for them" (Matthew 9:36).

LISTENING AND RESPONDING SKILLS

Listening well is not easy to do. Refraining from trying to "fix" the person or situation, preaching to them, or offering our advice requires self-restraint and the ability to bracket our own opinions. We may even subconsciously want to steer them away from their pain to try to quickly soothe them or ourselves. There are specific listening and responding skills we can employ to help others feel heard, seen, and understood—one of the goals of trauma care. These skills include focusing, active reflection of content and feeling, noticing body sensations, summarizing, providing context, and the use of silence.

Focusing. Focusing is a skill of selective attention. When trauma survivors share their stories, they often provide us with a significant amount of information, and focusing allows us to narrow in on specific facets of what they are sharing. Which aspects of the experience were most difficult for them? What are some themes, such as betrayal, isolation, or feeling powerless? What are some of their current needs? Consider where you would focus in the following example of a fourteen-year-old male sharing that his female youth leader, who was thirty-one years old, had sexually assaulted him:

> When I told my two best friends, Tony and Fred, what she did, they high fived me and congratulated me on "becoming a man." My face felt like it was burning up, and I hoped that they could not tell how I felt. My mother told me she was sorry that this happened and that I should be careful who I tell so that it does not cause other youth in our group to fall away from God. My dad just laughed and then looked at me with a weird grin—almost like he was proud of me. My own body even betrayed me. I guess my erection sent the message that I was okay with it and she could just do what she wanted to me. I hate that woman and hope she gets hit by a car. I guess that means I'm going to hell.

Where does your mind go first? You might have your own biases and wonder if the event was actually traumatic for him since he was a teenage boy and she was a woman in her early thirties. Do you focus on the assault or the friends or his parents or his spiritual condition? When people share stories, they can give us a lot of information at once, which can make it challenging to know where to start. One way to narrow focusing is to identify the theme that seems to be causing the most distress. In the above example, I would start with the idea that no one is acknowledging how this event hurt him. A focused response could be, "It sounds like no one around you really gets how traumatizing this assault was for you. I can see how painful this has been. Could you tell me more about what it has felt like to carry that pain with you these past few months?" Focusing, like many of the skills we will learn in this chapter, takes practice and will come more naturally as you practice identifying themes in conversations.

Active reflection. Reflecting back what you heard as someone shares their story shows them that not only are you tracking with the details of the story, you are also synthesizing the information they have given you in a way that invites deeper reflection. Reflection is a very *active* process and can feel like mental gymnastics to the safeguarder. It requires careful attention to the words others use, attunement to their emotional experience, and consideration of what to reflect back. Skilled reflection also includes discernment *when* to reflect to avoid interrupting and to remain silent when the survivor needs a moment to catch their breath or consider how to articulate their thoughts. We should listen more often than we speak, as the Scriptures instruct us: "Be swift to hear, slow to speak" (James 1:19). Active reflection takes practice but can produce significant results in all relationships. Our students who practice active reflection with friends, family, and coworkers frequently report back with great enthusiasm how it helped them feel more connected and facilitated more effective communication during conflict.

Reflecting content. Reflecting content involves repeating back a phrase or sentence based on the information you just heard. This reflection should not be verbatim what the speaker said (that would be annoying to have someone just keep repeating you) but a short paraphrase of the content. Consider the following examples:

> **Speaker:** When my ex-husband tried to hit me with his car, I thought I was going to die! I immediately ran as fast as I could into the nearest store to get help. The store owner waited with me until the police arrived.

> **Listener:** How frightening to have such a near-death experience!

In this example, repeating the fact that the client feared for her life reflected the essence of what she shared about her experience of the event. When a keyword is emphasized, you should use it in the reflection. You can also use a question with a curious tone to seek clarification of your reflection or express astonishment at the magnitude of the experience.

> **Speaker:** I was outside of a restaurant and apparently there was a bar fight between two women. I guess the one woman mistook me for the other, because she came running out of the nearby bar and attacked me while screaming, "How could you do this to me?" The woman hit me *repeatedly* without giving me a chance to respond.

> **Listener:** She hit you repeatedly before finding out if she had the right person?

Here, the question emphasizes your mutual shock at the woman's actions and further allies you with the speaker. You may not always reflect exactly what the speaker intended, but they can provide further clarification, so don't worry about perfection when it comes to your reflections.

Reflecting feeling. We are made in God's image and experience emotions such as anger (Deuteronomy 9:22), jealousy (Exodus 34:14), sorrow (Psalm 78:40), and joy (Zephaniah 3:17) as he does. Emotions also teach us and guide us. Experiencing fear when a tiger is near could prompt us to try to escape so that we are not killed. The key is that we know how to recognize emotions, identify the information they're giving us, and choose how to respond and act. Reflecting feelings, or the conscious interpretation of emotions, back to the person increases their awareness of the emotion and also names it. You could think of this interaction like a mirror, but instead of reflecting back an image, you are reflecting back the feelings embedded in their story. Some survivors will include feelings in their stories. For others, you may need to guess or ask them directly. Good listeners are not afraid of emotions but validate them as signals designed by God that help us explore our experiences with curiosity.

> *Speaker:* When my father came home stressed from work, he would hit my mother right in front of us.

> *Listener:* You must have been *so* frightened.

Sometimes clients will minimize their feelings, and our reflections can include a feeling they may not have considered.

> *Speaker:* Kelly died a few years ago so I'm pretty much over it. I went to counseling and dealt with all that. Of course, now I'm freaking out about "What the heck am I going to do with my life?"

> *Listener:* It sounds like you've processed the loss of your friend, but it is now hitting you how this might change your life. You seem scared and uncertain.

It is also crucial to correctly match the intensity of the words the speaker uses with our reflections. For example, if they tell you they were completely disgusted to hear that their supervisor had assaulted a young child, you should *not* reflect back "you were frustrated at that news." Here, *frustrated* does not match their emotional state. Listen not only to the words they are sharing but also to what you are observing in their reactions to the story.

Noticing body sensations. Trauma is often accompanied by physical sensations. The body can store memories that are outside conscious awareness, as the title of van der Kolk's (2014) bestselling book *The Body Keeps the Score* reflects. Think of the message sent if you experience a crushing pain in your chest and shooting pain up your left arm. That is feedback from your body that you could be having a heart attack. Just like physical pain, emotions, which are often experienced as bodily sensations, let our brains know when there is a wound that needs attention. For instance, when someone feels anxious, they might notice a tight feeling in their chest or the temperature rise in their face.

Connecting feelings with physical sensations enables trauma survivors to engage and regulate their emotional experiences more effectively. *Interoception* is the term for awareness of what is happening inside of us and connecting that internal experience with what our body is doing in that moment (Connell et al., 2018). Noticing the anger while balling up your fists or the anxious feeling when your shoulders are tense are examples of interoception. Awareness of our internal states and sensations is just as important as awareness of our thoughts. Once we notice these feelings and body sensations, we can give our body physical cues to help soothe those internal emotions, such as deep breathing and releasing the tension in those muscles. Interoception is also a skill that you can teach trauma survivors in order to increase their own awareness and regulation.

> *Listener:* How do you feel when we talk about what happened with your soccer coach?
>
> *Speaker:* I don't feel much of anything.
>
> *Listener:* Your emotions feel pretty numb. When we discuss those memories of him, where do you feel that in your body?
>
> *Speaker:* I feel it in my stomach. Like I just ate a poisoned meal.
>
> *Listener:* Can you describe that sensation further for me?

By expanding on the sensation of an upset stomach, the survivor can communicate their lived experience of the trauma and possibly connect with some dissociated emotions. It is also information you can use to help decrease their physiological distress. If someone tells you they feel nauseous as they discuss a traumatic event, you might invite them to take five deep breaths with you before going on, or you might offer some ginger ale.

Summarizing. Another active reflection skill is summarizing. Summarizing includes providing a few-sentence synopsis of a story that someone has just shared. Good summaries include not only the content information but also the emotions and themes of their stories. Summaries do not need to be done as often as short reflections of content and feelings, and they are very helpful to use at the end of safeguarding sessions. Here is an example.

Speaker: I felt really awkward being the only Black person at my wife's family gatherings at first. I could feel everybody holding back and watching me, but I soon realized that Asian and Black families have similar values. They wanted to know I would take care of her. I had to do a lot of work to understand them and prove myself, but they love me now.

Listener: It sounds like you've worked really hard to be accepted into your wife's family. You've had to figure out what being in a Black-Asian marriage looks like and build quite a few cultural bridges.

You may note that I have not asked any questions. You will find that a good summary acts like an unspoken question. Displaying that you are listening to their story with a summary prompts people to share more details, feelings, and thoughts.

Providing context. As we listen to trauma survivors' stories, it is often apparent that there are some distortions in the way they perceive themselves and the circumstances surrounding the abuse due to grooming behaviors of the perpetrators, shame, and false narratives from other people. This is an opportunity for safeguarders to validate the experiences of the survivors while countering false beliefs about themselves that have brought them shame, kept them stuck in their trauma, and held them captive from grace and truth. This scriptural principle applies perfectly here: "And you shall know the truth, and the truth shall make you free" (John 8:32). The perceptions and meaning derived from traumas can determine whether survivors move toward post-traumatic growth or whether they become stuck in the distortions of the context. The following narrative provides an example of a girl who was sexually abused by her parents' adult friend and the safeguarder using the skill of context.

Speaker: I guess I am partly to blame, because I really liked his attention and did not try to fight him off or tell my parents what was happening.

Listener: You feel responsible because part of you enjoyed feeling seen, but the abuse was in no way your fault. The only person who is responsible here is [name of perpetrator]. You are safe now, and I am with you. We will walk through this together.

In this scenario, the safeguarder can provide further context by helping the victim understand the power difference between a child and an adult and how it is the responsibility of adults to keep children safe. The safeguarder can also provide context through education about trauma responses if the girl has shame over her freeze response. Teaching victims about trauma responses can normalize their reactions and lead to greater self-compassion.

Use of silence. There is a time for everything under heaven (Ecclesiastes 3:1). As we have learned so far, good listening involves actively reflecting back thoughts and feelings to convey that we are tracking well with the person sharing their story. However, there is also incredible healing that can take place from occasional moments of silence. Using silence well not only means refraining from speech to allow survivors time to grieve or organize their thoughts, but it also means sitting comfortably with them in their pain. Several years ago, my (Lisa's) son was in the children's hospital to receive a feeding tube. It was a very difficult time in my life with many stressors attacking me at once. Two of my friends from college came to visit me in the hospital. They sat on either side of me while I waited on the cold wooden bench outside my son's room. We sat there in silence for a *long* period of time. I felt more love and support in those moments than if they had said a word.

Silence also creates time for reflection. The time we spend with survivors becomes sacred spaces where healing takes place. It is in those quiet times that survivors can hear the still, small voice of God as all other noise and distractions are minimized. It is not easy to allow this quiet space. Our defenses will want to stop the survivor (and ourselves) from sitting in the pain and despair. However, our role is to be patient, to grieve with them over losses, and to help them increase their tolerance for painful emotions by increasing our own ability to remain present and engaged.

NONVERBAL COMMUNICATION

Consider what it would be like to share something meaningful with a friend and then notice them check their watch, pick up their phone, or begin to look around the room. What would happen inside you? Most of us would stop sharing in that moment and feel less safe in our vulnerability. Our trust in that confidant would decrease and may also generalize to our ability to trust other people as well. We nonverbally invite or discourage engagement. We convey our listening with our whole bodies, including our posture, our voice tone, and our facial expressions. Inviting posture includes leaning forward with an open stance, while crossed arms can communicate a lack of interest or even anger. A voice tone that is gentle and warm can be soothing, while a raised voice or sarcastic tone can trigger danger to the listener. Facial expressions are directly tied to our central nervous system cues of safety. Smiles communicate compassion.

Safeguarders should note that trauma can lead to survivors' hyperawareness of danger cues. Therefore, we should pay close attention to our body language, the tone of our voice, and our facial expressions to promote a safe environment. Avoid looking shocked as survivors tell their story; we want to communicate grief but not disgust to avoid potential shaming. There are also multicultural considerations to be aware of for nonverbal cues. For example, maintaining direct eye contact may be considered attentive in some cultures and offensive in others. Notice how the survivor responds to your attempts at active listening, and express humble curiosity if you perceive a disconnect or miscommunication.

EFFECTIVE QUESTIONS

Not only are we paying attention to what someone is saying at the surface level, but there are also underlying emotions, messages, and meanings to observe. This is where good questions come in that can help both the survivor and helper gain more clarity and insight. Not all questions are created equal. An effective question elicits information while continuing to maintain empathetic connection. An ineffective question causes the survivor to feel interrogated and may put them on the defensive. Using *why* at the beginning of a question almost always implies some criticism. Questions can also communicate a judgmental tone if not worded properly. For example, asking a sexual assault victim, "How did you try to escape?" can convey an implicit message that you do not believe them or that you are blaming them for the abuse. Other questions that are commonly asked to victims that imply judgment are "What were you wearing?" and "Why were you alone with him?" These types of questions cause shame and further harm to victims.

Open-ended and closed-ended questions serve different functions in communication. Open-ended questions tend to elicit responses that provide more scope and context and encourage deeper reflection. Closed questions require the respondent to say yes, no, or a give a narrow answer and should only be used when specific details are needed, such as "Were you able to contact your doctor?"

An effective, open question example: "What did it feel like to experience such a betrayal from the mentor you had admired?"

An ineffective, closed question example: "Are you upset that he betrayed you?"

Observe how much narrower the response will be in the closed question example. By contrast, the open question gives the respondent a chance to tell you about sleep, eating, relationships, work, and anything else that trauma might impact for them. Some questions that are excellent prompts to trauma care include "Could you tell me more about . . . ?" "What does it feel like to . . .?" and "What strengths have helped you cope with the pain?"

POTENTIAL CHALLENGES IN COMMUNICATION

Potential for retraumatization. Questions should not be used to satisfy our own curiosity and should only be used in ways that avoid retraumatization. Retraumatization occurs when "an individual with pre-existing trauma is triggered by a new stressor" (Pazderka et al., 2021, p. 2). These intense reactions can cause survivors to relive aspects of the trauma. As safeguarders, our top priorities are the physical, emotional, and psychological safety of the survivor and the prevention of further harm—by the perpetrator, by the church, and even by our well-intentioned interactions. One way survivors are retraumatized is by questions that dig too deeply or too quickly into the details of their trauma. Although some information gathering is necessary for reporting abuse and other administrative tasks, we should not use questions to "go digging" for these details. Survivors should be free to share how little or how much they want to when they want to. They should feel in control of the dialogue, empowered to express their needs, and not obligated to answer questions that make them feel uncomfortable. Safeguarders should leave trauma memory reprocessing work to mental health professionals trained in providing additional layers of psychological and physiological protection.

Crises of faith. It is not uncommon for trauma survivors to question their faith. Trauma can feel like God betrayed us and can shatter our schema, or mental image, of a protecting Father. This cognitive dissonance in our belief systems often results in significant anxiety. Although some theological discussions, such as the topic of suffering, can be helpful, most existential questions such as "Why did God allow this to happen to me?" require our attunement as opposed to our quick answers. Provide space for survivors to wrestle with this question as opposed to preaching theology at them. God demonstrated an understanding of the human need for lament by devoting an entire book to it in the Old Testament. He is big enough to handle our anger, secure enough to tolerate our doubts, and strong enough to sustain our wrestling (Genesis 32:22-28).

You may serve in the role of spiritual leader and feel a responsibility to provide answers to "fix" spiritual doubt. Showing restraint in this instance and making space and time for the survivor to process through these difficult questions allows room for the gentle voice of the Lord to bring them answers. It is our role to be a safe listener who will not be offended by the questions and will validate how painful experiences can cause even the most spiritual persons to struggle and doubt. It is also our role to support them as they wrestle with their questions and to trust God that he will be faithful to answer their cries. "Safety does not consist of coming up with answers to the incomprehensible" (van der Kolk). Consider this example:

> *Speaker:* Me and God are in a fight right now. Why would he cause me to be born into a family that he knew would abuse me? Where was he when that man was harming me? I was just a helpless little kid!
>
> *Listener:* I can hear in your voice your struggle to understand where God was in all of this. Before we meet again next week, would you be open to spending time in a quiet place to ask him these questions and see what he says?
>
> [One week later]
>
> *Listener:* How did it go bringing those painful questions to God?
>
> *Speaker:* Well, I did not necessarily hear any specific answers, but he showed me an image of him sitting by my bed as I was being abused. He was sobbing . . . (she begins to cry).

In this scenario, the safeguarder stays attuned with her but silent until she speaks again. This allows her to direct the conversation where she wants it to go next and when she is ready to speak.

"He said/she said" of crimes. Victims' and perpetrators' stories usually do not line up. This is due to many reasons, including the fragmentation of

memories during a trauma, the perpetrator lying, and, in rare cases, the victims making false accusations. Thankfully, it is not the role of the safeguarder to play judge or jury. You can communicate to them, "This is not an investigation. I am here for you, and this is a safe place for you." The safeguarding role is to report what is required by law and to provide supportive care for the victim. There are other systems to investigate the validity of the allegations.

Survivors' language and expression. There are several cautions related to communicating with victims. First, avoid statements like "I totally understand." Even if you have experienced similar abuse, everyone's experience is different, and we want to hear their unique stories. Second, do not correct them if they swear. The pent-up anger and emotions that have been suppressed can come out strongly, like opening a shaken bottle of soda, and a swear word is sometimes the expression of that rage. One of my (Lisa's) parenting mistakes occurred when my son came in from playing outside and started swearing like a truck driver. I immediately launched into a stern lecture about how Christians should not use those words. During my tirade, I looked down and noticed blood pouring down his leg. One of the neighborhood kids had kicked him. Even many years later, the regret I have from correcting him instead of listening to him is very palpable. The survivor's expression of grief, anger, fear, betrayal, and sorrow can be uncomfortable but can also serve as a release for built-up stress hormones such as adrenaline. As long as survivors are not hurting themselves, you, or others, allow them to process these intense feelings without over-spiritualizing and correction.

Suicidal thoughts. Crisis situations include the presence of immediate or imminent danger. If someone shares that they are having thoughts about suicide, you should ask them direct questions in a compassionate and calm manner before moving on to any other topic. Here is an example of this dialogue:

Speaker: I want all this pain to end and hope I don't wake up tomorrow morning.

Listener: You sound like you are in an incredible amount of pain. Are you having thoughts of hurting yourself?

Speaker: Maybe, I just don't know.

Listener: I am thankful that you are sharing this with me. I want to keep you safe and to understand what you need. Have you thought of how you would hurt yourself?

These questions are nonjudgmental and direct. There is a difference in potential lethality between someone having a passing thought that they want their pain to end and someone who has a plan for suicide and the means to carry out that plan. While this is an oversimplification of an actual suicide assessment, it provides an example of how to use questions in a crisis. People often fear that they will put the thought into someone's head about killing themselves by asking the questions, but the reality is the thought is already there. They are alluding to it because they want help, and they want someone to talk to. Always take threats of suicide and homicide very seriously. Asking clear and direct questions will help you determine what actions to take next.

Imagine you are having a conversation with someone and they say:

Speaker: "Sometimes life feels so overwhelming. I just think about ending it all."

Listener: "When you say 'ending it all,' do you have thoughts of suicide or harming yourself?"

Speaker: "Maybe. Like, I haven't thought about how I would do it, but sometimes it sounds good to me to just take a long nap."

Listener: "Ok, so life is so overwhelming for you right now that you think of escaping. Do you have any access to anything that would hurt you if you got too overwhelmed?"

Speaker: "No, I would never do anything. I know I have too many people in my life that would hurt."

Listener: "You have a lot of important people in your life. Let's talk about some ways to help decrease your stress so that you don't get to that point of thinking of harmful ways of escape then."

Sometimes conversations about suicide and homicide do not get wrapped up that easily. If someone does express intent to harm or have a plan or method thought out, it is important to get help right away from a mental health professional or a nearby medical facility to do a more thorough risk assessment screening.

CONCLUSION

Providing support through attentive listening and reflective responses can bring healing to survivors through empathic connection and relationship. As you strive to attune to both your physical and emotional cues, you can also bring attention to the survivor's physical cues and emotions, which provide further awareness of their reactions and validate their experiences. Through strategic silence and reflective skills, you can communicate, "I am listening. I am here for you. I believe you. You are not alone. You deserve to feel whole and safe." As you help survivors unravel their thoughts and emotions with careful, open questions, you are setting them on a journey of healing, but you are not the only guide. You are not alone as you sit with survivors. The Holy Spirit is your guide and theirs as you minister. "And I will ask the Father, and he will give you another Helper, to be with you forever, even the Spirit of truth" (John 14:16-17 ESV).

PERSONAL REFLECTION

1. Consider a time when you shared a personal story about yourself, and you perceived the listener as distracted, uninterested, or unhelpful. What behaviors did you notice in the listener that communicated a lack of interest? What thoughts, feelings, and physical sensations do you remember experiencing as you told your story?

2. Consider a time when you shared a personal story about yourself, and you perceived the listener as present, attuned, and interested. What behaviors did you notice in the listener that communicated their interest? What thoughts, feelings, and physical sensations do you remember experiencing as you told your story?

3. Which of the listening skills do you anticipate being most challenging to implement as you practice your safeguarding role? Which of the skills come most naturally to you?

GROUP DISCUSSION

1. *Questions exercise.* Brainstorm questions you may consider asking an abuse survivor. Categorize these questions into effective, harmful, and borderline/gray areas. Discuss your rationale for your choice of categorization.

2. *Listening skills exercise.* Gather in groups of two or three. Assign a speaker, listener, and observer. The roles of each group member are as follows:

   Speaker—Choose a story that has some personal significance. For the purposes of this exercise, we do not recommend choosing a story that is emotionally intense and would be difficult or overwhelming for you to share. For example, an appropriate story for this exercise might be discussing your first day at a new job. There is some emotional significance (excitement, anxiety, uncertainty, etc.), but it is likely not traumatic for you to share. Tell the story to the listener, pausing every twenty to thirty seconds to give them the chance to reflect and summarize as you go.

Listener—Hear the speaker's story, paying attention to both the story's content and the feelings you perceive they may be experiencing. After twenty to thirty seconds of the speaker telling their story, practice giving a brief (1 or 2 sentences) summary reflecting content and feeling to show the speaker that you are following their experience. After your reflection, the speaker will continue their story. Do this for several rounds or until the story is complete. Be sure to practice nonverbal listening cues, including leaning forward, nodding your head, and making eye contact.

Observer—Your job is to provide constructive feedback. Listen to the speaker-listener exchange and notice strengths and areas for growth in the listener's responses. Be sure to communicate both what went well and where the listener could grow in their skills. (If only in groups of two, you may skip the observer role.)

Rotate speaker, listener, and observer roles so each group member can practice all three roles.

3. It is unfortunately not uncommon to come across someone who is having suicidal thoughts. What steps would you take next if someone shared with you that they were considering killing themselves?

REFERENCES

Connell, L., Lynott, D., & Banks. B. (2018). Interoception: The forgotten modality in perceptual grounding of abstract and concrete concepts. *Philosophical Transactions, 373*(1752), 1-9. http://dx.doi.org/10.1098/rstb.2017.0143

Lahousen, T., Unterrainer, H. F., & Kapfhammer, H. P. (2019). Psychobiology of attachment and trauma—some general remarks from a clinical perspective. *Frontiers in Psychiatry, 10*, 914. https://doi.org/10.3389/fpsyt.2019.00914

Pazderka, H., Brown, M. R. G., Agyapong, V. I. O., Greenshaw, A. J., McDonald-Harker, C. B., Noble, S., Mankowski, M., Lee, B., Drolet, J. L., Omeje, J., Brett-MacLean, P., Kitching, D. T., & Silverstone, P. H. (2021). Collective trauma and mental health in adolescents: A retrospective cohort study of the effects of retraumatization. *Frontiers in Psychiatry, 12*, 682041. https://doi.org/10.3389/fpsyt.2021.682041

RSA. (2013, December 10). *Brené Brown on Empathy* [Video]. YouTube. https://youtu.be/1Evwgu369Jw?si=IBqMELrRx4vJzoZM

Schore, A. N. (2021) The interpersonal neurobiology of intersubjectivity. *Frontiers in Psychology, 12*, 648616. https://doi.org/10.3389/fpsyg.2021.648616

van der Kolk, B. (1994). Foreword. In J.P. Wilson & J.D. Lindy (Eds.), *Countertransference in the Treatment of PTSD* (pp. vii-xii). The Guilford Press.

14

EMOTION REGULATION

DR. CINDY PALEN

TRAUMA IS EXPERIENCED as an emotional overwhelm that exceeds our ability to cope in that moment and often in the days, weeks, and, for some, years following the event. Even when the danger is past, external and internal stimuli can elicit strong emotional responses suddenly and without warning. Depending on a person's level of coping strategies and support network, emotional responses can be difficult to regulate. However, offering survivors exercises to help improve self-regulation can empower them and help them feel more in control over their emotional states. This chapter will briefly discuss sensory triggers and will give practical techniques that both survivors and safeguarders can use to assist in regulating intense emotional responses.

TRIGGERS AND RETRAUMATIZATION

Sights, sounds, smells, tastes, physical sensations, and specific emotions can remind survivors of a traumatic experience. These sensory stimuli are known as "triggers" because they activate survival responses in the body as if the traumatic experience were happening to the survivor again. Survivors might expect some events to be triggers, such as revisiting the scene of the trauma, but other triggers come on suddenly without any identified connection to the trauma. Any number of stimuli, including flashbacks and memories, can be triggers.

During traumatic experiences, the brain will record seemingly insignificant details associated with the trauma as cues of potential danger in the future. A train whistle that sounded in the background during the abuse might resonate as a trigger. A certain shade of blue could prompt vivid memories of abuse, because the survivor focused on a blue lamp in the room during the assault.

The smell of cologne, body odor, or cigarette smoke might be sensory reminders of the abuse. Due to the unpredictable nature of when and where
triggers will occur, they often catch a survivor off guard and may evoke panic
and emotional dysregulation. It is important for survivors to be aware of how
triggers can affect them and to have skills to self-regulate when they are triggered. It is during these moments when remembering the traumatic event can
cause a "reliving" of the trauma and lead to survivors being retraumatized.
Retraumatization happens when a survivor is taken back in their mind to the
moment of the abuse, and the memory is so vivid that the mind and body do
not recognize that the survivor is currently safe. During retraumatization, the
threat response system will activate a neurological reaction as if the danger
were still present. Self-regulating skills reduce this risk of retraumatization and
aid in returning the person's central nervous system to equilibrium.

Likewise, a safeguarder who hears of a survivor's traumatic experiences can
also experience psychological trauma. When a person experiences heightened
emotional responses to a traumatic event that did not happen to them, but that
they witnessed or heard about, it is called vicarious trauma. Safeguarders also
need self-regulating skills so that they can avoid vicarious trauma. The exercises in this chapter should be both used by the safeguarder and taught to the
survivor as a means to self-regulate emotional responses.

EXTREME EMOTIONAL STATES

Hyper/hypoarousal. In response to trauma, a person may be hyperaroused or
hypoaroused. In a hyperaroused state, the central nervous system is working
on overdrive to prepare the body for a way to escape the danger through
fighting or fleeing. A hyperaroused state may result in irritability, anger, impulsivity, hypervigilance, problems with concentration, insomnia, numbing,
withdrawal, and confusion (American Psychiatric Association, 2022). This
constant need to be ready to protect oneself can lead to hypervigilance, where
the person is jumpy and easily startled. Their heart rate increases and breathing
becomes shallower as if they have just done excessive cardio exercise. These
hyperarousal symptoms can become so severe that they lead to a panic attack,
which can feel similar to a heart attack. When survivors are unaware of the
physiological reactions to trauma stimuli, they may fear for their physical well-
being as well as their psychological state.

In a hypoaroused state, the coping strategy engaged is to shut down. In this state, a person feels numb and emotionless, and they may even disconnect from the present moment, a condition known as dissociation. They may desire to run or fight, but they cannot get their body to move. It feels like they are stuck and helpless to defend themselves. This automatic threat strategy is described as the freeze response. It is important to understand that the conscious mind does not decide which threat response will be activated, but rather it is an instantaneous decision from lower portions of the brain that determine which strategy has the most potential to promote survival.

Both hyper- and hypoarousal reactions are adaptive ways the brain and body react to a dangerous threat. When experienced briefly, these reactions are not necessarily problematic. For example, if someone jumps in front of you and yells "SURPRISE!" you may feel your heart race and breathing quicken in hyperarousal to prepare you if you needed to fight or run away. The key issue is whether your nervous system can return to a regulated state in a relatively short period of time. In this example, once you realize your friend dropped by to surprise you, you are probably able to catch your breath and have your heart return to a normal rate within minutes. For individuals who experience chronic exposure to trauma, this return to equilibrium may be more difficult. Some indicators of healing include being able to return to a regulated state as well as being able to tolerate emotions and triggers related to past trauma without entering these more extreme arousal states.

Window of tolerance. The *window of tolerance* (Ogden, Minton, & Pain, 2006) is a term used to describe the optimal arousal zone that exists between hyper- and hypoarousal. In this generally "balanced" condition, the person's threat response is low and therefore their defensive mechanisms are kept to a minimum. This is significant because the parts of the brain responsible for language, communication, reasoning, learning, and growth remain "online" within the window of tolerance as opposed to the more offline response during threat activation. Our goal as safeguarders is not only to stay within our window of tolerance while providing care but also to help survivors expand their own window of tolerance by tolerating stressors and triggers without moving into hyper- or hypoarousal. For example, Katia was an eight-year-old who had been rescued from a house fire by local firefighters. Katia came in to see me with her mother because they were both having trouble with anxiety after the fire. As we were talking, someone in my office lit a candle, and Katia became extremely agitated by the smell of the smoke. I told her that I could see that the smell of the candle was very upsetting for her and invited her to share what she was feeling. As she did, I took slow, deep breaths to ensure I stayed regulated, and when she was done describing what she was feeling, we practiced some of the relaxation strategies listed in the next section.

TECHNIQUES AND COPING STRATEGIES

A person experiencing emotional dysregulation will benefit from interventions that address either their hyperarousal state, in which they would require down-regulating (calming) techniques, or their hypoarousal state, in which up-regulating (energy-inducing) techniques would be more useful. The following examples can be used by safeguarders and survivors to modulate their state of dysregulation.

To help survivors return to a regulated state, grounding and mindfulness are beneficial activities that can be done anytime they experience a trigger. Grounding is a tool that utilizes a person's connection to this present moment in time on the earth as a way to encourage body awareness and physical and emotional stability (de Tord & Bräuninger, 2015). Grounding brings a person back to the present moment and instills an awareness of their surroundings and their body. Exercises encouraging grounding will remind the survivor of where they are physically in the present moment and will bring their thoughts and physical perceptions into an active state of noticing their physical presence. Mindfulness is an awareness without judgment of what someone is sensing and feeling in the moment. During mindfulness, a person has an awareness of negative and positive emotions and accepts them both, knowing that they have the skills to handle them. Both grounding and mindfulness combat emotional dysregulation. As you work with survivors, recognize that some people will prefer certain methods of self-regulation over others, so introduce them to several options and encourage them to find the ones that work well for them.

Expressive arts. Expressive arts are a way to communicate through music, movement, creative writing, drawing, sculpting, dancing, and other forms of creative expression. Artistic modalities are used to assist survivors of traumatic events in self-expression, personal communication, and emotional repair (Urquhart et al., 2020). Mimicking the natural childhood expression of play, expressive arts techniques allow for a positive safe space to interact with difficult content in a nurturing space (Urquhart et al., 2020). This section will give a few examples of how to incorporate expressive arts into emotional regulation techniques. Some items that you might want to have on hand for expressive arts include pencils, crayons, markers, acrylic paint, finger paint, watercolors, paper, clay or Play-Doh, ribbons, and/or flags.

Vertical regulation. One way to include expressive arts with regulation techniques is to combine art with breathing, which is the basic necessary element to emotional regulation. In this exercise, the survivors will draw in soothing repetitive motions as they breathe, so they are visualizing each breath as they include motion and art in the elemental experience of regulated breathing. Here is a script that you may read to teach this exercise.

> *Tape a piece of paper down in front of you so it does not shift when you are working. Choose two crayons or markers of any color and hold one in each hand. Start with your hands at the bottom of the page, and inhale as you draw upward strokes; exhale and draw downward. Continue with this up-and-down motion as you slowly breathe and draw up and down, up and down.*

Music and dance. Movement is another aspect of expressive arts that may help a person to self-regulate. If a survivor is in a hypoarousal state, upbeat music and movement can be used to energize. If the survivor is in a hyperarousal state, soft, slow music and movement can be used to have a calming effect. Worship and liturgical music may also be used to assist with the survivor's focus and positive thinking toward hope and restoration. This script can be used to direct a survivor in regulating movement.

> *I am going to turn on some music. I want you to take a ribbon* (or flag, or scarf) *in each hand. Imagine that your arms are tree branches, blowing in the wind. As you listen to the song, move your arms and wave the ribbons in any way you like. Ignore anyone present, and just allow your body to move with the music in any way it desires. You may feel like swaying back and forth, or moving up toward the sky and down to the earth. Your arms may move together, in sync, or they may each move separately. Listen to the music and your body and allow yourself to simply move.*

Creative writing. Creative writing is another expressive art form that allows survivors to feel more in control of their emotions. As survivors use their creative minds to write, they can express their thoughts and feelings in a "free flow" manner without judgment. Creative writing is beneficial in reducing stress and improving mental and physical wellness (Sloan & Marx, 2018; Zimmermann

& Mangelsdorf, 2020). This activity can also guide them in writing a dialogue between themselves and the Spirit of God.

> *Write a note to the Spirit of God. Write something like this. "Dear Holy Spirit, Thank you for filling my every breath. Thank you for filling me with peace as I inhale. You support me every moment and fill my lungs." And now, write back what the Holy Spirit might say to you. For example, "Dear Child of God, I am with you always. Even when you do not see me or feel me, I am there as a wind, and I am in your every breath."*

Encourage the survivors to use their own words as they write. The script is merely a suggestion to get them started.

Sculpting. Provide Play-Doh or clay and direct survivors to use it as a regulation tool.

> *Take the dough and mold it however you like. You do not need to create anything specific or anything recognizable. Feel the dough between your hands. Roll it back and forth, back and forth. Squeeze it, flatten it, roll it up. Use the dough to release tension and serve as a tool to help you focus on the texture and the way it moves.*

Grounding. The first set of grounding exercises we will discuss are breathing exercises. When dysregulated, people will often take shallow, short breaths. Slowing and deepening the breathing rates will help the central nervous system return to a more restful state. When people turn their focus to their breathing, they are also less likely to hyperventilate. They are providing their body with needed oxygen to slow the heart rate down to a resting rate. You may use the scripts in the following exercises to help survivors ground to present safety and achieve a calm state.

Balloon breathing.

> *Place your hand on your lower stomach. Imagine a balloon inside of you. As you inhale, picture the balloon inflating and with your hand feel your stomach rise as your lungs fill with air. After taking in a slow, deep breath, exhale slowly. As you exhale, imagine the balloon slowly deflating. Feel your stomach retreating back toward your spine. Notice how the slow exhale slows your heart rate and brings you to a calm state. Repeat this three to five times, each time bringing your awareness to your lungs and the air calmly entering and leaving your body.*

Square breathing.

Imagine a square with four sides. Begin on the right side of the square. As you imagine tracing the right side of the square from top to bottom, breathe in through your nose as you slowly count to four in your head. As you imagine tracing the bottom of the square from right to left, hold your breath as you count to four. Imagine you are tracing the square from bottom to top of the left side, and exhale slowly as you count to four. And finally, as you trace the top of the square from left to right, hold your breath for a count of four. Repeat this for three to four times around the square: Inhale, 2, 3, 4 . . . Hold, 2, 3, 4 . . . Exhale, 2, 3, 4 . . . Hold, 2, 3, 4 . . . Repeat.

You may also apply expressive arts to this exercise. Instruct survivors:

Draw the square as you breathe. Inhale, draw down; hold, draw across; exhale, draw up; hold, draw across. Continue to trace the square as you breathe.

Five senses. Once a person is breathing with some regularity, they can continue grounding by activating their five senses. The following script is an example of how to talk through activating the senses; it may be altered to fit the room and current situation.

We are going to work on grounding through an exercise called the Five Senses. The first sense is sight. Look around the room and notice what you see. Is there anything in the room that you did not notice before? How many different colors do you see? Turn your head around and notice the whole room. Look for details you might not have noticed—a spot on the carpet or a mark on the wall. Notice how you are bringing yourself into a state of present awareness.

If something with a pleasant scent is available, this can be used to assist with this section. Some might use anointing oil, essential oil, a candle, or other aromatic items, but even if nothing is available, you may still simply smell what is in the air, such as grass, dirt, or remnants of cooked food. Smells are also one of the strongest triggers so be aware of potential flashbacks, particularly with cologne and incense. If you are unsure of the potential triggering effect of a smell, ask the survivor before using it in this exercise.

The second sense we are going to activate is smell. Inhale slowly and deeply and take note of what you smell. Can you smell the lavender oil? Notice how it wakes your senses. Notice the sweetness of it and let it flow through your body as you relax into deep fragrant breaths. You may close your eyes and simply focus on the smells around you.

A piece of sour or peppermint candy can be used to help the body focus on the taste. This will also help them produce saliva, which dissipates during stress as the body shuts off the digestive system to prepare to flee or fight. A sweet or tangy drink may also be used. Be creative in the moment—the taste can be pleasant like a piece of chocolate or surprising like a bite of a lemon. If no physical food or drink is available, this exercise may be completed using only the imagination. The following script is for use when nothing tangible is available, but it may be altered when using a real drink or piece of food.

Imagine you have a lemon cut into quarters. This lemon is ripe and has the perfect combination of sweet and sour. You put it in your mouth and suck on its tangy flavor. Notice how your mouth begins to produce more saliva as you imagine sucking on this lemon. Your senses are activated, and you can imagine how this lemon smells and tastes. Its sour flavor creates an alertness in your senses. Notice this.

Another sense to use in grounding exercises is touch; however, be aware that physically touching a survivor of sexual abuse should never be done without their consent. Even a well-meaning tap on the hand or shoulder can cause a trauma reaction in a survivor.

Place your feet squarely on the floor. Notice how they connect to the floor and ground you to the present. Scuff them back and forth, paying attention to the friction as they brush against the floor's texture. Next, notice the chair you are sitting in. Can you feel its texture? Rub your hands along the armrests and feel the fabric. Notice it. Is it soft or rough? What other textures do you notice around you? Can you feel the smooth wood of the table or the rough teeth of the zipper on your jacket? Look around you and use your sense of touch to ground you in your present surroundings.

If a survivor is struggling with maintaining present focus or is dissociating, the sense of touch can be used with ice if it is available. Ask them to squeeze an ice cube or rub ice on their temples, wrists, or behind their ears. This cold sensation can help to ground them in the present. Another way to use touch is in combination with breathing. Many retailers now sell "calm strips," which are stickers with tiny bumps all over them which can be used as a grounding tool as people rub the bumps as a focal point. One might rub the sticker as they take breaths and try to self-regulate and reduce emotional dysregulation. Relics or religious items can also be used as a grounding tool. Stroking the Rosary or a cross around one's neck can be a useful grounding focal point.

Finally, sound can be used in the grounding process. For many people, music can have a calming effect. But even without music, just instructing someone to listen and notice what they hear will ground them in the present.

The following is an example of a script that could be used to help a survivor focus on the sounds around them.

> *Be still and notice what you hear around you. Take a couple of minutes to listen. What do you hear? Can you hear noises that you usually don't notice? Do you hear the buzzing of the lights? Do you hear a fly buzzing in the window? What else do you hear? Try to ignore the racing thoughts in your head and turn all of your focus to your ears and what you are hearing in the world around you.*

In all these sensory activities, the hyper- or hypoaroused person will be working to focus on the here and now and their body's reaction to the here and now, bringing them into the present moment and out of a dysregulated state.

5-4-3-2-1 Awareness. This next exercise helps the person to return from emotional activation to present awareness. The exercise is simple and can be done in any location. The following script may be altered to fit the available environment.

> *Look around you and notice five things that are white* (allow time for them to do this). *Once you have found five white things, look around and find four things that are yellow. Next, look for three things that are blue. Now, can you find two things that are green? And finally, can you find one thing that is red? Good. Notice how you are more aware of your surroundings and connected with the present space and moment.*

Containment. To help people feel a sense of control over their trauma memories and be able to take breaks from thinking about their trauma, use the tool of containment. The following script will help a survivor utilize an imaginary storage container to compartmentalize thoughts and images of their trauma by closing the "lid" of the container until they are in a safe place to process these memories such as with a counselor. A safeguarder can use the same exercise for themselves to contain the trauma narratives of the survivors as a way to avoid vicarious traumatization. You may apply expressive arts to this activity by instructing survivors to draw their container or create it out of clay.

> *Imagine a container. It can be a box, a chest, a cabinet, or any other container you visualize in your mind. Take a moment to find something that you can identify as a place to hold unwanted memories, thoughts, and images. The container should be sturdy and have a lock. When unwanted thoughts or memories invade your mind, imagine putting them in that container and locking them away. You are not simply stuffing your emotions away in this exercise. Instead, you are intentionally*

packaging the unwanted thoughts and feelings away until an appropriate time when you will get them out and process them with a person trained to help with trauma therapy. These thoughts are not allowed to interrupt your job, school, or home life. They belong locked away in the container, and you can replace those thoughts with Scripture and positive, hopeful thinking. As you lock those thoughts away, choose something hopeful to think about and stay with that thought.

Safe, calm place. Sometimes when a person is in a state of dysregulation, their mind races, and negative or anxious thoughts prevail. This activity clears the mind of intrusive thoughts and encourages the person to focus on an imagined calm, safe place. The following is a script used to help survivors locate a mentally calm space. You may apply expressive arts to this activity by having survivors draw their safe, calm place.

Take a moment to think about someplace where you feel the most content or calm. It can be a real or imagined place, such as a favorite chair in your home, a quiet place in the woods, a sunny spot on the beach, or a soft blanket in the clouds. Take a minute to think of a place that gives you a calm or neutral feeling. This should be a consistently safe spot for you, so you may not want to include other people in it. You may imagine God or angels there with you. When you have the place in mind, we are going to use all of our senses to really bring us to that spot.

For the purpose of this text, we will proceed with a script based on the beach as our imagined place; however, as you conduct this exercise with yourself or a survivor, alter the script to fit their chosen safe place.

Now, close your eyes and picture your safe place. Look around in your mind and imagine what you see. Do you see the waves crashing gently on the shore? Do you see the birds calmly soaring in the sky? Is it sunny or overcast? Are you in a chair or on a towel? As you look left to right, what do you see?

Next, think about what you feel. Do you feel the sun warm on your skin? Do you feel a soft cool breeze? Do you feel the sand on your feet, or do you just feel the softness of the chair? Take a moment and sit in that space, noticing all of the sensations of touch around you.

Now listen. What do you hear in this calm place? Do you hear the waves crashing or the birds chirping? Does the wind make a sound as it graces your skin? Or are you listening to music in this place? If so, what type of music is playing?

And finally, what do you taste in this place? Do you taste the ocean's saltiness in the air? Are you sipping on a favorite drink, and can you imagine what it tastes like? Is it sweet, tangy, or bitter?

Take a couple of minutes to take deep, slow breaths as you continue to imagine yourself in this place. (Allow them to take four to five breaths as they relax in this safe, calm place.) *Now you may open your eyes and come back into the room. Look around and notice where you are in this present moment.*

Once people know how to do this exercise, they may do it on their own any time they wish to help them relax or if they are beginning to feel dysregulated. Safeguarders may do this exercise after hearing a trauma narrative as a way to turn their focus away from ruminating on the trauma.

Butterfly hug. The butterfly hug is a tool developed by Lucina Artigas while she was working with survivors of a hurricane in 1997 (Artigas et al., 2000). In this exercise, the survivor crosses their arms over their chest and taps on their clavicle area in a method like a butterfly's wings. This self-hug with tapping can be done while the survivor is thinking about a safe, calm place, and it helps to reinforce positive thoughts and feelings (Jerero et al., 2008).

Talk a survivor through this exercise in this way.

We are going to do an exercise called the butterfly hug. It is a way to self-soothe and regain a state of emotional regulation. Take your arms and wrap them around yourself like you are giving yourself a hug. Your hands should be on your clavicle area or your shoulders. Now, slowly tap your hands left, right, left, right, as you settle into this self-hug. This is called the butterfly hug because the gentle tapping of your hands is similar to a butterfly's wings gently flapping back and forth. Do this for one to two minutes, taking slow breaths as you tap.

SPIRITUAL INTEGRATION

Many times, incorporating a survivor's spiritual beliefs into emotional regulation can be beneficial. However, use caution when adding this spiritual component. First, check in with the survivor to find out about their spiritual beliefs. Second, assess by their responses if spiritual content is a trigger for them. For those who were abused by priests, pastors, and others in the church, spiritual exercises can be associated with the trauma instead of bringing peace. If the survivor reports that they benefit from prayers, Scripture, and religious music, you may incorporate those things into their emotional regulation skill set. Here is one such exercise.

We are now going to combine the breathing exercises that you have learned with Scripture. You may close your eyes if you wish. You may speak this next part verbally or in your mind, whichever you prefer. We will use Psalm 46:10 for this exercise. Now, say, "Be still" as you slowly inhale. And say, "And know that I am God" as you exhale. Do this four to five times as you breathe in and out, repeating the phrases "Be still" and "And know that I am God."

Another variation of this exercise is to say, "I am God's," on the inhale, and "Nothing can separate me," on the exhale. Survivors can also choose to meditate on scriptural truths to help them regulate and return to their window of tolerance, including:

- God is good and faithful and always with us (Isaiah 41:10; 1 Corinthians 1:9).
- Our present suffering does not compare to the glory coming (Romans 8:18; James 1:12).
- God wins against evil (Deuteronomy 20:4; 1 John 5:4).
- We will be rewarded for our perseverance and doing his work (Mark 9:41; Colossians 3:23-24).

CONCLUSION

The impact of trauma is not only psychological but also physiological. Therefore, it is necessary to provide trauma survivors activities that promote regulation of all bodily systems. "*Physiological strategies* address physical needs such as maintaining hydration, blood sugar levels, and nutrition and providing regular physical and sensory activities. These strategies are important for stabilizing moods and behavior and optimizing cognition and self-regulation" (Purvis et al., 2014, p. 357). Wellness for survivors includes this level of physical self-care as well as attention to central nervous system activation. As triggers can cause threat responses to activate with a hyper- or hypoarousal state, the survivor is more vulnerable to emotional dysregulation and potential retraumatization. The activities in this chapter provide specific tools to reduce these activations.

Safeguarders can personally be affected by hearing the trauma narrative of survivors and may experience some of the same states of emotional dysregulation. Safeguarders can learn to self-regulate using these same relaxation and grounding activities and practice staying in their own window of tolerance.

PERSONAL REFLECTION

1. How can you recognize when you are emotionally dysregulated? What are your symptoms and signs?

2. As you consider staying regulated and grounding with a survivor, are there any areas in your own life that could make you vulnerable to dysregulation?

3. What are some signs that you may be experiencing vicarious trauma?

GROUP DISCUSSION

1. How does breathing help in emotional regulation?

2. What are some signs that would indicate survivors are moving out of their window of tolerance? Practice in a group a few of the methods listed to help someone feel more grounded and return to a calmer, more regulated state.

3. How could we incorporate some of these exercises in our work settings?

REFERENCES

American Psychiatric Association. (2022). *Diagnostic and statistical manual of mental disorders* (5th Ed., text rev.). https://doi.org/10.1176/appi.books.9780890425787

Artigas, L., Jarero, I., Mauer, M., López Cano, T., & Alcalá, N. (2000, September). *EMDR and traumatic stress after natural disasters: Integrative treatment protocol and the butterfly hug.* Poster presented at the EMDRIA Conference, Toronto, Ontario, Canada.

de Tord, P., & Bräuninger, I. (2015). Grounding: Theoretical application and practice in dance movement therapy. *The Arts in Psychotherapy, 43*, 16-22. https://doi.org/10.1016/j.aip.2015.02.001

Jerero, I., Artigas, L., Montero, M., & López, L. (2008). The EMDR Integrative Group Treatment Protocol application with child victims of a mass disaster. *Journal of EMDR Practice and Research, 2*(2), 97-105.

Ogden, P., Minton, K., & Pain, C. (2006). *Trauma and the body: A sensorimotor approach to psychotherapy.* Norton.

Purvis, K. B., McKenzie, L. B., Becker Razuri, E., Cross, D. R., & Buckwalter, K. (2014). A trust-based intervention for complex developmental trauma: A case study from a residential treatment center. *Child & Adolescent Social Work Journal, 31*(4), 355-68. https://doi.org/10.1007/s10560-014-0328-6

Sloan, D. M., & Marx, B. P. (2018). Maximizing outcomes associated with expressive writing. *Clinical Psychology: Science and Practice, 25*(1), e12231. https://doi.org/10.1111/cpsp.12231

Urquhart, M., Gardner, F., Frederico, M., & Sanders, R. (2020). Right brain to right brain therapy: How tactile, expressive arts therapy emulates attachment. *Children Australia, 45*(2), 91-96. https://doi.org/10.1017/cha.2020.30

Zimmermann, N., & Mangelsdorf, H. H. (2020). Emotional benefits of brief creative movement and art interventions. *The Arts in Psychotherapy, 70*, 101686. https://doi.org/10.1016/j.aip.2020.101686

15

COMPLEXITIES OF SAFEGUARDING CARE

DR. DANIELLE H. JOHNSON, DR. LISA COMPTON, AND DR. KRISTY M. FORD

THERE ARE MANY COMPLEXITIES to your role as a safeguarder. Awareness of the ethics and boundaries surrounding safeguarding is a protective measure both for the people you help and for your own wellness. Recognizing these as vital practices protects those we serve, creates space between our personal and professional lives, and supports our ability to help others in the future. One key question to consider when providing services is, "What is my role in this situation?" As safeguarders, we are not fully responsible for every aspect of the lives of those we help and should not try to play the role of savior. On the other hand, we can make a significant difference by extending care and compassion and effectively communicating the parameters of what we can offer. This chapter will cover many of these safeguarding challenges, including informed consent, power differentials, dual relationships, professional boundaries, confidentiality, approaching forgiveness, and knowing when and how to refer.

INFORMED CONSENT

Every form of ministerial care should begin with an explanation of the services being provided and the parameters of the relational engagement. The notion of informed consent is consistent with Christian principles of respecting an individual's freedom to choose and operating in full honesty and transparency (Tan, 2022). Before moving forward, explicit or implicit acceptance to proceed with the proposed care plan should be obtained verbally and, ideally, also in writing. Consent must be freely given. This includes the absence of pressure that could compromise the individual's ability to make an independent decision. Safeguarding relationships should prioritize the victim's right to make choices for themselves, even if their decisions go against what others believe to be in their best interest (except in cases of imminent harm).

Providing safeguarding services to minors should only be done with a parent or legal guardian present. Typically, informed consent of the scope of safeguarding services should be clearly communicated by the safeguarder to both the minor and the caregiver. Because they are minors, children and adolescents (with a variable cutoff age) are unable to provide consent for their own treatment, as they are not considered competent to make this decision for themselves. Typically, the primary caregiver is required to provide consent on behalf of the child. By requiring a capable adult to give consent on behalf of the child, the child is then protected from pressure to participate in a program or treatment they do not or cannot understand. Even with parental consent, it remains critical to provide developmentally appropriate explanations of the services provided, making allowances whenever possible for the child to assent to the treatment. As a vulnerable population, children and adolescents are susceptible to coercion, and it is important for helpers to acknowledge the role of power, even if the intentions are aimed sincerely toward helping.

On the other hand, it is also important to be aware of the influence of power dynamics within the family system, particularly if the caretakers are suspected as perpetrators of abuse. These caretakers may be motivated to dismiss the abuse or avoid exposing the details of the abuse, actively denying the child or adolescent access to resources for help. If this is the case, it is important for helpers to know the laws that protect children's rights for safety and utilize the services of governmental agencies or other organizations to assist with intervening as needed.

The informed consent is an opportunity to discuss at the onset of the helping relationship what they can expect from you in your role as the helper. Topics may include who you will share information with, how often you will meet, how to contact you or another designated person in an emergency, and what your part may be if there is an investigation into the abuse claims. This is also a great opportunity to see if they have any questions about the care or specific needs they would like you to address. Ensuring informed consent in safeguarding relationships is not merely a procedural formality but an expression of respect for the autonomy and dignity of those we seek to serve.

WORKING WITHIN POWER DIFFERENTIALS

The next challenge in safeguarding is awareness and consideration of power in the safeguarding relationship. Power differentials are inherent within faith communities (Droogers, 2010). Accordingly, individuals in positions of trust and authority, such as spiritual mentors, must recognize their influential role and exercise responsibility when defining boundaries. When trauma victims seek the help of a safeguarder, they are placing themselves in a position of significant vulnerability. Safeguarders should be aware of their inherent power when performing their role, both with child and adult victims. It is the safeguarder's responsibility to steward this power faithfully. Not only is there a potential power differential between adult safeguarders and children, but there is also a differential with adult survivors due to the vulnerability around their sharing the intimate details of their lives and painful experiences. Because the safeguarder holds significant power and influence in their relationships with trauma survivors, it is their responsibility to monitor the relationship and maintain appropriate boundaries to promote the health and safety of the victim.

DUAL RELATIONSHIPS

Another challenge to safeguarding relationships is the occurrence of dual relationships, or the overlap between roles the safeguarder and survivor may have with each other. In religious settings, dual relationships are often unavoidable. For example, a safeguarder may attend the same church or be a neighbor to the individual they are helping in their safeguarding role. Dual roles, such as balancing a friendship and a professional helping relationship with the same person, present benefits and risks. Dual relationships can be beneficial in breaking down barriers for those seeking help, offering a familiar and comforting presence during their recovery. However, these dual relationships can challenge safeguarders to uphold distance and objectivity, which are necessary for effective trauma care.

Juggling multiple roles with a person can lead to role confusion and burnout and can potentially cause conflicting feelings when reporting abuse. For example, if a safeguarder reported abuse and the perpetrator was a friend of their family in the community, the report may lead to fallout for the safeguarder's family members in their social circles. These multiple roles can complicate or enhance the dynamics and expectations within their relationship. When possible, a team approach to safeguarding can not only help bear the emotional burdens of trauma work but also avoid dual relationships by providing alternative safeguarders when someone has a conflict of interest or an existing relationship. To mitigate dual relationship risks, safeguarders should establish and maintain clear boundaries.

PROFESSIONAL BOUNDARIES

Relational boundaries. Boundaries are the limits between two people that define their interactions to promote healthy relationships and self-care (Cloud & Townsend, 2017). We have already covered some important boundaries, such as transparency about the nature of the safeguarding services through informed consent and careful management of power differentials. Boundaries are a crucial way to promote safety in relationships. It should go without saying that safeguarders should not enter into any physical or romantic relationship with the individuals they are helping. This would violate both the sanctity and safety of safeguarding. The potential for romantic feelings to develop in either the safeguarder or the helper is increased by the private nature of the information shared and the empathetic feelings expressed. It is *our* responsibility to protect against this through taking preventive steps. The first step is safeguarder self-awareness of our own thoughts/feelings, trauma, impulse control, sexuality, and even the potential of arousal to trauma stories. The next step is supervision from a trusted professional colleague. The final step is to ensure the survivor is safe and to refer them to another safeguarder if necessary.

Another relational challenge occurs when the perpetrator is someone the safeguarder thinks highly of, respects, or even loves as a brother or colleague or is known as a "good person" in the community. The cognitive dissonance of how someone can act so kindly in some areas of their lives and then act abusively in others is overwhelming and confusing. This is even more complicated when the perpetrator is a spiritual leader. There may be fears for the safeguarder of being viewed as not "covering" their spiritual leaders' sin and not being compassionate to someone "falling" into temptation. Nevertheless, no matter how kind or respected one is, harming others is never justified or acceptable behavior. If abusers are not stopped, they will more often than not continue to harm and seek out additional victims.

Work vs. personal life boundaries. Safeguarders should also strive to keep their helping roles separate from their personal lives for the sake of their own wellness. We caution you to limit when possible giving out your cell phone number, participating in social media with survivors you are supporting, and meeting in your home to maintain some separation between work and personal life. If you recognize that boundaries have been crossed or situations challenge these principles, it is essential to promptly seek advice from a trusted colleague or supervisor. Safeguarders who understand and manage relational complexities such as boundaries optimize the relationship's health and supportive functioning for all parties involved. Remember to reassure the helpee of your care and commitment to help them when setting boundaries so they do not feel rejected or abandoned.

Case Study: Navigating dual relationships and boundaries

Miguel shared with Carlos that he had been physically and sexually abused by a family friend when he was a child. Miguel is now fifty years old and struggling with his mental health. Carlos is not just Miguel's friend but also a safeguarder within Miguel's church community.

Carlos understands his dual roles with Miguel and explicitly acknowledges their twofold relationship. He reassures Miguel that anything shared during their conversations will remain confidential except for suspicions of child abuse or threats to harm himself or others, in which case he must report this information to local law enforcement or mental health services. Carlos and Miguel set up times when Miguel can meet with Carlos privately to discuss his mental health.

Carlos notices Miguel's increasing distress and potential signs of depression and recommends mental health resources and professional counseling, demonstrating his role as a helper and resource navigator. Since he does not meet any of the criteria for mandatory reporting, he keeps all information private—even the fact that he is meeting with him for current distress. In the church and community settings, Carlos ensures he does not use or share the personal information Miguel shares in their safeguarding relationship. This separation maintains Miguel's privacy and avoids potential discomfort or embarrassment.

Throughout the process, Carlos checks in regularly with Miguel about their relationship, making sure that Miguel feels comfortable managing their dual roles. When uncertain, Carlos seeks advice from a trusted colleague to maintain appropriate boundaries. Carlos carefully navigates power differentials, dual relationships, and boundary setting within their faith community through these actions.

Workload boundaries. Boundaries for heavy workloads are often nonexistent within churches and ministries. There are high expectations from pastoral staff, the congregation, and even our own desire to please God and not appear sluggish or disobedient to take on enormous responsibility for the total care of congregants' psychological, emotional, relational, and spiritual well-being. Although Jesus took time to rest (John 4:6) and encouraged his disciples to do so as well (Mark 6:31), many safeguarders miss this wellness opportunity and will inevitably experience burnout. Burnout not only is harmful to the safeguarder but also may cause impairment in their ability to provide effective and ethical trauma care.

Competency boundaries. Safeguarders should only provide services within the limits of their training and competencies. This means safeguarders should never cross the line into providing mental health counseling unless they are also licensed as mental health professionals. While safeguarders can assist survivors in building the skills covered in previous chapters, such as coping, grounding, relaxation, and containment, they should never attempt psychotherapy to reprocess trauma memories or implement reckless spiritual interventions that attempt to "quickly get rid of trauma" from the victim's mind. These types of interventions have the potential to cause destabilization, further memory suppression, and retraumatization. Instead, safeguarders should function only within their competencies and allow survivors to safely share their stories at their own pace in a safe environment.

CONFIDENTIALITY

In the safeguarding role, individuals will share very intimate details of their lives that they may not have shared with anyone else. Safeguarders must act as a "locked vault" with their private information and not break their sacred trust by sharing it with anyone else, except in the cases of mandatory reporting and harm to themselves or others. Even when breaking confidentiality due to suicidal thoughts, it is vital to only communicate with the individuals or agencies needed to provide intervention. Some people in the church share another's business to elicit prayer for the person they are helping. However, this is still a form of gossip, because it is not their story to tell.

The circumstances around confidentiality should be clearly expressed and strictly followed. For example, if you suspect a child is being abused, this should immediately be reported based on local laws and guidelines. Conversely, if someone shares with you that they had an affair, no known laws require a safeguarder to share this information. The limits of confidentiality, similar to other boundaries, should be discussed at the onset of the safeguarding relationship so that the survivor is aware of these limits. This is an example of how to explain the limits of confidentiality:

> We need to ensure that you and others are not harmed. Therefore, I will keep private everything you share with me but will need to disclose any suspicions of child or vulnerable adult abuse to law enforcement. If there are any threats of harm to yourself or someone else, I must also take steps to ensure safety.

If you work with a supervisor, you should also disclose to the survivor that you may share information with them to receive consultation on the case. However, you and your supervisor should keep confidential all information outside the above-mentioned exceptions. This means you do not share *any* information with your spouse, pastor/priest, friends, or anyone else. Breaking confidentiality is a serious violation of trust.

FORGIVENESS

Forgiveness is an area that many victims of crimes and their loved ones will wrestle with, possibly for years. There are several factors relative to forgiveness that are pertinent to safeguarding:

1. Bringing a perpetrator to justice is not an act of unforgiveness.

2. Although God is capable of not remembering our sins (Isaiah 43:25), we are not capable of forgetting. Trauma stays with us.

3. Forgiveness does not mean reconciliation. No victim should ever be forced to reconcile with a perpetrator. In fact, all efforts should be made to ensure that the victims do not need to interact with the perpetrator again. This may mean having a different office location if providing services to both the victim and perpetrator. Any inconvenience should be put

on the perpetrator, not the victim. For example, a victim should not be forced to leave their school if the perpetrator works there. The perpetrator should be removed (and given due process through the legal system).

The Scripture in Mark 11:25 tells us to forgive others. However, forgiveness will be a process for victims, and safeguarders should never push the speed of this process. Many victims need to experience anger and grief before they can move toward forgiveness.

REFERRAL: KNOWING WHEN, HOW, AND TO WHOM

While faith community members can provide significant emotional and spiritual support to those experiencing trauma, it is essential to recognize when the victim's needs surpass the safeguarder's expertise. This acknowledgment is not just about understanding one's limitations but also demonstrates the virtue of humility. Humility prompts us to recognize our scope, competency, and strengths while honoring the unique training of experts, specialists, and advocates, and acknowledges the diverse giftings and strengths in the body of Christ. A multidisciplinary approach that prioritizes collaboration with mental health providers, pastors, physicians, and law enforcement is required to care for and advocate for trauma survivors.

When necessary, making appropriate referrals and maintaining relationships during and after the referral process becomes paramount to ensuring individuals receive the holistic care they need. These situations include severe depression, hallucinations or delusions, thoughts of suicide or homicide, drug or alcohol addictions, or violent tendencies. The safeguarder should go to local professional mental health services if they are available in their area or through virtual formats. The safeguarder, echoing the virtue of humility demonstrated by Moses in the face of Jethro's counsel (Exodus 18), should recognize that they are not equipped to handle every crisis alone. Just as Moses acknowledged the wisdom of delegating tasks to capable leaders, safeguarders must prioritize the well-being of victims by recommending appropriate professional support when faced with situations that surpass their expertise.

The referral process. The referral process involves identifying the appropriate service or professional to handle the individual's needs, explaining why the referral is necessary, and helping them make the initial contact. Safeguarders may provide the person they're supporting with contact details and location information or accompany them to the first appointment if they both feel comfortable with that plan. It is important to maintain a current list of local resources such as health centers, emergency hotlines, shelters, and mental health response units to have quickly on hand for crisis situations such as someone who is suicidal.

Ethical and practical considerations. Ethical considerations during the referral process include respecting the individual's autonomy and privacy. The safeguarder should ensure the individual understands why the referral is needed and agrees with the selected referral source. For practical considerations, safeguarders should consider factors like the professional's expertise, location, costs, and the individual's personal preferences or needs.

Relationship maintenance during and after referral. Maintaining the relationship with the individual during and after the referral process is crucial. Safeguarders can follow through with the referral process by checking in regularly, offering support during transitions, and continuing to provide spiritual and emotional care within their capacity. After the referral, safeguarders should also respect the boundaries of the professional referral's role and not try to intervene in their work. Knowing when, how, and to whom to refer an individual experiencing trauma is critical for any safeguarder within a faith community. Becoming a referral conduit ensures that individuals receive appropriate care while maintaining their dignity, autonomy, and supportive relationships within the community.

Case Study: Knowing When, How, and to Whom to Refer

Jenn, an active congregation member, has taken on the role of mentoring new church members for several years. Her mentorship is characterized by her resilience and empathetic nature. During a recent mentoring session, her new twenty-five-year-old mentee, Rosa, confided in her about a sexual assault that occurred within the past month. Rosa described symptoms such as sleep disturbances, flashbacks, physical pain, and pronounced distress around certain triggers.

Jenn, though compassionate and well intentioned, recognized that Rosa's traumatic experiences and symptoms surpassed her mentoring capabilities. The depth of Rosa's trauma required a more comprehensive support system than mentorship could offer. Rosa's physical and psychological symptoms pointed to the necessity for a holistic team of professionals, each specializing in their respective fields.

Jenn informed Rosa about the benefits of a multidisciplinary approach while reassuring her that she would continue to provide her safeguarding support. She suggested that Rosa consider a physician evaluation to address her physical symptoms, a consultation with a therapist experienced in trauma counseling, and, if Rosa desired to do so, contact with law enforcement to ensure her safety and a lawyer to explore her legal options. Jenn provided Rosa with a resource list, including a trauma-informed therapy center, a medical clinic familiar with treating assault survivors, the local police department's special victims unit, and a law firm that provides pro bono services.

From the onset of their discussion, Jenn placed a significant emphasis on confidentiality, ensuring that Rosa felt safe and that her personal experiences would remain private. Jenn reiterated to Rosa that she had a right to privacy and that her story would not be shared with others without her explicit consent. Jenn also highlighted the informed consent, ensuring that Rosa felt empowered in her decisions, understood her choices, and knew Jenn's obligations and limitations as a safeguarder. Recognizing the complexities of Rosa's situation and understanding the boundaries of her own expertise, Jenn believed that a specialized, professional approach would best address Rosa's needs. Importantly, she made sure to provide Rosa with resources that also prioritized client confidentiality, always putting Rosa's choice and privacy at the forefront of every step.

As Rosa made the brave choice to seek out various services, Jenn remained a steady source of spiritual support. She continued offering mentorship and confidentiality about the assault and her healing process, ensuring Rosa always felt cared for and safe. Although Rosa began trauma healing with multiple professionals, Jenn exercised the virtue of humility and maintained a clear boundary. She avoided interference in their specialized roles while reminding her of the congregation's unwavering love and support—even if they did know about her trauma.

Jenn demonstrated the importance of recognizing one's limitations and the necessity of a holistic, multidisciplinary approach. Her actions encapsulated the essence of safeguarding, ensuring Rosa felt empowered, informed, and cared for throughout her healing process.

CONCLUSION

The challenges presented in safeguarding can feel frustrating and difficult to navigate. The roles and relationships within your communities can add to the complexities. Thankfully, some tools and guidelines can help steer your decision making. Potential pitfalls can be mitigated by ensuring you stay within your scope of practice, understand power dynamics, and uphold boundaries. The conversation about effective trauma care in the church should be ongoing. As safeguarders, staying committed to continual learning and growth is vital through participation in regular training, consultation with trauma-informed Christian mental health providers, and dedication to your own spiritual health and wellness.

Remember that you only need to play the part God calls you to do, and that he will equip others to do the rest. Paul wrote to the Corinthians, "Praise be to the God and Father of our Lord Jesus Christ, the Father of compassion and the God of all comfort, who comforts us in all our troubles, so that we can comfort those in any trouble with the comfort we ourselves receive from God" (2 Corinthians 1:3-4). This passage underscores a helper's role—as we walk alongside those in pain, we share the comfort we have received from our own experiences of God's faithfulness. Be encouraged and motivated as you serve as the salt and light of trauma prevention and support within your communities, always seeking to preserve and reflect God's love and compassion.

PERSONAL REFLECTION

1. What are some boundaries in your role as safeguarder that you anticipate will be the most challenging?
2. Who do you feel most responsibility toward?
3. What are some strengths you have when setting boundaries?

GROUP DISCUSSION

1. Role play with your group how you would present the limits of confidentiality based on your local laws.
2. Create a list of "hats" you wear as a safeguarder and the hats you would need to avoid in order to not cross professional boundaries. Then, come

up with an action plan to manage a specific type of dual relationship that someone in your group may face in their safeguarding role.

3. Develop a list of local resources with various scenarios and referrals, including helping someone who is suicidal, someone who needs shelter from a violent home, and someone who is dissociating and needing professional mental health services.

REFERENCES

Cloud, H., & Townsend, J. (2017). *Boundaries: When to say yes and how to say no to take control of your life*. Zondervan.

Droogers, A. (2010). Towards the concerned study of religion: Exploring the double power-play disparity. *Religion, 40*(4), 227-38. https://doi.org/10.1016/j.religion.2010.07.001

Jones, S. (2019). *Trauma and grace: Theology in a ruptured world*. Westminster John Knox Press.

Tan, S. Y. (2022). *Counseling and psychotherapy: A Christian perspective* (2nd Ed.). Baker Books.

SECTION VI

CARE FOR SAFEGUARDERS

16

HAZARDS OF PROVIDING CARE

DR. LISA COMPTON AND
TAYLOR PATTERSON

EXTENDING COMPASSION FOR THE PAIN and suffering of others is a divine calling. Jesus modeled care for others through many acts of kindness and mercy, including healing sickness, feeding the hungry, and forgiving sins. However, these acts of service are not just physical motions but also involve emotional engagement. Jesus was "moved with compassion" (Matthew 14:14)[1] as he healed the sick and "wept" (John 11:35) at the news of Lazarus dying despite the fact that he would soon raise Lazarus from the dead. This emotional connection helps us build trusting relationships but can also create vulnerability for us as care providers as we empathize with painful trauma stories.

EMPATHY

Empathy is our emotional connection with the pain of others. *Compassion* is our response to this empathy that creates a drive to do something to heal the pain. Both empathy and compassion are necessary characteristics for safeguarders to have the motivation to engage with suffering and the ability to honor God while effectively caring for the wounded. Our service to others, like Jesus', must be genuine and mirror their emotions: "Rejoice with those who rejoice, and weep with those who weep" (Romans 12:15). As the body of Christ, we do not have the freedom to emotionally detach from suffering. We are called to go to the dark places and to bear witness to stories of grief, loss, and trauma. We have already covered in previous chapters the value of empathetic attunement for trauma survivors. However, our empathetic engagement also

---

[1]Scripture quotations in this chapter, unless otherwise indicated, are from the NKJV.

makes us vulnerable to vicarious trauma symptoms if we do not learn how to steward it correctly. Helping as a vocation requires consistent engagement with suffering—hour after hour, one heartbreaking story after the next. While there is certainly satisfaction that comes from helping others and obeying divine callings, our emotional connections with pain and our cumulative exposure to trauma create a vulnerability to our own potential suffering.

OCCUPATIONAL HAZARDS

The topic of vicarious trauma (or personal distress resulting from exposure to others' trauma stories) for professional helpers has been a research focus in the mental health field over the last several decades. There are many terms in the literature related to vicarious trauma and some overlap between them. *Burnout* (Freudenberger, 1986) describes the emotional exhaustion and stress reactions primarily from work environment factors such as a difficult supervisor, heavy caseload, long hours, lack of sufficient resources, and other variables that contribute to cumulative work stress and reduced work satisfaction. *Compassion fatigue* (Figley, 2002), or secondary traumatic stress, refers to a professional helper experiencing posttraumatic stress symptoms similar to those experienced by the trauma victims themselves. These can include intrusive thoughts like nightmares and/or flashbacks of trauma images and avoidance of people, places, things, and/or memories associated with the trauma. Helpers, like trauma survivors, can experience hypervigilance, rage, sleep disturbance, difficulty concentrating, and isolation from others. *Absorption vulnerability* (Compton & Patterson, 2024) is the newest term in vicarious trauma literature and describes the risk of professional helpers "absorbing" or being personally impacted by the trauma of the people they help. Absorption vulnerability will be discussed in greater depth later in this chapter.

Changes to beliefs and world assumptions. Exposure to trauma changes the way we think and perceive the world. I (Lisa) can vividly remember coming home from work one night after several years of counseling and screaming at the top of my lungs (thankfully, no one else was home at the time), "Has everyone on this planet been sexually abused?!" Safeguarders and mental health workers hear a disproportional number of horrible reports about the world we live in. According to world assumptions theory, exposure to trauma can shatter the previously held beliefs we have about the fairness and predictability of the world, perceptions of safety, views of the goodness of other people, and the meaningfulness of life itself (Janoff-Bulman, 1992). Providing safeguarding care can negatively impact our thoughts and distort the way we view the world, resulting in *vicarious traumatization* (Pearlman and Saakvitne, 1995). These changes can manifest as a negative outlook on life, mistrust, fear, pessimism, cynicism, helplessness, and hopelessness.

Existential crises and impact on faith. The potential impact of indirect trauma exposure on safeguarders is not only cognitive but also spiritual. Safeguarders may experience existential crises and struggle with how a loving God can allow his people so much suffering. We may question Scriptures that promise safety and protection. Our sense of justice may feel shattered, particularly when the victim is a child. When the perpetrator is someone with a position of authority in the church and is supposed to represent the character of God to the people, we may feel disillusionment, anger, and disgust that can taint our faith. These feelings that arise in us as safeguarders often mirror those of trauma victims. We can feel betrayed by people who are supposed to lead, protect, and serve as shepherds of the flock. We can feel hardened toward the suffering of others, the goodness of God, and the pleasures of life. The embodied, empathetic care for the suffering takes us a step too far when we begin to display similar symptoms of those who have been wounded.

Other vicarious trauma symptoms. Hearing stories about the reality of trauma within the church and the awareness of such atrocities can cause a variety of symptoms for safeguarders. These symptoms may develop gradually over long periods of time or come on suddenly, manifesting themselves in our bodies, minds, emotions, and relationships with others and God. These symptoms can show up in our physical bodies through headaches, digestion issues, muscle tension, sexual difficulty, and sleep problems. Our thoughts and minds may feel burdened by the belief that we are powerless, flashbacks of trauma stories, and difficulty separating our work and personal life. Emotionally, we may feel intense rage, heavy guilt, overwhelming sadness, anxious or on edge, and detached numbness. These reactions may cause dysfunction in other areas of our lives. We might isolate ourselves from close relationships or feel like we're constantly in conflict with those we love. We may experience increased fear causing us to restrict our normal behaviors. For example, after working with many abuse survivors, I became overprotective with my own children and did not want them to go to sleepovers or have babysitters for a period of time. Even our spiritual life can become affected by experiencing anger toward God, doubts about his goodness, loss of meaning, and avoidance of the religious activities we once found fulfilling. It is crucial to explore our personal reactions with curiosity and self-compassion.

A few months ago, I received a cortisone shot in my foot to reduce the pain from a pinched nerve. The shot worked so well that I decided to do a high-impact workout the following week. However, my foot still had an injury despite the fact that I did not feel the pain, and quickly returning to intensive exercise caused me to break a bone in that foot. The Lord reminded me in my prayer time that pain is an important indicator of an injury that requires our attention. When numbing the pain, there is less motivation to attend to the initial injury. Dr. Kenyon Knapp (2023) states that "symptoms in our body notify us that something is wrong and needs to be changed" (p. 2). Pain—whether it is a physical tightness in our chest or feelings of dread about our safeguarding role—is a red flag indicating the need to stop and attend to our well-being.

Here are a few questions to consider when reflecting on how your work with trauma has impacted you (Compton & Schoeneberg, 2021):

- Do I see danger, evil, and a lack of safety everywhere?
- Am I withdrawing from my relationships?
- Do I frequently think about the trauma stories of the people I am helping when I am not at work?
- Am I often angry and irritable?
- Do I often feel powerless, hopeless, or helpless?

While not all safeguarders will experience these symptoms, it is important to be aware of the potential for these reactions and continue to self-monitor.

ABSORPTION VULNERABILITY

As mentioned previously, absorption vulnerability (AV) is the individual risk of being negatively impacted by indirect exposure to trauma. There are many factors that can increase this risk, such as a lack of support system at work or at home, heavy caseloads, long working hours, and lack of trauma-informed training and supervision. Three of the most significant risk factors we will examine are (1) the indirect trauma exposure itself, (2) a personal history of trauma, and (3) relationship triggers from family of origin.

Traumatic indirect exposure. It is normal to respond to horrific stories of trauma with strong emotional reactions. If we were not angered and repulsed by hearing a story of a person using their spiritual authority to abuse a child or vulnerable adult, we would not have a heart after God and certainly should not be in the protective role of safeguarder. These short-term reactions are normal and common as we empathetically engage with trauma victims and experience sorrow for their pain. However, absorbing the pain of trauma victims as if it were our own pain or that of our loved ones leads to personal distress and impairment that can affect our health, our relationships, and our ability to provide effective, long-term safeguarding services. If we allow our empathetic engagement with the suffering of others to be experienced as a direct hit, as if the trauma happened to ourselves or to the people in our inner circle, our threat response system will engage as if we are in present danger. Although safeguarders are called to empathize and extend compassion for others' pain, we are not called nor capable of carrying all that suffering and taking every tragedy as a direct hit to our hearts. Instead, we should extend compassion with a degree of therapeutic distancing to provide empathy without personal threat activation. Our longevity in the helping role is significantly dependent on our ability to care for our own well-being and to be aware of our trauma absorption levels.

Personal trauma history. Having our own history of personal trauma, particularly during childhood years, can also increase our absorption risk. Experiencing trauma does not disqualify us from safeguarding work and can even be an asset in allowing us to understand and connect with similar pain. Issues can arise, however, when our central nervous system reacts to aspects of stories we hear when helping others that trigger our trauma memories, especially memories or experiences that have not been processed through counseling or other means. God divinely designed our bodies to promote survival, and he created our minds and bodies with built-in mechanisms to attempt to keep us safe at signs of danger. As we mentioned in previous chapters, when our brain detects danger in our environment, an alarm (our amygdala) sounds in our brain which creates a response throughout our body to prepare to deal with that threat. Our brains subconsciously select a response such as fight, flight, or freeze and release stress hormones to prepare the body to complete these actions. Hormones such as cortisol and adrenaline rush through the body, increasing heart and breathing rates and slowing functions not immediately necessary for survival, such as digestion and sexual function.

For example, I (Taylor) was riding in the passenger seat of a car while my husband was driving seventy-five miles per hour on the interstate. Suddenly, we saw brake lights in front of us and cars swerving into the adjacent lane. As the cars in front of us pulled aside, we saw a large, white truck barreling toward us in the opposite direction of traffic. My husband had a split second to react, his choice determining whether we lived or died. In an instant, his brain directed all its resources to assessing the threat and protecting us. He skillfully swerved into the adjacent lane, avoiding the truck speeding toward us and the semi-trailer to our right. As we processed the threat, our hearts were racing, aware of how close we were to a life-threatening car accident. These reactions are very useful in the face of real danger. However, our brains do not necessarily differentiate between present danger and triggered memories of past traumas. If the event had not been sufficiently processed, my husband could feel the same kind of amygdala-driven fight, flight, or freeze response every time he drove on an interstate, which could prevent him from wanting to drive at all.

A safeguarder may be sitting with a trauma victim and hearing his story of sexual abuse may trigger his own memories of childhood abuse. He may experience heart pounding and shortness of breath as well as an upset stomach. It is possible that these reactions could occur without explicit thoughts of his own abuse or awareness of the connection to past events. These physiological reactions may significantly interfere with his own health and ability to provide care if he does not recognize what is happening and take action to reduce that response (more on intervention and prevention in the next chapter).

Relationship triggers. The relationships we had during childhood also impact our absorption vulnerability. We have learned in this text that attachment, or the degree to which our primary caregivers bonded with us and met our needs during our early years of life, is one of the most significant influences on our ability to emotionally regulate later in life. Our attachment figures provide a template in our minds for the expectations we can have from our external world, a model for self-soothing, and a sense of safety and security. Insecure attachment can lead to increased absorption of traumatic stress and reduced ability to emotionally regulate in the presence of dysregulated trauma victims.

Our other relationships in childhood and adulthood, such as siblings, extended family, and friends, can also impact our relationship triggers both positively and negatively. Negatively, damage from relationships with others can increase relationship triggers, leading to higher levels of indirect trauma absorption.

Relationship triggers do not necessarily require physical harm or abuse. For example, a woman's parents may have felt very uncomfortable with the feeling of sadness. So, every time she cried as a child, her parents would scold her or withdraw from her, leaving her to manage her sadness by herself. As an adult, she may feel severe discomfort when listening to a trauma survivor who is expressing their deeply felt grief over their abuse. She was never taught how to sit with and tolerate the feeling of sadness. Without intervention, that discomfort can build up over time, magnifying her absorption of the trauma exposure.

Though family-of-origin dynamics play a significant role in our template for relationships, it is possible to compensate for attachment deficits through developing healthy relationships outside the family, a term known as *earned-secure attachment*. Forming close relationships with people who can serve as surrogate attachment figures, such as teachers, counselors, and safeguarders, can provide safe, secure, and nurturing connections that promote healing from insecure attachment and also reduce relationship triggers. This is one of the many reasons that abuse from mentors and leaders is so devastating. They have the potential to provide earned-secure attachment for those who have been wounded or have lacked care; however, their abusive behaviors compound pain instead of ministering healing.

INVOLVEMENT EXTREMES IN TRAUMA CARE

Avoidance. Family-of-origin issues can cause a desire to run away from those who are in need. For example, if someone was parentified, or forced into a responsible role for other family members as a child, the idea of caring for others may triggers feelings of overwhelm and anxiety. For these individuals, helping may be subconsciously associated with functioning in a role beyond their abilities and a lack of being able to attend to their own needs. In these cases, they may engage avoidant behaviors and subconsciously steer clear of people who are struggling or appear "needy." While avoidance and underinvolvement in helping occur for many people, for those drawn to the ministry, overinvolvement without appropriate boundaries is a much more common occurrence.

Overinvolvement. While safeguarding inherently requires personal involvement with the lives of trauma victims, there is also the potential for overinvolvement, which is another trauma absorption vulnerability risk. There are two main reasons that safeguarders become overinvolved with the individuals they are trying to help. The first cause for overinvolvement is a potential "savior complex" where we believe our role is to rescue trauma victims. While there is merit in our aims to protect victims from further harm, ensure action is taken against perpetrators, provide empathy and comfort for their pain, pray for them, and help them in their healing journey, we must continue to recognize that God is their sustainer and healer. He is the one who will "redeem their life from oppression and violence; and precious shall be their blood in His sight" (Psalm 72:14). Trauma may cause us to doubt whether God sees their pain and will act on their behalf. This distorted thinking elevates our role beyond what we can achieve or sustain in the lives of others and leads to poor boundaries and burnout. It represents a lack of faith in who God is and confusion in our own level of responsibility for others. It is our role as safeguarders to walk alongside trauma victims as one part of their healing journey and trust God that he is faithful to complete the work he has begun in their lives (Philippians 1:6) and bring their healing to completion.

The second cause for overinvolvement involves wounds from our past. We may have grown up in a family where our role was to ignore our own needs in order to meet the needs of others (such as being expected to meet the emotional needs of our parents or parent younger siblings). We may receive praise and validation for selfless giving to others and feel our value comes from being needed. Our past fawn trauma responses and relational triggers may motivate our overinvolvement. Many of us seek out the helper role of safeguarder due to our personal experiences. We may subconsciously continue old patterns of codependency through poor boundaries, enmeshment, and enabling behaviors. Although we are called to serve, our identity and self-worth should come from our who we are in Christ, not from our service.

OUR CAPACITY

As safeguarders, you are not only a valuable resource for others, but you are made in the image of God, valuable in his sight, and worthy of your own protection from injury. As humans, we are limited by capacity. We need rest and nourishment every day and can only give out a finite amount before needing to be filled back up ourselves. The Lord commanded us with the sabbath rest for this exact reason. We need to attend to our own care while we care for others. It is very easy to become overwhelmed by the enormous need to help those who suffer and extend beyond our personal limits to meet those needs. However, we are called to be led by the Holy Spirit, not by needs. Jesus modeled this in Matthew 9 as he gazed upon a crowd of people who were "weary and scattered, like sheep having no shepherd" (Matthew 9:36). In his compassion for the crowd's suffering, Jesus stated, "The harvest truly is plentiful, but the laborers are few. Therefore pray the Lord of the harvest to send out laborers into His harvest" (Matthew 9:37-38). The need was too great for the disciples to meet alone, so rather than instructing them to work tirelessly until they were burned out, he encouraged them to take the need to God in prayer.

The Lord has a specific role for each of us in our service—not to help everyone in every way but as he leads and directs. He also does not want us to bear the weight of other's sorrows: "Cast your burden on the LORD, and He shall sustain you" (Psalm 55:22). Taking sabbath rest and giving him our burdens are not suggestions but divine commands, because he knows our limitations and cares for our well-being.

REWARDS OF CARE

Although there are several hazards to consider with safeguarding work, there are also significant rewards. Compassion satisfaction is the joy and sense of fulfillment that comes from helping others (Stamm, 2002). In addition to the gratification of caring for individuals who suffer, safeguarders can also participate in the same positive aspects of growth and healing that many trauma survivors experience. Traumatic experiences can result in increased resiliency (the ability to bounce back from adversity) and posttraumatic growth (making meaning from experiences and gaining new perspectives and insights from the healing process). Safeguarders can gain vicarious resiliency and vicarious posttraumatic growth from their work with trauma survivors and by witnessing survivors' healing journeys (Hernandez et al., 2007; Tedeshi & Calhoun, 1996). There are also eternal rewards for our work. When the Lord returns, he promised to bring reward with him: "And behold, I am coming quickly, and My reward is with Me, to give to every one according to his work" (Revelation 22:12). When describing the final judgment, Jesus welcomes the compassionate and generous, stating, "Truly, I say to you, as you did it to one of the least of these my brothers, you did it to me" (Matthew 25:40 ESV). Our service to the most vulnerable has the joy and reward of service to Jesus himself.

CONCLUSION

The role of safeguarding is heroic work with both potential hazards and rewards. While we can enjoy the satisfaction of doing the Lord's work and making a difference in the lives of other people, it is also important to be aware of the impact this significant work can have on us personally. As safeguarders, we should seek to understand our own vicarious trauma absorption risk and what our potential triggers may be. The following chapter will explore ways to improve our emotional regulation, self-screen for compassion fatigue, reduce our absorption risk, increase our boundaries, and metabolize already experienced trauma.

PERSONAL REFLECTION

1. Reflect on a time you felt particularly drained or overwhelmed by the emotional demands of your work or relationships. What contributed to those feelings? How did you manage them?

2. Reflect on your personal history. What experiences or relational dynamics do you think could contribute to your absorption vulnerability as you do the work of safeguarding?

3. Do you find yourself more prone to avoidance, overinvolvement, or both? How does this show up in your life?

GROUP DISCUSSION

1. How can you equip your ministry to identify the signs of compassion fatigue or the factors contributing to their absorption vulnerability?

2. What are some ways to decrease community avoidance of trauma issues and increase active participation in trauma care?

3. What are some ways the church has contributed to overinvolvement and diffuse boundaries? What are some ways to change this culture to a healthier one?

REFERENCES

Compton, L., & Patterson, T. (2024, March 14). Absorption vulnerability: A new look at compassion fatigue. *Traumatology*. Advance online publication. https://dx.doi.org/10.1037/trm0000503

Compton, L., & Schoeneberg, C. (2021). *Preparing for trauma work in clinical mental health: A workbook to enhance self-awareness and promote safe, competent practice.* Routledge.

Figley, C. R. (2002). *Treating compassion fatigue.* Routledge.

Freudenberger, H. J. (1986). The issues of staff burnout in therapeutic communities. *Journal of Psychoactive Drugs, 18*(3), 247-51. https://doi.org/10.1080/02791072.1986.10472354

Hernandez, P., Gangsei, D., & Engstrom, D. (2007). Vicarious resilience: A new concept in work with those who survive trauma. *Family Process, 46,* 229-41. doi:10.1111/j.1545-5300.2007.00206.x

Janoff-Bulman, R. (1992). *Shattered assumptions.* Free Press.

Knapp, K. (2023). *Healthy depression.* Wipf & Stock.

Pearlman, L. A., & Saakvitne, K. W. (1995). *Trauma and the therapist: Countertransference and vicarious traumatization in psychotherapy with incest survivors.* Norton.

Stamm, B. H. (2002). Measuring compassion satisfaction as well as fatigue: Developmental history of the compassion satisfaction and fatigue scale. In C. R. Figley (Ed.), *Treating compassion fatigue* (pp. 107-22). Routledge.

Tedeschi, R. G., & Calhoun, L. G. (1996). The posttraumatic growth inventory: Measuring the positive legacy of trauma. *Journal of Traumatic Stress, 9,* 455-71. doi:10.1002/jts.2490090305

17

STRENGTHENING THE SAFEGUARDER

TAYLOR PATTERSON AND
DR. LISA COMPTON

CARLOS GREW UP IN A SMALL TOWN where both his parents had to work two jobs to provide for him and his four siblings. He loved spending time at their local church and was very close with one of the priests whom he had known since he was an infant. This priest mentored him through his adolescent years. Carlos considered him a surrogate family member until the day the news broke that this priest had molested several other boys at their parish. Carlos wondered how he had escaped such a fate as those other boys and could not believe that the priest had been capable of both kindness toward him and evil toward others. That night, Carlos felt a strong calling from God to try to prevent abuse from happening again within his community. After a few years of pursuing other careers, including working at a restaurant and the local bank, Carlos answered this calling and was hired as a safeguarder at a parish an hour from his hometown.

Carlos found his safeguarding profession very fulfilling. He enjoyed meeting with individuals and their families and being a listening ear for those who were hurting. Carlos worked hard at administrative duties as well. He developed church policies and procedures that were adopted not only in his parish but in other surrounding ones as well. During that time, he fell in love with a woman named Taley, and they were married in their local church with many of the people he had helped in attendance at the wedding. Several years passed and Carlos and Taley welcomed their first child, a baby boy named Leo. As Leo became a toddler, Carlos began having nightmares about Leo being molested by a priest. While Carlos sat with parishioners who shared their stories of trauma and abuse, his mind often wandered to fears of a similar scenario happening to Leo. He would not allow Leo to attend children's ministry at church nor allow anyone to watch him except Taley. This created tension between him and Taley since she did not share these same concerns and wanted her son to have healthy socialization with others.

Carlos began to have several health issues. He fell asleep quickly from exhaustion but then woke up during the night and had difficulty falling back asleep. He also experienced digestive issues and had to switch to a very restricted diet. Taley told him that he was more irritable than usual, and she also noticed that he no longer took pleasure in going to church picnics, which he used to enjoy. Taley pleaded with Carlos to talk to his supervisor about what he was experiencing. With some reluctance, Carlos agreed and met with his supervisor, John, the following week.

John helped Carlos make sense of the feelings he was experiencing. They discussed concepts such as vicarious trauma and compassion fatigue and the fact that many people in helping vocations deal with compassion fatigue at some point in their careers. Carlos was able to share the story about the priest who had molested some of his friends and the conflicting feelings he had when he thought about that man. John listened empathetically and shared some of his own experiences that made his role as safeguarder more challenging. John helped Carlos assess his absorption vulnerability and how he could reduce this risk. They met together for the next few months to build skills to manage the impact of safeguarding work.

As Carlos discovered, developing skills to build resilience and experience growth amid trauma exposure is an essential component of preparing for the work of safeguarding. It is emotional and mental labor to be empathically attuned to trauma survivors, make ethical decisions, and advocate within our communities. To do this labor faithfully and sustainably, we must be aware of our needs through self-assessment, steward our personal limits, manage our relational triggers, and practice emotion regulation skills.

SELF-ASSESSMENT

Arousal self-screening. God created us with emotions that function as responses to the world around us. Jesus displayed many emotions, as described in the Gospels, including sorrow and anger. Experiencing and processing our emotions is necessary for our health and wellness; however, allowing emotions to overtake us or dictate our behaviors can be detrimental. The apostle Paul wrote, "Be angry, and do not sin" (Ephesians 4:26 NKJV). For example, hearing the painful stories of victims may cause us to rightly feel horror and rage, but impulsively acting on these emotions and seeking to physically harm the perpetrator ourselves would circumvent the justice system and could result in our own imprisonment. Ignoring or suppressing these feelings could also lead to our own distress and mental health issues. In this section, we will cover the necessary skills to recognize our own physiological cues of distress so that we can identify when and how to self-regulate and avoid causing harm to ourselves or others.

We have explored the concepts of hyperarousal, hypoarousal, and the window of tolerance in previous chapters as they relate to the experience of trauma survivors. However, these same processes occur in safeguarders in response to our work. When our brains perceive a threat in the environment, whether there is a real, current danger or our systems are responding to perceived threats from secondary trauma exposure or issues from our past experiences, physiological responses occur in our bodies. The first step in managing these reactions is to recognize when our fear responses are triggered and to maintain a keen awareness of our internal states.

The term *window of tolerance* (WOT) describes the optimal zone of emotional arousal for us as safeguarders as well, avoiding the extreme states of both hyper- and hypoarousal (Larsen & Stanley, 2021). In other words, it is our state of equilibrium between these two extreme emotional states where our threat response activation is low and higher-order thinking parts of the brain are accessible. Staying within the WOT allows us to feel our emotions from safeguarding while maintaining a state of relative calm and balance in our minds and bodies. We will explore several quick self-screening tools to assess our emotional states before moving on to intervention strategies.

Window of tolerance color zone. The WOT color zone (Compton & Patterson, 2023) is a tool to recognize whether we are in the optimal arousal zone (represented by the color green), the hyperarousal zone (represented by the color red), or the hypoarousal zone (represented by the color gray). The green zone indicates that we have a "green light" to proceed forward with our daily activities knowing that we are within the realm of equilibrium. The red zone indicates that we need to stop and engage in calming activities to cool off the fire of our emotional intensity. The gray zone indicates that our systems are shut down and that we need to induce movement and healthy activities to become reenergized.

Body scan. The body scan is a form of interoception, or the ability to recognize and attune to physiological sensations, that helps us practice conscious awareness of our physiological cues and bodily sensations. Starting with your head, pay attention to each part of your body, noticing areas that may feel tense, numb, or painful. As you move down your body, notice if you have tight muscles in your back, a heavy feeling in your chest, or an upset stomach. Awareness of these cues can help you notice when you are feeling distressed and can equip you to relax areas of tension intentionally.

SUDS. The subjective units of distress scale (SUDS) is a self-report tool often used in healthcare settings to assist patients in considering and quantifying their levels of physical pain. This measure can also be useful in reflecting on levels of emotional distress. Consider your current distress level on a zero to ten scale, with zero representing no distress at all up to ten representing very high levels of anxiety, depression, panic, or other distressful emotions.

SELF-CARE AS STEWARDSHIP

There is a popular term in the helping professions, *self-care*, that refers to strategies employed by helpers to recuperate from or sustain their work. This can often be oversimplified and misunderstood as self-indulgence, suggesting that the only way to recuperate from a challenging day is to hide away alone, take a bubble bath, and drink a glass of wine. While we are not against bubble baths, there are more robust perspectives on the concept of self-care. In Christian circles, self-care has sometimes been reframed in the language of "stewardship" (Spurlock, 2021). This perspective highlights that God intentionally granted us limited resources (such as time, energy, talent, emotional capacity, physical abilities, and finances) that we are entrusted to invest and steward faithfully. Each of us has different capacities in these areas, which are fluid and change in and out of season. This is one reason why self-assessment is a crucial first step to self-care. Managing the areas within our God-ordained limits helps us to flourish as it recognizes God's design as *good*. These habits alone are insufficient to manage the unique consequences of secondary trauma exposure (Rivera-Kloeppel & Mendenhall, 2023). However, they are important for our well-being as people made in the image of God, and it can cause us significant harm to ignore them.

Stewarding your mind. Empathic engagement is emotional and mental labor, much like running and lifting are physical labor. When you practice the attunement and reflective listening skills described in this text, the cognitive and emotional "muscles" you exercise can become exhausted. Recovery from this work requires intentional mental rest. Intentional rest from the highly attuned, cognitively demanding work of safeguarding looks different for everyone, but it typically requires thoughtful application of Paul's exhortation in Philippians 4:8: "Finally, brothers, whatever is true, whatever is honorable, whatever is just, whatever is pure, whatever is lovely, whatever is commendable, if there is any excellence, if there is anything worthy of praise, think about these things."[1]

Strategy: Monitor your unnecessary trauma exposure. Be discerning about the entertainment you consume. Television shows, podcasts, movies, and books can have disturbing scenes that trigger thoughts of one's own trauma or the trauma of survivors they have encountered. I (Taylor) worked for several years with survivors of domestic violence, sexual assault, and human trafficking. While working with this population, I realized I had to be diligent about limiting my trauma exposure at home. Every scene in a television show that depicted trauma sparked my attuned, problem-solving mind and reminded me of survivors' stories. I was emotionally and mentally exhausted, and every reminder of trauma at home disrupted my mind's ability to rest. Monitoring your unnecessary trauma exposure honors the truth that you were not designed to engage with tragedy twenty-four hours a day. These limits help you create space for rest, delight, playfulness, and connection with others.

Stewarding your body. Abraham Heschel (1951) writes, "If you work with your hands, Sabbath with your mind; if you work with your mind, Sabbath with your hands." An important aspect of resting from the emotional and mental labor of safeguarding is attuning to our physical experience and caring well for our bodies. Your emotional response to survivors' stories is experienced in your body. For example, when you feel angry over a perpetrator's abuse of power, you may feel heat rise in your face. When you feel anxious about how you will respond to survivors' difficult questions about the character of God, you may notice your chest get tight. It is necessary to process these emotions with our mind by acknowledging and naming them, but it is equally necessary to engage our bodies. Reading a good book may not feel rejuvenating, as it is "Sabbath with your mind." Instead, you may find it more

---

[1]Scripture quotations in this chapter, unless otherwise noted, are in the ESV.

effective to practice hobbies that are tactile, like knitting, cooking, gardening, or woodworking. Psalm 103:14 reminds us that God "knows our frame; he remembers that we are dust." Eating nourishing foods, prioritizing restful sleep, and exercising our muscles help us to remember that we are merely humans called to steward a body with limits.

Stewarding your time. God did not make you infinite. He has provided each of us twenty-four-hour days that he himself has numbered. Therefore, our time is a limited resource that also must be stewarded. People's needs will extend beyond your hours in a day, which means you will *have* to say no to some requests no matter what. So, it is not a question of whether or not you refuse a request, but rather when and how you choose to say no. This can have many challenges, as there may be real or perceived negative consequences of not complying with every request, especially requests from spiritual leaders or others in positions of authority.

There are many situations where we simply must say no out of care for the places God has called us to be faithful. This is why it is crucial to serve alongside others on a team. When we know there is someone else to call or fill in the gap when we need to tap out, we can feel much freer to pull back and take a break. However, saying no may not always be a feasible option for a variety of reasons, such as significant personal consequences, lack of resources, or cultural expectations. In these instances, it is helpful to reframe all-or-nothing thinking that requires you to accomplish all aspects of the task by yourself immediately. Instead, it may be wise to consider what accommodations would alleviate the burden of the task or responsibility. For example, it may be challenging to do what is being asked in the requested time frame because of other time-sensitive responsibilities. In this case, a person could request more time, find someone else to delegate some of the tasks to, or break the responsibility into smaller parts.

Stewarding your relationships. We were designed by God to be in relationship with him and others. A study of several "highly resilient" trauma counselors found they all were grounded in a "strong web of vibrant connectedness" (Hou & Skovholt, 2020). The importance of connection does not only apply to mental health workers but is essential to anyone in a helping role. Hou and Skovholt (2020) described this connectedness as the connection to oneself (or self-awareness), loved ones, colleagues, and values. We have already highlighted the importance of self-awareness to help sustain you in the work of safeguarding. It is equally important to maintain healthy, meaningful relationships with your friends and family. Too many helpers have devoted their lives to serving others while neglecting their relationships with those closest to them.

Additionally, it is wise to build relationships with colleagues, or other people who are committed to the work of safeguarding. In a study examining counselors' experiences of grief following a client's suicide, the authors highlighted the impact of "confidential grief," or grief that a helper experiences in the loss of someone whose identity and circumstances are protected by confidentiality (Salpietro et al., 2023). The confidentiality restraints with many of our cases limits our ability to share our thoughts and feelings about our day the way we normally would with family and friends. However, it is possible to discuss our reactions with trusted colleagues who understand the nature of our safeguarding work without sharing the personal details or identifying information about their case. While you must care well for the privacy of trauma survivors, you will experience your own grief over their suffering, feelings of betrayal if you knew the perpetrator, and potential doubts about the character of God. These feelings cannot be processed alone. Connection to other safeguarders and a well-trained counselor can help you manage this grief.

Lastly, we must steward our relationship with God. Exposure to suffering challenges our perception of God's character and his church. We do not need to turn away from or stuff down our questions that arise from suffering. Scripture is filled with faithful people of God crying out to him, begging for answers to their own or others' suffering. It is an act of faith to trust God with the fullness of our anger, doubt, and grief. Neff and McMinn (2020) connect this to biblical lament, highlighting four distinct characteristics of lament: (1) experiencing suffering, (2) crying out to God, (3) exclaiming the world is not as it should be and asking God to make things right, and (4) trusting that God hears and is moved by our lament. They describe this lament as an act of faith, writing, "Our divine protest can be an indication of our attachment and the trust we experience with God. Protest is birthed in the hope that we believe God to hear and be impacted by us" (Neff & McMinn, 2020, p. 55). Stewarding our relationship with God does not mean we do not wrestle with him; in fact, our wrestling can be evidence of our intimacy with him.

MANAGING RELATIONAL TRIGGERS

We have explored how attachment to caregivers in infancy and childhood forms the relational templates through which people view and engage in connection with others and applied this to the way you experience the "occupational hazards" of the work of safeguarding. You as the safeguarder have a lens through which you view relationships with others, triggers based on past wounding, and learned ways of managing unmet needs and emotional dysregulation that will inevitably impact how you engage in this work. How do we notice and address this? Here are a few questions that may help guide your reflection:

- When do I find myself reacting out of proportion to what is happening in the present moment?
- What thoughts, feelings, and physical sensations do I experience in those out-of-proportion reactions?
- When I reflect on those thoughts/feelings/physical sensations, when do I remember experiencing something similar in the past?

While in my graduate program, I (Taylor) noticed myself experiencing more intense exhaustion and dysregulation after meeting with married couples than my colleagues did. I discussed this with my supervisor, telling him that I worried I just was not cut out for the work of counseling. He encouraged me to slow down, take a few deep breaths, and reflect on my emotional experience while working with couples. As I reflected, I realized I often felt "trapped" and had a tight feeling in my chest, fueled by fears that it was impossible for me to make both people in the room happy. I felt obligated to be perfectly attuned to two individuals who needed or wanted opposite responses from me simultaneously. My supervisor encouraged me to express curiosity about my feeling of responsibility and fear of misattuning. This curiosity allowed me to identify connections to the roles I played in my own family of origin and how similar fears and coping mechanisms were being triggered in my interactions with couples. Noticing this enabled me to identify the feelings I was experiencing with couples, practice strategies in the moment to soothe my dysregulation, and pursue counseling to process my triggers more thoroughly. The questions above can help you foster a similar curiosity and identify unhealed wounds to be explored in your own counseling.

MANAGING EMPATHY

Growing in your ability to endure secondary trauma exposure is not only the way you *recuperate* from the exposure but also the way in which you *engage* with the exposure. We have explored the importance of empathic attunement to trauma survivors, but there is some fear that experiencing this kind of emotional connection with people who have suffered will cause us harm. The research is split on this. Some studies argue that empathy is correlated with compassion fatigue, while others claim it is correlated with compassion satisfaction (Hansen et al., 2018). This has led to further exploration of our understanding of empathy. Is all empathy created equal? Or are there certain ways we can identify and connect with the suffering of others that promote healing relationships while protecting the heart of the listener from long-term impacts?

Zhang and colleagues (2021) explore the construct of empathy, specifically distinguishing between self- and others-oriented empathy. Self-oriented empathy (not to be confused with the concept of self-compassion, which is a good thing) is experiencing another's suffering as a "direct hit," or as if their suffering were happening to you or someone you love. This kind of empathy has a positive correlation with compassion fatigue (Zhang et al., 2021). This makes sense. Of course it would be unsustainable to experience every story of abuse as if it were happening to you. But what is the alternative? We are taught that we grow in empathy when we "walk a mile in another's shoes." Others-oriented empathy, or empathic concern, provides us with a feasible alternative to this perspective. Others-oriented empathy includes genuine concern for another's suffering, but there is some measure of emotional distance from that suffering. Zhang and colleagues (2021) describe it as the ability to "understand the suffering belongs to clients/patients rather than caregivers themselves" (p. 3). This type of empathic concern, or the ability to connect with others' suffering without significant personal distress, has been shown to increase a person's ability to build a strong alliance with the one who is suffering (Kim & Han, 2018).

How do we cultivate others-oriented empathy and avoid self-oriented empathy? Researchers have described others-oriented empathy as "compassion in action" that has an affective, cognitive, and active component (Bentley, 2022). The affective component is what we typically think of when we consider empathy; it is the ability to feel *with* someone. But others-oriented empathy allows us to feel their pain and then create a degree of emotional distance so that we are not stuck in that feeling. It uses the affective "feeling *with*" to inform a thoughtful conceptualization of the person's suffering and how to alleviate it. This cognitive component externalizes our felt awareness of another's suffering, allowing us to maintain a thoughtful awareness that their suffering belongs to them and to develop strategies for how to best engage with their story. The last component of others-oriented empathy is action. This is *not* to say that it is wise to dive into problem-solving mode with trauma survivors to try to rescue them from their suffering. Instead, this type of action involves moving toward someone's suffering in a meaningful and beneficial way (Bentley, 2022). This can be as simple as silently praying they would be relieved from their suffering. This triggers the reward circuits in our brain, facilitating an increased sense of compassion satisfaction (Bentley, 2022).

Shortly after coming across this research, I (Taylor) worked with a trauma survivor who had recently been sexually assaulted. As she described her story, I felt *with* her. I thought to myself, *I cannot imagine if that happened to me*. I recognized this thought as self-oriented empathy. Immediately, I took a deep breath in through my nose and out through my mouth to regulate my personal distress and used my emotional experience (affective) to inform my under-standing of her experience (cognitive). This helped me to notice that she might have felt lonely and helpless during her assault. I reflected those feelings back to her using the reflective listening skills described in an earlier chapter (action) and silently prayed that she would feel the Lord's nearness in her suffering and that he would help me to remain grounded as I continued talking with her (action). This small shift, made possible by self-assessment and the use of self-regulation techniques, reduces our risk of absorbing a survivor's pain as our own and enables us to attune to their experience more effectively.

The Emotional Distancing Target (Compton & Patterson, 2024) is a visual-ization exercise allowing us to conceptualize whether we are functioning in healthy others-oriented empathy or crossing boundaries into self-oriented empathy. Picture a target in your mind such as one used for archery. All "arrows of empathy" need to hit somewhere on the target in order to compas-sionately connect with the pain of other people. The bullseye area, however, should be reserved only for "direct hits" or traumatic situations experienced by us or our loved ones. If we take all the arrows as a direct hit, we will inevitably experience compassion fatigue. When you are ruminating on a story that you heard from someone in a safeguarding or other work capacity, consider where the arrow of their story is hitting. If it is not even on the target, you may be avoiding all emotional connection. If it is a direct hit to the bullseye, you may need to create some emotional distance while still maintaining supportive connection with them.

EMOTION REGULATION SKILLS

In recognition of the limits of the self-care model that emphasizes how we *recuperate* from exposure to trauma, Miller and Sprang (2017) developed the Components for Enhancing Clinician Experience and Reducing Trauma model (CE-CERT) that details skills to utilize *during* secondary trauma exposure that can reduce the long-term impact on the helper. Miller (2022) expanded on this model in his book *Reducing Secondary Traumatic Stress: Skills for Sustaining a Career in the Helping Professions*. This model provides a unique and practical roadmap for engaging with secondary trauma exposure that we have adapted to incorporate spiritual disciplines and fit the work of safeguarding. CE-CERT has five components, but we will explore three that are particularly relevant to your work as a safeguarder: (1) experiential engagement, (2) managing rumination, and (3) parasympathetic recovery.

Experiential engagement. Emotions themselves are not dangerous. By design, emotions come and go like waves—rising, strengthening, and eventually settling (Miller & Sprang, 2017). God created us to experience the full range of emotional experiences—from intense joy to intense sorrow. When we suffer a significant loss, our nervous system begs to experience significant grief. Our avoidance of emotions we deem negative, like grief or anger, fosters a multitude of unhelpful coping mechanisms that intensify, rather than reduce, compassion fatigue and secondary traumatic stress. It may seem counterintuitive that leaning into the experience of emotions will actually decrease their intensity in the long term. Miller (2022) addresses this as he writes,

> If you avoid a feeling or experience, those feelings aren't really evaded; they are merely dampened. The energy of the emotion will linger, and the emotion that we were attempting to escape will incubate and actually increase in duration. The anxiety that we add through our avoidance may actually intensify the feelings. (p. 36)

Our willingness to allow our emotions to rise, fall, come, and go as they please opens us up to feel both the fullness of grief *and* the fullness of joy. To numb one is to numb the other.

Strategy: Allow and notice. The strategy of allow and notice is simple in concept but can be incredibly challenging in practice. In order to allow and notice our emotional experience, we must be attuned to our thoughts, feelings, and physical sensations as we engage with trauma survivors and remain regulated enough to make choices about how we respond to the emotion. For example, imagine you are meeting with a trauma survivor who is expressing intense anger at God. She tells you that she believes God must be evil if he sat idly by as he watched her get assaulted repeatedly. If you are choosing to allow and notice your emotional experience, you might notice your chest tighten as you hear her raise her fist to the heavens in anger. You may notice feelings of defensiveness and an urge to protect the character and reputation of God. You might feel your stomach turn in knots as images arise involuntarily of her assault. You feel disgust, rage, confusion, and grief. Allowing and noticing these feelings does *not* mean that you act on them with the trauma survivor. This is not a license to ignore the reflective listening or empathic attunement skills described in earlier chapters. Instead, we are inviting you to simply notice the truth of your experience in the moment, bringing the fullness of your emotional response to God.

Managing rumination. Rumination occurs when we find ourselves unable to shake a specific thought or memory long after the initial wave of emotion has come and gone. Have you ever had trouble sleeping because you were replaying a difficult conversation over and over again? Or had difficulty feeling present with your children because you were repeatedly reviewing your to-do list in your head? Our brain latches on to experiences or thoughts it believes are left undone, hoping that bringing them to the forefront of our minds will help us solve the problem (Miller, 2022). This is helpful when it elicits creative problem-solving or alerts us to potential danger. However, this cognitive replaying does not always lend itself to problem solving, but instead can intensify our distress. There are many problems that are not immediately solvable when we lean into the work of safeguarding. We have to be able to manage our tendency to ruminate so we can be totally present in the aspects of our lives that are rejuvenating, such as time with family and friends, worship, and sleep. Sometimes, shifting into an activity or conversation that requires our full attention, such as interacting with our children about their day at school, helps break us out of the ruminating thoughts. If that does not help, consider the following exercise:

Strategy: Journaling exercise. One of the goals of exercises aimed at reducing rumination is to help turn our wandering mind, which intensifies our distress, into goal-directed thoughts that remind our brain that we are okay and it can release its grip on the unsolved problems. When you notice ruminating thoughts, consider practicing the following journaling exercise to release the unfinished pieces to God.

Write out each thought or memory that is "sticking," followed by Jesus' words "My yoke is easy, and my burden is light" (Matthew 11:30). For example, if you are replaying an interaction with a trauma survivor in which you wish you had attuned more effectively, you might write down, "I fear I dismissed his anger." Then write, "My yoke is easy, and my burden is light." Write the next thought that comes up, such as "I am scared he won't trust me anymore." Again, repeat, "My yoke is easy, and my burden is light." As you do this exercise, you might notice thoughts of tasks to accomplish emerging. Similarly, write these down followed by the reminder, "My yoke is easy, and my burden is light." Keep going until each "sticking" thought has been expressed.

This exercise is designed to help you notice and respond to ruminating thoughts. Rather than telling yourself to "just stop thinking about it," this exercise directly addresses the thoughts that are hard to let go.

Parasympathetic recovery. In Miller's (2022) CE-CERT model, parasympathetic recovery refers to the use of strategies *throughout your day* that bring your nervous system back into a state of equilibrium, or back into your window of tolerance, after a feeling of dysregulation. We discussed the importance of experiencing the fullness of your emotional experience, but it is equally important to let the emotion pass as it wishes. For example, I (Taylor) recently had a trauma survivor express significant frustration toward me when I was unable to reschedule a missed appointment until the following week. This survivor feared this meant I was "too busy for her." I reflected back her feelings of anger and fear that I would abandon her, connecting these fears to her experience of childhood trauma and unreliable caregivers. The survivor left feeling connected and reassured and had increased insight into the source of her reactivity. However, I experienced her anger as deeply dysregulating. As she expressed her frustration, I noticed myself feeling defensive, fearful, and misunderstood. I silently noticed and acknowledged these feelings in the moment (experiential engagement), but I noticed myself continuing to feel "wound up" after our meeting. This is the moment to practice intentional parasympathetic recovery, or attunement to our nervous system with the goal of regulating back into the window of tolerance. The strategies presented in the earlier chapter on emotional regulation can also be valuable to you as the safeguarder. In addition to those techniques, consider the following strategy to help regulate your emotions after a stressful event.

Strategy: Breath prayer. In her book on breath prayer, Jennifer Tucker (2022) provides a brief overview of the regulating value of breath prayer and its use throughout church history. She provides several exercises based in Scripture that help regulate your nervous system and attune to the presence of God. These can be used before, during, or after interactions with trauma survivors to regulate our breathing and remind us of the presence of God. We have listed a few below, but for further exploration read Jennifer Tucker's *Breath Prayer: Calm Your Anxiety, Focus Your Mind, and Renew Your Soul* (2022). As you practice these exercises, breathe in through your nose as you say the "inhale" phrase to yourself, and breathe out through your mouth as you say the "exhale" phrase.

God is our refuge and strength, a very present help in trouble. (Psalm 46:1)

> Inhale: "You are my refuge and strength"
> Exhale: "A very present help in trouble"

Cast your burden on the LORD, and he will sustain you; he will never permit the righteous to be moved. (Psalm 55:22)

> Inhale: "I give my burdens to you"
> Exhale: "You will take care of me"

And the peace of God, which surpasses all understanding, will guard your hearts and your minds in Christ Jesus. (Philippians 4:7)

> Inhale: "Guard my heart and mind"
> Exhale: "With your indescribable peace"

GOD AS SUSTAINER

At the beginning of the book, we cautioned that the work of safeguarding is challenging and it *will* be difficult at times even with self-care practices.

Exposure to our own suffering and the suffering of others changes us. That change can be positive and meaningful, making us more compassionate to the needs of others; or it can be damaging, prompting us to withdraw from goodness or drown in tragedy. While these strategies will not remove the pain of bearing witness to another's suffering, they will hopefully help us to see that "when I sit in darkness, the LORD will be a light to me" (Micah 7:8). God has called us all to the hard work of advocating for the vulnerable, and he is faithful to sustain us through it.

PERSONAL REFLECTION

1. Considering the *self-care as stewardship* perspective, how do you believe God is calling you to steward your limited resources, particularly your time, emotional capacity, and physical abilities?

2. When have you noticed yourself experiencing care for someone who is suffering that felt like a "direct hit" (self-oriented empathy)? When have you noticed connection with someone that felt attuned but with emotional distance (others-oriented empathy)? How can you tell the difference?

3. Reflect on the relational triggers questions to help identify areas of vulnerability. Develop a plan for processing this with a safe person (friend, family, counselor, pastor, etc.).

GROUP DISCUSSION

1. How can your church more effectively support its leaders and members in practicing faithful stewardship of their time and resources?

2. Take a moment to do a self-body scan, check your WOT zone, and assess your SUDS level. If you are comfortable, share some of these with the group. Next, implement one of the strategies you have learned and see if you can decrease your SUDS score by at least one number.

3. Pretend your group is a collaborative team of safeguarders helping Carlos, the person in the case study at the beginning of the chapter. What are some specific interventions you would use to help him?

REFERENCES

Bentley, P. G. (2022). Compassion practice as an antidote for compassion fatigue in the era of COVID-19. *The Journal of Humanistic Counseling, 61*(1), 58-73. https://doi .org/10.1002/johc.12172

Compton, L., & Patterson, T. (2023, September). Essential skill development for meaningful social connection. *Counseling Today, 66*(3), 41-45.

Compton, L., & Patterson, T. (2024, March 14). Absorption vulnerability: A new look at compassion fatigue. *Traumatology.* Advance online publication. https://dx.doi .org/10.1037/trm0000503

Hansen, E. M., Eklund, J. H., Hallén, A., Bjurhager, C. S., Norrström, E., Viman, A., & Stocks, E. L. (2018). Does feeling empathy lead to compassion fatigue or compassion satisfaction? The role of time perspective. *The Journal of Psychology, 152*(8), 630-45. https://doi.org/10.1080/00223980.2018.1495170

Heschel, A. J. (1951). *The Sabbath.* Farrar, Strauss & Giroux.

Hou, J.-M., & Skovholt, T. M. (2020). Characteristics of highly resilient therapists. *Journal of Counseling Psychology, 67*(3), 386-400. https://doi.org/10.1037/cou0000401

Kim, H., & Han, S. (2018). Does personal distress enhance empathic interaction or block it? *Personality and Individual Differences, 124,* 77-83. https://doi.org/10.1016/j.paid .2017.12.005

Larsen, K. L., & Stanley, E. A. (2021). Leaders' windows of tolerance for affect arousal—and their effects on political decision-making during COVID-19. *Frontiers in Psychology, 12,* 749715. https://doi.org/10.3389/fpsyg.2021.749715

Miller, B. (2022). *Reducing secondary traumatic stress: Skills for sustaining a career in the helping professions.* Routledge.

Miller, B., & Sprang, G. (2017). A components-based practice and supervision model for reducing compassion fatigue by affecting clinician experience. *Traumatology, 23*(2), 153-64. https://doi.org/10.1037/trm0000058

Neff, M. A., & McMinn, M. R. (2020). *Embodying integration: A fresh look at Christianity in the therapy room.* IVP Academic.

Rivera-Kloeppel, B., & Mendenhall, T. (2023). Examining the relationship between self-care and compassion fatigue in mental health professionals: A critical review. *Traumatology, 29*(2), 163-73. https://doi.org/10.1037/trm0000362

Salpietro, L., Ausloos, C. D., Clark, M., Zacarias, R., & Perez, J. (2023). Confidential grief: How counselors cope with client suicide. *Journal of Counseling & Development, 101*(4), 461-74. https://doi.org/10.1002/jcad.12484

Spurlock, R. (2021). Self-care: A stewardship perspective. *Journal of Christian Nursing, 38*(2), 98-101. https://doi.org/10.1097/CNJ.0000000000000688

Tucker, J. (2022). *Breath as prayer: Calm your anxiety, focus your mind, and renew your soul.* Thomas Nelson.

Zhang, L., Ren, Z., Jiang, G., Hazer-Rau, D., Zhao, C., Shi, C., Lai, L., & Yan, Y. (2021). Self-oriented empathy and compassion fatigue: The serial mediation of dispositional mindfulness and counselor's self-efficacy. *Frontiers in Psychology, 11,* 613908. https:// doi.org/10.3389/fpsyg.2020.613908

18

EDUCATION, COLLABORATION, AND RESOURCES

DR. CRISTA GLOVER, DR. DANIELLE H. JOHNSON, AND CYNTHIA FISHER

He has shown you, O mortal, what is good.
And what does the LORD require of you? To act justly and
to love mercy and to walk humbly with your God.

MICAH 6:8

SAFEGUARDERS PROVIDE CARE FOR VICTIMS and advocate for systemic change to prevent future harm. As safeguarders, we remain cognizant of power differentials in relationships and vulnerabilities in children and other populations. We recognize the signs of abuse and the devastating impact of trauma while also acknowledging the resiliency of survivors and the importance of their support systems. Safeguarders give voice to those whose cries have gone unheard and use our influence to stop the corruption of power and the weaponizing of religion. We take self-inventory of our motives and actions and seek accountability for ourselves and others. We never conceal the abuse of an individual, no matter the cost to our organizations.

In our efforts to be the salt and light to a broken world, we will encounter those who have experienced pain and suffering. The Lord's compassion for those who suffer is evident, as illustrated in Psalm 34:18, which states that he is close to the brokenhearted and saves those who are crushed in spirit. Accordingly, as the hands and feet of Christ (1 Corinthians 12:27), we strive and equip ourselves to understand, support, and gently guide the wounded to opportunities for healing in a way that allows them to use their voices and welcome God into their pain. Downie (2022) emphasizes this duty of the church, stating, "The responsibility for naming such experience and changing social power structures which not only harm but also protect those who harm others from accountability lies with the entire religious community, not with those who have been harmed" (p. 7). Through trauma-informed ministry, we can build compassionate and resilient faith communities, always prioritizing the safety and well-being of victims. As safeguarders, we must listen to and support the afflicted, recommend resources pertinent to a hurting person's needs, and promote communal knowledge and healing to prevent injury and reinjury.

TRANSPARENCY AND SHIFTING CULTURE

There is nothing concealed that will not be disclosed, or hidden that will not be made known. What you have said in the dark will be heard in the daylight, and what you have whispered in the ear in the inner rooms will be proclaimed from the roofs.

LUKE 12:2-3

Transparency. Truth and open, honest communication build trust and credibility. These qualities are essential for the church as it proclaims the gospel to the world. The way the church manages issues such as finances, relationships, and safety influences whether those who are unsaved view the church as a beacon of light or a whitewashed tomb. When the church conceals the sin of abuse, it increases the likelihood of future abuse, lessens the pressure on the perpetrator to come to repentance, and communicates to the victim that their pain is irrelevant. In the sanctuary of secrecy, sin and darkness flourish. Even when the church publicly discloses sexual misconduct, true transparency should be free of any coercion. As we learned earlier, trying to control the thoughts, feelings, and reactions of the congregants is not helpful to healing and is coercion and abuse of power as opposed to honest transparency and walking in truth.

However, the light of Christ shines in the darkness, and his truth brings freedom (John 1:5; 8:32). This is where healing begins. According to Dr. Judith Herman (2023), abuse survivors seek truth about the severity of harm inflicted on them and repair for the damage caused by the abuse. She writes, "Survivors want the truth to be recognized and the crime to be denounced by those in their communities who matter" (Herman, 2023, p. 15). The demand for repair and justice should come not just from the victim but from the outrage of their community.

Accountability. For survivors, holding perpetrators accountable for wrongdoing and preventing future harm are critical ways to restore safety. The first step to accountability is to acknowledge any power dynamics that lack checks and balances, making abuse easier to occur. No one should be absolved from rebuke or correction simply because they are in authority, nor should leaders require blind, unquestioned submission from others. Rather, the entire body of Christ is to submit one to another out of reverence for the Lord (Ephesians 5:21). The second step is to follow through on mandatory reporting to law enforcement when applicable. The third step in accountability is to provide consequences for the offender and care for the victim(s). Fourth, we must implement changes to prevent the abuse from happening again.

Early intervention. Early intervention should begin with self-awareness and an emphasis on character formation at the beginning of every ministry leader's career and ongoing throughout their lifespan. Awareness of how family-of-origin issues and trauma history may impact them and influence their vocational roles is essential to professional development. Spiritual mentors who provide supervision to ministry leaders should continuously monitor the leader's stress levels, their ability to emotionally regulate, the health of their relationships, their personal boundaries, and how their past issues may be affecting their present functioning. We are all new creations in Christ, but our attachment styles and trauma responses can still impact us, particularly when stress levels are high.

The sin of abuse does not just happen overnight. It occurs over time. As James 1:15 says, "After desire has conceived, it gives birth to sin; and sin, when it is full-grown, gives birth to death." It begins in the heart and thought life. It begins with crossed boundaries, off-the-record interactions, and blurred lines. It begins with suggestive conversations and putting "feelers" out there to gauge the target's response. It begins when leaders fail to avoid the appearance of evil (1 Thessalonians 5:22) and no longer live above reproach (Titus 1:6). It is vital that ministry leaders are self-aware and committed to their inner, private lives matching their outer, public ones. To prevent abuse, leaders must regularly examine themselves and be able to recognize and respond early to red flags when they see them. Therefore, just as counselors must receive annual ethics training to prevent client injury and professional impairment, ministry leaders need regular training as well.

EDUCATION AND AWARENESS FOR MINISTRY LEADERS

Promoting safety through understanding. Leaders in the church are the first people that those who are struggling with mental health needs go to, even before counselors and doctors (Lehmann et al., 2022). Every ministry leader should be trained on recognizing and addressing how trauma impacts individuals, families, and communities and implementing protective measures. This understanding should be incorporated into all areas of church life. Trauma survivors do not "just get over" their suffering, and trauma memories are not something that can merely be "cast out" or "rebuked." Abuse was committed at the hands of people acting selfishly and ruthlessly, and, as an antidote, healing comes through people who act empathetically and compassionately and demonstrate true righteousness. As leaders become mindful of trauma care, they can model to the congregation concrete ways to support survivors and not minimize their pain.

Trauma-informed leaders are also aware of the potential shame and isolation that abuse can cause in many lives. This is amplified in a church setting as other church members often hide their own struggles. Historically, personal problems and mental health issues have been hidden from public view, and when asked how someone is doing, church members will often answer "Blessed!" despite their own distress. Some abuse survivors feel further alienated by feeling everyone else looks "happy and normal." The perception of not fitting in with a happy, healthy, and shiny church community exacerbates feelings of shame and isolation, often resulting in their pulling away from their faith community.

This feeling of disconnection can also extend to how abuse survivors think God perceives them and how they perceive God. What compounds isolation are comments from uninformed individuals who do not understand the effects of trauma, as well as sermons and small group teaching that cause undue condemnation or weaponize Scripture to foster abuse. Because trauma is so prevalent, every church will have trauma survivors sitting in their services. Therefore, trauma-informed awareness and teaching within the faith community is necessary to develop sensitivity to the needs of those who are deeply hurting. This support and care from the body of Christ can help abuse survivors feel connected, understood, and less isolated.

Promoting safety in church teaching. As counselors, we can recall getting voicemails from survivors of abuse on a Monday morning asking for an appointment to process what had been spoken in the sermon the day before. Certain philosophies and teachings can significantly impact those who have endured abuse either as children or as adults. For example, a preacher recently taught on the topic of God's sovereignty. While the sovereignty of God (the belief that he is a supreme power and no one controls him) is a biblical principle, the preacher made statements such as "every event that happens on this earth is God's will." The relationship between the sovereignty of God and the free will of mankind is a complex theological discussion in which faithful Christians often disagree; however, we can be clear and certain that God is not the source of abuse. Someone hearing this sermon could easily misinterpret that to mean that God caused them to be sexually assaulted. This is against the character of God and also negates the fact that people have a free will (John 7:17; Galatians 5:13) and that there is a devil who seeks to steal, kill, and destroy (John 10:10). Being intentional and mindful of trauma when drafting sermons and educating the congregation on how Scriptures can be misused by evildoers to groom and enable abuse could help survivors feel protected and validated.

EDUCATION AND AWARENESS FOR THE CONGREGATION

All members of the body of Christ, not just church leaders, are given gifts and abilities to provide ministry and healing (1 Corinthians 12). Trauma-informed training should, therefore, extend to the whole body. These trainings can include classes for parents on attachment, discipline, and how to support children who experience trauma, as well as classes for children on coping skills, healthy boundaries around their body, and how to tell a safe adult when they need help. Members of the congregation should also receive training in recognizing signs of abuse and how to provide support to trauma survivors as lay ministers.

So many victims are reinjured by a lack of compassionate response after abuse is disclosed. This amounts to betrayal trauma, which occurs when a person, a group of people, or an institution violates the expected trust or commitment to someone's safety or well-being (Freyd, 2008). In other words, the entire faith community becomes compromised when there is complicity in ignoring victims and protecting predators. Imagine people who claim to love and care for you know your secret, the most painful violation that has ever happened to you, and do nothing. A nonresponse to injustice is not something the Lord takes lightly. In fact, he makes it very clear that "whatever you did for one of the least of these brothers and sisters of mine, you did for me. . . . Whatever you did not do for one of the least of these, you did not do for me" (Matthew 25:40, 45).

Bystander intervention. Safe church environments ideally include everyone in the church community taking responsibility for promoting safety and acting against abuse. Bystander intervention training can provide direction on what to do if someone becomes aware of an abusive situation. Bystanders are people who witness signs of danger or dangerous events, and they can have a significant influence not only on the physical safety of the victim but also on the psychological impact of the trauma. Many of our counseling clients have shared that the pain caused by those who could have protected them but did not or who did not believe them was more damaging than the abuse itself! The concept of bystander effect, or the inactions of those witnessing a dangerous situation without intervening, was studied by Darley and Latane after thirty-eight neighbors failed to timely act when witnessing the 1964 rape and murder of Kitty Genovese (Darley & Latane, 1968; Madden & Loh, 2020). A lack of action by bystanders in this case led to sexual assault and death. Passivity in the face of abuse could also lead to perceptions of abuse as an acceptable behavior and create a climate in which bystander complicity fuels the ongoing powerlessness of victims.

There has been significant research since the 1960s on what causes the bystander effect. Studies have found that higher numbers of bystanders (diffusion of responsibility), ambiguity of the perceived threat of the situation, avoidant coping strategies, minimal perceived personal responsibility, negative attitudes toward the victim(s), lack of close relationship with the victim, fear of retribution from the perpetrator, and not knowing what to do to help all led to bystanders being less likely intervene (Brody & Vangelisti, 2016; Haynes-Baratz et al., 2022; Liebst et al., 2019; Madden & Loh, 2020; Pozzoli & Gini, 2013). This is important information when developing training programs for congregations. Educating church members on how to advocate for vulnerable persons and encouraging intervention demonstrates a unified force against abuse. Herman (2023) highlights the impact of empowering the whole community, writing, "Once bystanders begin to take a righteous stand in support of survivors, the powers of the tyrant [perpetrator] begin to crumble" (p. 37).

Other ways to help. There are practical things that members of the church can do to address potential abuse. One church I (Cynthia) visited had small business cards in each bathroom stall with information on a Christian ministry to help women who are trapped in abusive relationships, and another church provided literature on support groups for people needing healing from trauma. Churches can provide information from the pulpit and through small groups on topics such as healthy relationships, mental health and wellness, and how to support others who are in crisis. Part of implementing a trauma-informed ministry is increasing collaboration with other ministries and connecting people with community resources. Ministry collaboration and maintaining a thorough list of referrals and resources facilitate safe church environments.

RESOURCES

Implementing mental health and self-care practices within the church to assist those at risk and prevent abuse of children and vulnerable people is a top priority that can only successfully be accomplished through interdisciplinary efforts from various community systems. When the church partners with law enforcement, legal assistance, social services, medical professionals, and other groups to provide care and prevention, the community becomes better together. Just as the strands of rope are stronger when tied together, we are more effective when we are knit together in God's love, stand in the strength of unity with fellow believers, and collaborate with others in our communities. Ecclesiastes 4:12 illustrates this: "A person standing alone can be attacked and defeated, but two can stand back-to-back and conquer. Three are even better, for a triple-braided cord is not easily broken" (NLT).

All referrals should be checked for safety, reputation, and current status of contact information on an ongoing basis. Local resources should include professional mental health services for crisis intervention as well as outpatient counseling. Support groups, both ministry-sponsored and professional psychotherapy groups, can also be extremely helpful for trauma survivors and anyone dealing with mental health challenges. In the United States, there are several state and national organizations providing trauma-related services such as Called to Peace Ministries, Survivor Network of Those Abused by Priests (SNAP), and Stop Child Abuse Now (SCAN). Godly Response to Abuse in the Christian Environment (GRACE) is a very active organization, providing safeguarding policy-making assistance for development of best practices within churches, onsite risk assessment, independent investigations into abuse allegations, and consultations for addressing abuse, harassment, and other misconduct allegations (netgrace.org).

There are many excellent resources to continue your education on the topics of trauma and abuse. Here is a brief list of suggestions:

- *Homecoming: Overcome Fear and Trauma and Reclaim Your Whole, Authentic Self* by Thema Bryant (self-help for trauma)
- *God Made All of Me* by Justin and Lindsey Holcomb (talking to children about protecting their bodies)
- *Preparing for Trauma Work in Clinical Mental Health* by Lisa Compton and Corie Schoeneberg (training for mental health professionals)
- *Redeeming Power* by Diane Langberg (abuse of power and coercion)
- *Safe People* by Henry Cloud and John Townsend (boundaries and healthy relationships)
- *The Body Keeps the Score* by Bessel van der Kolk (trauma responses)
- *The Child Safeguarding Policy Guide for Churches and Ministries* by Basyle Tchividjian and Shira Berkovits (policy and procedures)
- *A Church Called Tov* by Scott McKnight and Laura Barringer (church culture)
- *The Deepest Well* by Nadine Burke Harris (understanding childhood adversity)
- *The Garden Within: Where the War with Your Emotions Ends and Your Most Powerful Life Begins* by Anita Phillips (faith-based neuroscience perspective on emotions, anxiety, and trauma)

- *The Soul of Shame* by Curt Thompson (a neurobiological/theological lens)
- *The Whole-Brain Child* by Daniel Seigel and Tina Payne Bryson (child neurodevelopment)
- *Transforming the Living Legacy of Trauma* by Janina Fisher (healing steps for survivors)
- *Truth and Repair* by Judith Lewis Herman (justice for survivors)
- *Try Softer: A Fresh Approach to Move Us out of Anxiety, Stress, and Survival Mode and into a Life of Connection and Joy* by Aundi Kolber (self-compassion in suffering)
- *The Wounded Heart* by Dan Allender (adult survivors of childhood sexual abuse)

CONCLUSION

As we come to the end of our training on safeguarding, we commend you for not turning away from this heavy subject of abuse but rather leaning in to be an advocate for vulnerable members of society. You have learned why safeguarding is essential for the body of Christ and also gained skills to complete this mission. Remember to see the good in the world as you participate in the army of God to fight against evil. Take breaks, walk in the sunshine, and connect with others. "Whatever you do, work at it with all your heart, as working for the Lord, not for human masters, since you know that you will receive an inheritance from the Lord as a reward. It is the Lord Christ you are serving" (Colossians 3:23-24).

PERSONAL REFLECTION

1. How can mentors and supervisors best help leaders continually assess their own wellness, boundaries, and relationships, and overall healthy functioning?
2. Have you witnessed the church manage a scandal? What are some actions that you found helpful and/or some that you found potentially harmful?
3. Why is it important to allow people to grieve at their own pace?

GROUP DISCUSSION

1. What are some ways the church can reduce the likelihood of the bystander effect?

2. Consider what grade you would give to your faith community on how responsive it is to mental health and to trauma care. If the grade is less than an A, what steps can be done for improvement?

3. Pick one book, podcast, movie, or class you would like to use to continue your professional development. Share these with the group.

REFERENCES

American Psychological Association. (n.d.). Bystander intervention tip sheet. https://www .apa.org/pi/health-equity/bystander-intervention

Brody, N., & Vangelisti, A. L. (2016). Bystander intervention in cyberbullying. *Communication Monographs, 83*, 94-119. doi:10.1080/03637751.2015.1044256

Darley, J. M., & Latane, B. (1968). Bystander intervention in emergencies: Diffusion of responsibility. *Journal of Personality and Social Psychology, 8*, 377-83. doi:10.1037/ h0025589

Downie, A. (2022). Christian shame and religious trauma. *Religions, 13*, 925. https://doi. org/10.3390/rel13100925

Freyd, J. J. (2008). "Betrayal trauma." *The encyclopedia of psychological trauma* (G. Reyes, J. D. Elhai, & J. D. Ford, Eds.). John Wiley & Sons.

Godly Response to Abuse in the Christian Environment. (n.d.). www.netgrace.org.

Haynes-Baratz, M. C., Bond, M. A., Allen, C. T., Li, Y. L., & Metinyurt, T. (2022). Challenging gendered microaggressions in the academy: A social-ecological analysis of bystander action among faculty. *Journal of Diversity in Higher Education, 15*(4), 521-35. https://doi.org/10.1037/dhe0000315

Herman, J. L. (2023). *Truth and repair: How trauma survivors envision justice.* Basic Books.

Lehmann, C. S., Whitney, W. B., Un, J., Payne, J. S., Simanjuntak, M., Hamilton, S., Worku, T., & Fernandez, N. A. (2022). Hospitality towards people with mental illness in the church: A cross-cultural qualitative study. *Pastoral Psychology, 71*(1), 1-27. https://doi .org/10.1007/s11089-021-00982-1

Liebst, L. S., Philpot, R., Bernasco, W., Dausel, K. L., Ejbye, E. P., Nicolaisen, M. H., & Lindegaard, M. R. (2019). Social relations and presence of others predict bystander intervention: Evidence from violent incidents captured on CCTV. *Aggressive Behavior, 45*(6), 598-609.

Madden, C., & Loh, J. (M. I.). (2020). Workplace cyberbullying and bystander helping behaviour. *The International Journal of Human Resource Management, 31*(19), 2434-58.

Pozzoli, T., & Gini, G. (2013). Why do bystanders of bullying help or not? A multidimensional model. *The Journal of Early Adolescence, 33*(3), 315-40. doi:10.1177/0272431612440172

SUBJECT INDEX